politics
of the
imagination the life
work and
ideas of
charles fort

colin bennett

Critical Vision
an imprint of Headpress

A Critical Vision Book
Published in 2002
by Headpress

Critical Vision
PO Box 26
Manchester
M26 1PQ
Great Britain
fax: +44 (0)161 796 1935
email: info.headpress@telinco.co.uk
web: www.headpress.com

Politics of the Imagination
Text copyright © Colin Bennett
This volume copyright © 2002 Headpress
Cover artwork: Rik Rawling
Photo on p. 4 courtesy Fortean Picture Library
World Rights Reserved

British Library Cataloguing in Publication Data
A catalogue record for this book is available from the British Library

ISBN 1·900486·20·2

contents

Charles Fort aged nineteen

foreword

Forever perusing journals of scientific interest, Charles Fort (1874–1932) came across a letter to *Land and Water,* of June 4, 1881, in which a correspondent wrote that during a violent thunderstorm, tons of periwinkles had fallen from the sky, covering fields and a road for about a mile. He comments:

> Upon May 28th, 1881, near the city of Worcester, England, a fishmonger, with a procession of carts, loaded with several kinds of crabs and periwinkles, and with a dozen energetic assistants, appeared at a time when nobody on a busy road was looking. The fishmonger and his assistants grabbed sacks of periwinkles, and ran in a frenzy, slinging the things into fields on both sides of the road. They raced to gardens, and some assistants, standing on the shoulders of other assistants, had sacks lifted to them, and dumped sacks on the high walls. Meanwhile other assistants, in a dozen carts, were furiously shovelling out periwinkles, about a mile along the road. Also, meanwhile, several boys were busily mixing in crabs. They were not advertising anything. Above all there was secrecy. The cost must have been hundreds of dollars. They appeared without having been seen along the way, and they melted away equally mysteriously. There were houses all round, but nobody saw them.
>
> Would I be so kind as to tell what, in the name of some slight approximation to sanity, I mean by telling such a story?
>
> But it is not my story. There was, upon May 28th, 1881, an occurrence near Worcester, and the conventional explanation was that a fishmonger did it. Inasmuch as he did it unobserved, if he did it, and inasmuch as he did it with tons upon acres, if he did it, he did it as I have described, if he did it.[1]

This is the kind of tale appreciated by people who call themselves Forteans. All readers of this almost Chaucerian story, whether Forteans of not, will have some idea of what may happen next. A world of periwinkles will appear momentarily on the reader's horizon, a kind of bubble world. He or she will experience invasions not of humanoid aliens, but of a kind of periwinkleness. For all the world just like the *Gremlins* films, objects and people who look a bit like periwinkles will laugh, smile, and even threaten a reader from advertisements, television shows, and books. Periwinkle-forms will peer from behind bus shelters, be seen driving cars, and waving from trains. Periwinkles will enter perceptions like a giggling family in a TV game. For a short time, the essence of periwinkleness will dominate that stage show called reality. Reports of the mysterious arrival of periwinkles from all over the world will for a short time be seen as a kind of joker's code a reader will never solve.

When we have recovered from this alien invasion, we may realise with a terrible shock that Charles Hoy Fort, the teller of the periwinkle tale, towers above Winston Churchill, Albert Einstein, Tom Edison, and all the other alleged giants of the hundred years. Fort made us realise that despite the protestations of science and all common sense, we still live in a world of incredible magic with frogs and fish falling from the skies, and countless charitable fishmongers appearing suddenly from nowhere and subsequently disappearing without trace.

After some youthful travels, and before he left America for an eight-year stay in Britain in 1921, Fort spent most of his time in the New York Public Library, quietly starving and quietly thinking. Browsing through scientific journals, newspapers, and magazines, he came across many odd and unexplained items. He discovered reports of strange creatures seen in the sky, weird creatures and machines rising out of the world's oceans, peculiar foreign objects falling from the sky — everything ranging from great quantities of raw meat and blood to hand-carved stone pillars as well as periwinkles. People and things were often disappearing suddenly, only to reappear halfway around the world. Human footprints and man-made objects were repeatedly turning up in coal mines and geological strata dating back millions of years.

Fort wrote down his findings in his own special code on scraps of brown paper, which he stuffed into cardboard boxes. Day by day, month by month, year by year, the notes accumulated until he had thousands of them, and his small apartment was strewn with piles of boxes. In 1915, at the age of forty-one, he started to organise these stories into a book he planned to call *X and Y*. He never finished it, discarding it for another idea — a book that eventually appeared as *The Book of the Damned*. In May 1916, his uncle, Frank Fort, died leaving him a small inheritance, sufficient to support him and his wife Anna in a minimal way.

Theodore Dreiser, one of America's most famous and most influential novelists, took the manuscript of *The Book of the Damned* to his own publisher, Horace Liveright, and dumped it on his desk. Liveright reluctantly read it and then complained, "I can't publish this. I'll lose money." Dreiser told him flatly,

"If you don't publish it, you'll lose me."

Contrary to Liveright's expectations, the literary world greeted *The Book of the Damned* with awed enthusiasm. Newspaper and journal reviewers heaped praise upon the strange opus. Men like Booth Tarkington, John Cowper Powis, Ben Hecht, and Tiffany Thayer, all big names in their time, applauded. "I am the first disciple of Charles Fort," Ben Hecht wrote in the *Chicago Daily News*, "He has made a terrible onslaught upon the accumulated lunacy of fifty centuries. Whatever the purpose of Charles Fort, he has delighted me beyond all men who have written books in this world."

But despite these positive reactions, Fort believed that *The Book of the Damned* was a flop (sales were slow) and that he had wasted his life. He burnt 40,000 of his notes, quit America, and sailed for England with his wife Anna, an Englishwoman from Sheffield.

The Forts lived in London for eight years. During the day, he spent almost all his time in the British Museum pouring over old books and crumbling magazines, compiling reports of all kinds of cracks and fissures in the mundane world constructed by rationalism and common sense. In the evenings he often went to Speaker's Corner in Hyde Park and spoke there himself. His stay in London produced one book, *New Lands,* and much material for two other books. Though Fort and Anna arrived back just in time to witness the Wall Street crash, Fort had safely invested his meagre inheritance. Moving back to the Bronx, this income gave him enough time to complete his last two books, *Lo!* and *Wild Talents*.

Colin Bennett is correct in his thesis that the four books of Charles Fort present the world of conscious experience as being built essentially of advertising structures. We hear a lot about the *facts* concerning the present perilous situation of the world. But Fort warns us that the idea of *fact* itself is a late and rather callow arrival on the historical scene. Our present problems are "caused" by the life and death struggle between separate accounts of Creation, rather than facts. These stories, in their everlasting struggle for the prime time of consciousness, drag the "factual" economics, politics, and culture of the so-called "real" world behind them like tin cans on the tail of a cat. It appears that significant wars are waged for command of the high frontiers of applied mystique rather than anything more tangible.

Yes, I use facts to pull on my socks in the morning, but by evening I am thinking why the American Warren Commission of 1964 was an identical entity to the American Condon Report of 1969. Fort was the first writer to coin the phrase *the system;* meaning change of tribal individuals does not change the species of organisational animal. The latter report struggled with just as much energy to eliminate the truth about UFOs as the former commission struggled to obscure the truth about John Kennedy's assassination. Both used "facts" as a mundane control in a crisis management of wonders. Fort was the first writer to show that this was a common cultural vanishing practice, whether the particular tribal wonders consist of walking on the water, being cast out of Paradise, hovering over Jerusalem on a winged horse, or being abducted by aliens.

In our own time for example, the biggest astronomical scam of the 1970s was the black hole. It began as a minor element in a science fiction story published about thirty years ago. Basically, it is the notion that a dying star shrinks to a very heavy mass — so heavy that light can't escape from it. Therefore it is invisible and we have no way of detecting its presence. Science writer Fred Warshofsky[2] put it this way: "The physicist outside the black hole cannot get any information from inside it and has no way to understand the laws which govern it. Without that understanding he need not seek the laws since they are impossible to understand."

The black hole is a foolproof theory because there is no way of testing it, of proving or disproving it. Perfect fodder for the Walt Disney studios. Sciences other than astronomy were equally amusing to Fort. He suggested that archaeologists were just as busy burying things in their way as digging them up, in order to fit their pet theories. For example, they tell us that North America was uninhabited by anyone except Indians before the Europeans arrived. They overlook all the stone towers and structures found all over this continent (including miles of paved roads) when pilgrims arrived. Fort catalogued all kinds of metal objects from swords and axes to coins that have been found and dated as pre-Columbian. Somebody was mining ore and coal in this country, and pumping oil into Pennsylvania, before Columbus set sail. Rather than tussle with the problem of identifying those mysterious North Americans, the archaeologists have chosen to ignore these artefacts.

Wild Talents is a book about just how magical human possibilities are. We are most definitely not the sum of our parts, and "paranormal" talents emerge almost accidentally rather like slops from a shaken bowl of liquid. Fort's view is that unconscious fire-raising, telepathy, levitation and impossible human strengths, all these are lost powers ridiculed, falsified and restricted by science. *Lo!* is yet another assault on scientists — in this case astronomers. It lists many strange reports of unidentified aerial objects. Sitting in his study, Fort picked out two simple sentences that would identify the flying saucer mystery, define it and touch upon the only possible explanations.

> "Unknown, luminous things, or beings," he observed, "have often been seen, sometimes close to this earth and sometimes high in the sky. It may be that some of them were living things that occasionally come from somewhere else in our existence, but that others were lights on the vessels of explorers, or voyagers, from somewhere else."

Charles Fort perceived a truth that has been ignored by scientists and historians. Our world has two sets of natural laws. One set tells us stupidly simple things about gravity and nature. The other tells us that space and time are constantly distorted in our reality, and that we are all subject to the still unidentified laws of that second set. We never know when we might step through that magic door that will suddenly transport us 10,000 miles away.

We never know when we might encounter a beast or a being from "some-where else in our existence." Fish may rain on us, or red snow, or clouds of insects that no scientist can identify. Flying saucers will continue to buzz our farms and swamps, just as they have for thousands of years. Science attempts to work with the first set of laws and they come up with Black Holes. Magicians, occultists and psychics strive to manipulate the second group of laws. As Colin Bennett points out, in a media age, science and magic are becoming almost indistinguishable. When Fort studied the bizarre events of this super-spectrum, he was obliged to ask, "If there is a Universal Mind, must it be sane?"

In his vastly intriguing book on Charles Fort, Colin Bennett asks this very same question, and takes us on a dramatic voyage to seek answers to it.

—John Keel

What is a house?

It is not possible to say what anything is, as positively distinguished from anything else, if there are no positive differences.

A barn is a house if one lives in it. If residence constitutes houseness, because style of architecture does not, then a bird's nest is a house: and human occupancy is not the standard to judge by, because we speak of dogs' houses; nor material, because we speak of snow houses of Eskimos — or a shell is a house to a hermit crab — or was to the mollusc that made it — or things seemingly so positively different as the White House at Washington and a shell on the seashore are seen to be continuous.

The Book of the Damned

introduction

The American Charles Hoy Fort (1874–1932), the "foe of science" as the *New York Times* called him in its obituary, is certainly the most frequently acknowledged influence behind countless popular New Age books on magic, occultism, earth and sky mysteries, and the paranormal. Authors Louis Pauwels and Jacques Bergier acknowledge their debt to Fort in their influential book *The Morning of the Magicians*,[1] and science fiction writers such as Robert Heinlein, Theodore Sturgeon and James Blish have acknowledged their debt to Charles Fort's four books: *The Book of the Damned, Wild Talents, New Lands* and *Lo!* The books of John Michell, John Keel, Brad Steiger, Jacques Vallee, and Aimé Michel, also show the influence of Fort's ideas.

He was certainly a very important thinker. He created also the idea of paradigm-shift as the basis of cultural change some fifty years before Thomas Kuhn's epoch-making book on scientific philosophy, *The Structure of Scientific Revolutions*.[2] Though Fort's fame is now spreading rapidly, and his work is becoming known world-wide, it has taken over sixty years to secure his reputation as a major thinker and writer, and often in the face of vicious opposition from those individuals and institutions he opposed.

Though he was no hermit in the very fullest sense, he spent most of his time in reference libraries in his native town of New York, and later for some years in London after WWI. There he compiled thousands of notes of records of strange and unexplained phenomena, including spontaneous combustion, unidentified flying objects, poltergeists, telepathy, and extra-sensory perception. He was perhaps the first writer in history to bring these things together and subject them to a quite unique and integrated analysis. Though some Fortean enthusiasts stand on their heads to try and show he was sympathetic to science, his main object was plainly to demonstrate that not only is the world we live in far stranger than scientific culture will allow, but that science is as much about active concealment as discovery.[3]

In this respect, Fort is first and foremost a politician in the widest possible sense. It was what he regarded as an oppressive arrogance based on shaky "absolutes", "accuracies" and "certainties" which originally deeply offended both his moral and intellectual sense. As distinct from other more cautious natural philosophers, scientists have throughout history been very aggressive in their self-elected role of universal demystifiers. We are daily bombarded in our own time by claims from laboratories and research institutes for "facts", "objective truths", "improvements", and even "reality", this latter being a late and rather callow arrival on the historical scene. It would have pleased Fort to know that, as in his own time, most of these offered "scientific" wonders have a life as long as an average commercial break, and are just about equal in substance.

Ever since science appeared on the cultural stage, such intriguing and often comic claims for perfectly revealed truths have been with us. We might compare two observations some two hundred years apart, the first of William Hazlitt, reflecting the views of the early scientists of his day, and the second of Nobel Prize physicist, Murray Gell-Mann,[4] of our own time:

> We are so far advanced in the Arts and Sciences... the accumulation of knowledge has been so great that we are lost in wonder at the height it has reached. What niche remains unoccupied? What path untried?[5]

> Gell-Mann's conviction is that it is indeed possible to know it all, that in principle there is nothing to prevent the future day when sovereign science will be able to explain absolutely everything, in a single coherent picture of how the universe works.[6]

Such claims are not unusual. In 1887 the great chemist Marcelin Berthelot wrote, "from now on there is no mystery about the Universe." In 1895 the celebrated Professor Lipmann told one of his pupils that physics was a subject that was "exhausted". Even the great Heinrich Hertz wrote to the Dresden Chamber of Commerce saying that research into the transmission of Hertzian waves (that were eventually to become the foundation of wireless) should be discontinued, as they could not be used for any practical purpose.

This kind of scientific absolutism continues in our own day. How do we resist such ludicrous absolutism, even from such extremely brilliant men? Taking a hint from Charles Fort, we do it by feeling, with patience and total dedication, for those myriad hairline cracks in the scheme of things that science cannot account for.

In *The Book of the Damned*, Fort describes how he found such anomalies. He discovered contradictions and paradoxes, endless inexplicable curiosities on earth, sea and air. What might be termed a First Fortean Law emerged from his studies. This law is that the fantastic is the rule rather than the exception, and that the idea of the "factual" is more a limiting psychological device to allow us to get some sleep at night than anything else.

Fort's gathered information showed that throughout the nineteenth century there were countless reports from all over the world of material falling from the sky. Salt, vegetable substances, coal, sand, fibres, red worms, alkaline substances fell together with rains of blood, tons of spider webs and shards of iron and quartz. Most of this material could be named, but the technical identity of some of the material was never completely settled. Indeed, some of the stuff could not be named at all because nothing like it had ever been seen before. Then there was that material which could be partially identified, and also the stuff whose almost-identification caused controversy amongst the many scholars and experts of the time. There was also the material which disappeared in a manner as mysterious as it came, such as the countless strange mushroom formations, jelly-like substances and curious mould cultures, all of which appeared to have fallen from the sky in a partly developed form.

As if lacking proper credentials of perfect solidity, these events were "damned". They were cast out, like Milton's Satan, from those mighty courts of proper affairs that were busy building the great nineteenth-century systems of cultural reference, of which ideas of moral certainty and scientific determinism were the keystone. Such events as Fort describes were almost always officially declared never to have occurred, or if it was acknowledged that something very strange did occur, then frequently it was said to be of no importance to anyone. Fort was the first to point out that this was the kind of ultra-professional vanishing practised in almost every society as a crude form of imagination control, and hence social control.

The main Fortean principle is not so much one of the real versus the unreal, or truth versus falsehood, but the question of what as a society we decide we shall *allow* ourselves to experience. When, say, Mrs Bentley, night-cleaner, clocks off at dawn and sees a massive Adamski-type UFO hovering over the boiler house, more often than not, a powerful and intimidating process begins immediately to convince her that she has seen absolutely nothing. She may fear ridicule, fear for her own state of mind, fear that she has by chance seen something forbidden, or fear that she may be dismissed, for whatever reason. Amidst these fears she knows one thing that is far more important — she knows that Authority will not help her. What she may not know is that the only thing Authority ever wishes to conceal *is that it almost certainly has the same fears as she.*

These very old and powerful uncertainties relating both observer and the guardians of a body of received experience, are all forces which combine to de-scale such anomalous experiences, either to clothe them with overt normality (a "military experiment", or even the planet Venus), or to vanish them completely; Mrs Bentley has had an "hallucination". Here then is a deep implicit conditioning — nothing to do with economics, class, or "objective" social forces, but both an explicit and implicit conspiracy at the heart of cultural and political

formation and control. In this respect, readers new to Fort are often disappointed to find out that in a Fortean universe, there are hardly such things as
occultism, the paranormal, or whatever; *all* things are equally fantastic. In such
a world model, there exists only the politics of combative scales of fantasy
limitation of which individual sectors are the battlegrounds.

The high-level professional denial by authority (whether concerning UFOs,
arms sales, or moving lights seen on the moon) has become such that it is a
unique twentieth-century institution, part of the media rituals of techno-mythol-
ogy that now constitutes what might be termed Entertainment State. Science,
being almost exclusively a heavily institutionalised activity, is implicitly involved
in these matters at every stage, despite its frequent protestations of innocence. Ever-evolving Authority therefore still finds experimental science a useful culture to work alongside faltering and antiquated systems of state religion,
royalty-mysticism, and Camelot-republicanism as a means of effective control
of human emotional resources. Science, like Authority again, is equally good at
such Darwinian ideo-adaptation. As if taking a leaf from Fort's book, only
recently has science itself created fuzzy logic and chaos theory as more
anomaly-sympathetic disciplines in order to try and avoid the deadlock of
classical Aristotelian true-or-false absolutes as absorbed by Victorian science.
As Fort might have said, perhaps the equations of the advertisements of such
adaptive cultural bough-plumage have yet to emerge.

Ironically, Fort's work parallels relativity in that it found the Achilles heel
within facile scientific illusions posing as absolute and omnipotent permanence. Evolving in almost exactly the same historical dimension, like relativity
again, and indeed quantum theory, Fort's books contain a unique phenomenol-
ogy founded on observation of exceptions rather than rules. The sociology of
Einstein's work has yet to be written, but both Fort and Einstein provided
weapons for resistance against a mass of burgeoning *systems* that descended
upon early twentieth-century folk like a plague, some of which still prevail. In
the sense that the institutionalisation of many of these "absolute" systems
dictated the destiny (and frequently the deaths) of countless millions, Charles
Fort has now become a very important interpretative philosopher. Though in
essence pre-electronic,[7] Fort's thinking is particularly relevant to our own time
as both the consumer society and the electronic village blend to become Entertainment State. With powerful new technology, this emerging society, in its
structured mass-appeals, relies heavily on imagination control of a scale and
depth of which not even Fort could have had a conception.

Fort describes a tragicomedy not of stupidity, but of the fallible nature of
the highest levels of trained perception and intelligence. Should anyone have
doubts about anomaly theory being socio-political dynamite, Damon Knight[8],
Fort's biographer, talking of Immanuel Velikovsky's[9] books, gives a good
picture of the kind of forces involved:

The uproar over the books came as an unpleasant revelation to those of us who had thought of scientists as disinterested seekers of knowledge. A group of astronomers led by Harlow Shapley, then Director of Harvard College Observatory, mounted a campaign to prevent the publication of *Worlds in Collision;* failing that, to discredit it; finally, to force Macmillan to cease publication of the book by boycotting its textbook division.[11] Macmillan, which depended heavily on textbook sales, found so many heads of college departments refusing to see its salesmen that it was forced to give in. In June 1950, although the book was a bestseller, Macmillan turned it over to Doubleday (which has no textbook division). James Putnam, the Macmillan editor who signed the original contract for the book, was summarily dismissed from a post he had held for twenty-five years. Gordon Atwater, who had championed Velikovsky, was fired as Curator of Hayden Planetarium and Chairman of the Department of Astronomy of the American Museum of Natural History.[11]

Similar quotations could be given illustrating what happened at about the same time to orgone theorist Wilhelm Reich[12] and acid guru Timothy Leary.[13] In Britain, Fort himself was dealt with in a much more effective and less messy way — he simply was not published here until Sphere issued *The Book of the Damned* and *New Lands* in 1974, and the titles went rapidly out of print. Fortunately, since then, the Fortean flag has been flown by a small but dedicated group of brilliantly gifted people whose work over the years has resulted in the highly successful magazine *Fortean Times*. This magazine in particular has helped create and develop part of a culture of dissent sorely needed in an increasingly conformist society, whose accountancy-driven input/output assumptions would stifle all creative life.

The briefest look at the contents of this magazine (and others like it), will demonstrate how any single scientist (like any single TV programme), may be fine, but his profession as practised is inextricably involved with different kinds of power interests, massive market investments, and military, industrial and technological intrigue. What happened to the much-vaunted Attic idea of "disinterested objectivity" in this vicious context is anybody's guess. Fort shows the typical scientist forced to work within this structure as a kind of hapless librarian receiving new categories that are constantly subverting traditional systems of reference, which therefore will not stay still for a minute. What is this librarian to do? Somehow the library must be kept going, if only for national image, rather than profit, still less for knowledge. Therefore the librarian has to create endless lists of complicated approximate speculations, some of which vary in quality, such as the many contradictory astronomical claims described in *New Lands*. Moreover, as this kind of difficult work proceeds, there are accusations of inaccuracy and misrepresentation. There are even charges of fraud and downright lying, such as in the recent dispute about cold fusion.

There occur also such unfortunate affairs as that of the scandal surrounding the influential psychologist Sir Cyril Burt,[14] and also the mathematician Samuel Soal,[15] the former having exercised a profound influence on the planning the somewhat nationally important 11-plus examination! There are also endless rows about naming things. The trouble lies in the overlapping. The scandalous business of Blondlot's N-rays,[16] polywater,[17] and intelligence testing in general, shows that hard definitions and categories just will not stay separate. Against a background of cultural change, such definitions and categories appear to fight amongst themselves as if they were more live information-animals rather than dead ideology. Many contradictions appear as regards accuracy, definition, etymology and proper semantic relation. Fort comments on this in *Lo! :*

> I have never heard of any standard, in any religion, philosophy, science, or complication of household affairs that could not be made to fit any requirement. We fit standards to judgements, or break any law that it pleases us to break, and fit to the fracture some other alleged law that we say is higher and nobler. We have conclusions, which are the products of senility, or incompetence, or credulity, and then argue from them to premises. We forget this process, and then argue from them to premises, thinking we began there.[18]

Fort himself was in a unique historical position to see scientists transfer from the tightly closed circles of upper-middle class leisured gentlemen of independent means of the nineteenth-century who could quote Homer and Virgil, to the more industrially-pressured scientists of the emerging manufacturing world to whom quotations only meant price-lists in good plain Anglo-Saxon. In this new cost-effective, project-oriented world, the problems of scientific credibility were multiplied. One new difficulty was that actual constructs tended to get out of date before they were even manufactured. That is a problem we in our own time are more than familiar with than the Victorians, to whom the idea of being "out of date" was largely incomprehensible. Their sense of time was very different to ours; our Project Time will hardly wait for the next exhausting phase of industrial and research-definition tasking. The result of such pressure and forced directions is more guesses and crossed fingers than are ever admitted.

Finally, below decks, ignoring fancy philosophers on the bridge, the practical folk get impatient. They are not concerned that there may be no such thing as absolute randomness, or that experimental methodology is never ever logically tight enough, or that the pristine fact appears to be a Grail as elusive as a perfect translation of Proust. Finally, the hammer-and-chisel folk send something made of good guesses to the moon, cross their fingers again, and leave the public relations department to call it a triumph of "exact" science. Just how exact it is, we can judge by Norman Mailer's description of astronaut Michael Collins' comments on the behaviour of the LEM (Lunar Expedition Module) aboard Apollo 11:

Something mysterious was going on when Collins reported: "The LEM wants to wander up and down... several minutes ago I was steadily on data and since then I have been moving forward, the LEM pointed straight down towards the radius vector, and that's been despite a number of down minimum pitch impulses." Ten minutes later Collins was reporting again, "the tendency seems to be to pull the LEM down toward the centre of the moon... interesting data on thruster firing versus pitch angle. It looks like that LEM just wants to head down towards the surface."

"I have a comment here" replied the Capcom, "that says that's what the LEM was built for, I believe."

Collins was grinding through the anxiety that the LEM was behaving most peculiarly, not unlike a dog on a leash who keeps leaning in the direction of a new and fascinating scent. There were unsatisfactory explanations for the inexplicable. The moon had mascons, mass concentrations of dense material buried irregularly in its sphere. So its gravitational effects were a hint displaced. So the mascons might pull on the spaceship itself. But why pull on the LEM in preference to the Command and Service Module?[19]

If, on the other hand, it was a computer mistake (as it could have been), then the mistake in any case was such an indicator of the heart of the situation as to cause more than second thoughts about what Mailer calls the "the psychology of machines".

Countless other such examples could be given, but no matter how many such incidents occur in any field, they are still nowhere near affecting the broad roads of official science. The highly respected Bernard Heuvelmans thoroughly analysed 587 sightings of marine monsters in his 1968 book *In the Wake of the Sea-Serpents*, but it made no difference to conventional zoology. In Professor John Hastead's laboratory at Birkbeck College,[20] London, hundreds of children, in tests, distorted metal strips in sealed containers that they could not possibly have had access to. But as far as official physics goes, they might as well have been playing football in the park.

To Fort's mind, the scientist is like the librarian who thinks he has a solution to all this. Some categories are rarer than others. Therefore better to stick to the mainstream and imply that is all there is, and not say anything at all about the missing sections. If something new and odd occurs (as frequently happens), then attempt to drag it into the mainstream, even if it is like trying to drag a large object through a cat-door. Perhaps, that way, a little something of the extremely large whatever-it-is will get through to give the thing some scrap of an approximate name and nature, and thus calm everyone down. If this scientist-librarian sounds a little like a character from Kafka or Borges, it might be borne in mind that both these men were young when Fort was writing. Although it is extremely unlikely that they knew one another's work, perhaps the *Zeitgeist* works in Fortean ways.

One step beyond this tragicomedy of attempts at absolute categorisation, and the plot thickens. Fort's *Wild Talents* deals with anomalies within human actions, thinking, and general behaviour rather than with external nature's inconsistencies. Here, human beings themselves are the centres of curiosity. We come across mysterious woundings, mass hysteria, poltergeist activities and spontaneous combustion. These things often show the same characteristics. They appear to be highly selective. In normal circumstances, if A wishes to damage B, there is usually a blow to the face, shoulder, stomach, or ribs. Human beings, when in combat, do not hit one another on the bottom, or the soles of the feet. Neither, it appears, do these quite *invisible* assailants; most hit *as human beings would hit*.

As regards the phenomenon of spontaneous combustion, Fort's explanation of dresses, socks and shoes being left intact whilst a temperature sufficient to calcine bone destroys intestines, is that when A imagines destroying B, the image hardly includes the destruction of B's surely innocent socks!

Thus Fort concludes that certain aspects of such events are as if parts of the scene had been *imagined*.

All these ideas are united by a single quest that unites all the many themes that run through the books of Charles Fort. The quest is to try and rediscover the universe as a live animal. That this idea has been stolen, falsified, curtailed and restricted is behind his implicit political anger. This is the force creating the raw emotional energy running about in a Fortean world model, which is a structure in which feelings can disembody themselves and effect whatever areas are convenient or accessible as symbolic foci of resentment:

> I feel the relatability of two scenes:
> In Hyde Park, London, an orator shouts: "What we want is no king and no law! How we'll get it will be, not with ballots, but with bullets!"
> Far away in Gloucestershire, a house that dates back to Elizabethan times bursts into flames.[21]

This sheds some light on the mechanics of sets of coincidence clusters, such as the death of a number of British hunting folk within a short time,[22] twelve men suffering falls on separate building sites in one morning,[23] and even a mass rage against lace curtains. We may not know we are spinning such tragic-comic webs, it may frighten us, but we *do* do it. Even the dullest humans cannot help imagining many thousands of times per minute, on all kinds of levels and intensities, according to their mood, if nothing else. That our images may have a separate life unknown to us and can indeed act at a distance is an idea which modern society finds extremely difficult to accept. In demythologising ourselves of such "primitive" beliefs, a good part of our rich emotional life has been curtailed, falsified and restricted. If that is not political control in the deepest sense, then nothing is. Fortunately perhaps, we give love and compassion through the same route in transfers of both matter and emotion. There is a touching moment in an otherwise macabre tale where Fort tells us that water was found in a coffin from which noises had emanated. He adds that perhaps that the water was "sent" to make a quick end of it.

Of course the "sending" of water for such a particular purpose gives most modern minds unprecedented intellectual difficulty. But certainly Shakespeare would have no problem with such a relationship between water and need. For him, mind and nature were a single entity. In Lear's court and in Hamlet's castle an atmosphere exists which performs as a complete character whose name is not on the list of *dramatis personae.* If we regard such an anonymous entity as merely being an historical curiosity, then perhaps this accounts for our unprecedented difficulties when we meet the mysteries of disappearing ships, aircraft and people. The mysteries of the major American assassinations, the Holocaust, the death of Diana, Princess of Wales and the events of September 11, 2001, in New York would have Fort saying certainly that there is no such thing as a *single* anything, never mind a single philosophy, and even less a single assassin. Chapters of this book will attempt to show how the anomaly acts as an unnamed character within human situations, just as do crypto-geographic landscapes in Shakespeare and Thomas Hardy.

Fort's structure of quite original ideas would have been an achievement in itself, were it not that he is also one of the great comic stylists of his age. He uses laughter as a weapon against comics certainties of science, and eventually, his four books comprise a twentieth-century *Inferno* that will surely be put alongside James Joyce's *Ulysses* or Laurence Sterne's *Tristram Shandy.* His work has the same circumlocutory psychological interiors, the same feel for the infinities within a moment, and convey a questioning narrator voyaging through a cosmos of ever-unfolding dimensions of questions, rather like a chaos fractal. His style is quite unique. Following the chain of his thought is rather like following a jazz chorus. He moves sideways, takes backwards steps, allows himself (like many a good mind) to get completely lost, and then rights himself quickly, only to chase immediately some wild goose that has appeared from a totally unexpected direction. But like following the often discontinuous ramblings of Coleridge, Rabelais, Cervantes, or even Charlie Parker, it is all very much worthwhile. The wonderfully comic story of the debacle at the Swanton Novers Rectory in *Lo!* gives an idea of Fort's modern, almost up-against-the-microphone performance style, pioneered in fume-filled basements by Lenny Bruce. The style is close also to the stream-of-consciousness technique of James Joyce's *Ulysses*, and is a good illustration of the principle that we prefer that version of events that is most comfortable to live with, or one that satisfies the current paradigm.

From time to time there appear brilliantly conceived systems (such as that advanced by Rupert Sheldrake, for example,[24] or David Bohm[25]) put forward as accomplished attempts to reconcile some anomalistic ideas with a science desperate to re-propagandise itself. Fort would not have approved. The last thing wanted in a Fortean world is yet another system. He sees all such dialectical animals as different forms of oppression. In this sense, he sees science, no matter how re-imaged as liberal and interesting, as essentially the religion of secular Authority in different disguises. In this sense, the much-vaunted "objective facts" of science are nothing more than masks for almost-living programmatic tissues of information. Fort presented such things as ritualistic and devotional viruses trying desperately to re-advertise themselves. In this view, science is a deceptive *mysterium,* with its practitioners having the morals of all advertisers in constructing almost irresistible glamorous stage-fronts of the intellect for the purposes of social control.

It is thus understandable that Fort is the *bête noire* of most scientists. He teases to death both their linearity and their blushing protestations of correct and worthy moral purpose. He reveals them as always forgetting something, committing some absurd blunder, making claims of a phenomenal accuracy within a scheme of things whose high strangeness makes the very idea of simple objective accuracy quite meaningless. Nevertheless, he frequently suggests that we need the mythology of ever-increasing approximations to the truth to keep us at least partly sane. Therefore the state of our mental health is engineered around, rather than anything being "solved" in the scientific sense. In this sense, science to Fort is about presentation of information rather than investigation. It seems we need, indeed consume, explanations whose equivalent structures of fishmongers are much more fantastic than the phenomena they seek to explain.

Fort always taps patiently along the line of accounts of causal reasoning until he finds some fresh version of the same super-energetic and super-charitable fishmonger who gets up early in the morning before anybody is around and strews Sussex with millions of periwinkles. Perhaps Gell-Mann's quark, Smoot's gravity waves, or the "black holes" of Professor Hawking[26] or indeed the atom and the electron, being pure conventions in themselves, are such Fortean fishmongery. After nearly a hundred years, the wave-particle controversy still leads right under the hill to the quite mythological realms of modern particle physics. In pointing this out when science was still young and somewhat innocent, the Fortean view broke open sealed systems of conscious cultural advertisements to reveal to us what is being hidden rather than what is revealed. His method might be applied to an article in a recent issue of *The Sunday Telegraph,* which commented on astronomer Fred Hoyle's book, *Home is Where the Wind Blows:*

> According to [Hoyle's] theory, there never was a Big Bang but instead an incredibly slow, continuous creation of matter through the cosmos at the rate of about one hydrogen atom in each cubic yard per billion years.

For the sake of the cause, perhaps we shouldn't ask what, in the name of Einstein, "incredibly slow" means, or ask what, in the name of Planck, "continuous" means, and certainly not what, in the names of Schrödinger, Rutherford, and Bohr, what "matter" is, and perhaps, in the name of Groucho Marx, how relative is the word "incredible". And in the name of the gods of embarrassment, perhaps we should not even think about asking what the cubic yard mentioned above is *of*. A cubic yard of space, perhaps? What is space? Like just what happens between the two quite separate windings of any transformer, no one really knows. We have a choice of Euclidean space, the space of Einstein, and some pretty peculiar views on space from Reimann, Minkowski, and the curious "metaphysical" space of the great mathematician George Cantor, to name but a few. Not that Hoyle's enemies from across the Atlantic are any better. Here's that indefatigable instigator of incredible indices, George Smoot:

> The weak, strong, and electromagnetic forces behave differently in the universe as we experience it. But long ago, at the unimaginable temperature of the first instant of the universe (within 10^{34} seconds, or one ten-millionth of a trillion of a trillion of a second after the Big Bang), they were all essentially the same and operated in the same way on particles.[27]

A nice performance, and such marvellously decadent "factual" accuracy is a good example of the disease which now affects science, as it frequently presents such phenomenal niceties of what a cynic might well term intellectual junk-culture. Here's another example of such from science writer Fred Warshofsky:

> The physicist outside the black hole cannot get any information from inside it and has no way to understand the laws which govern it. Without that understanding he need not seek the laws which govern it.

After such blushing precision, let there be no more accusations of eccentricity. The worst excesses of French post-modern thought are nothing compared to these attempts by science to explain itself. All this would be splendid Fortean fun, were it not that our technological society, from electric kettles to cyclotrons, is based on such well-managed and glossy propagandising of certainty and accuracy in which manufactured facts become commodities within an ecology of equally fashionable reassurances. Fort attacked the industry that produces such pseudo-information. Scientists to him are like naked men trying put on torn rags and patches of clothes in a raging hurricane. He ridicules their obligatory *gravitas,* their inevitable social conformity, their relatively safe jobs, their frequent pomposity, and the intimidating gloss of the corporate identity behind which almost all hide, for science will not tolerate non-conformists within its own structures. Should any happen to come along, then they are got rid of by being either rejected or ignored, like Alan Turing, Barnes Wallis, Charles Babbage, George Boole, or indeed the many constructors of fuelless motors, such as Keely, Spear, and Hendershot, described in *Wild Talents.*

Being such a complete original of course, and having such relatively subversive views for his time, Fort found it quite difficult to get his work published. His friend, the writer Theodore Dreiser (he wrote *Jenny Gerhardt* and *An American*

Tragedy), was instrumental in getting him a publisher, and he sent a copy of
The Book of the Damned to H.G. Wells, whom he rightly regarded as being one
of the more far-seeing men of his time. But Wells was not interested because
he still had (at that time) a deep faith in science as the one philosophy which
would (like the popular Marxism of his day), give positive social solutions,
and construct a world free of war, disease, and human misery and strife.
Wells' reaction gives us the key to Fort's almost completely isolated position
as a thinker and writer. He was a mite too dangerous for his age. He asked
too many disturbing questions at once, and had the infernal cheek to laugh
out loud at the intellectual oppression dished out by more linear and humourless minds. In our own era, he remains to this day still a controversial
author as far as intellectual influences are concerned. Like Genet, Céline,
Henry Miller, or Leon Bloy, there is hardly hope yet of seeing Charles Fort on
any A-Level syllabus.

At the time The Book of the Damned appeared in 1919, there was almost no
intellectual opposition to science as the dominant mode of experience. The
seemingly total success of its fearful instrumentation, its mighty machines, the
intrigue of its fascinating theories, and the glamour of its main figures, together with the (alas, illusory) successes of its philosophical bed-mate, "scientific" Communism, seemed to sweep aside once and for all mysticism, magic
and religion.

The great warning films such as Fritz Lang's Metropolis (1926) and Modern
Times (1936) are virtually dramatisations of Fort's Book of the Damned.[28] But
as far as an intellectual analysis of any Achilles heel of science was concerned,
there was practically no work at all which compared to the work of Charles
Fort. The intelligent occultists and esoteric thinkers of Fort's time, such as
Madame Helena Blavatsky, Aleister Crowley, the circles of Gurdjieff and
Ouspensky, and indeed the Yeats group, were driven into cultural isolation,
many reduced to posturing, scandalous eccentricities, and hole-in-corner obscurities. If T.S. Eliot and Ezra Pound had at this time introduced "real thinking" into poetry, there really was no equivalent to this as regards opposition to
science as a new mythology; the then young Society for Psychical Research
was ever its cautious, snooty and narrowly-clever upper-middle-class self, and
avoided controversy, as it still does today. The great characters of occultism
(such as Eliphas Levi) were long dead, as were the great nineteenth-century
figures that were suspicious of the absolutism of science, such as Oliver Lodge,
Crookes and Conan Doyle. The coming age belonged more to the hopeful and
pragmatic Bernard Shaw, Julian Huxley and Bertrand Russell. Carl Jung, a man
who might well have understood Fort's work, was almost equally isolated. Jung's
essay, Synchronicity: An Acausal Connecting Principle, though hardly available to
Fort, would doubtless have fascinated him, and would have shown him that he
was not quite as isolated as he thought.

Hemingway and James Joyce had nothing to say about science. Joseph
Conrad was indeed suspicious of the "wooden-faced panjandrum"[29] but only

D. H. Lawrence, alone, like Keats a hundred years before, condemned it outright. Thus science out-advertised easily all and everything. With Aldous Huxley, Orwell and Koestler yet to write, no writer saw science as a deceptive or threatening philosophy still less as a set of intellectual conditions for a unique form of social control. There would have been no prizes for anyone in the 1920s and 1930s, for example, who claimed (as Fort claimed) that the new scientific accounts of causation contained the same mythological flat-earth phantasmagoria and the epicycles-within-epicycles confusions of the early astronomers. Neither would it have been good for a career in any field at all to have suggested that Rutherford's achievement in splitting the atom was the fulfilment of over a thousand years of an alchemical dream. Science was therefore unique in that it successfully propagandised itself as a complete historical break from all such nonsense, which it viewed as belonging to a Neanderthal past. Unlike religion, science offered rewards in this life, but although like religion it desperately needed mass belief, it was very careful to keep itself as a very small club, somewhat difficult to join without going through the rituals of applied rationalism.

What society was going to have to pay for these first promises of science early in the century was therefore not a leading question of Charles Fort's day. When Fort was a young man, Marie Curie had only just begun to take a deeper interest in the strange spots on her hands, and the first discoloured fish had only just begun to appear belly-up in the canals by the new chemical works. But like Faust, humanity had signed an agreement with its blood, and the deal was on.

Fort was unfortunate in the sense that he died without seeing his prophecy about scientific decadence come to pass. Whilst he was alive, science was still a breathlessly exciting adventure. Like Marxist communism again, science as a kind of millennial cult of rationalism, promised an Aladdin's cave full of the very best of human expectations. Fort would have been most interested to see the failure of communism exactly at the same time as the failure of major scientific constructs such as nuclear power. He would also have been fascinated by the way that redundant weapons software is being turned into massive games systems, that the wonder of outer space has become an expensive and obsolescent boy-scout wonderland, and the desperate attempts of the new cosmologists to re-advertise and sell their faltering profession. He would also have been intrigued to see many of the science departments of respectable universities become the technological support base for toy-culture, mass entertainment and media, as science struggles to join the new ideo-anthropological games systems.

Recent examples of what Fort might have called ideological tooth and claw abound. Dr Fenwick, neuro psychiatrist at the Maudsley hospital in South London, announced on the front page of *The Sunday Telegraph* that he had found the location of the human soul within the brain. Such grey-scale confusions within the octave of appearances of matter and spirit mirror the similar deep confusions now raging in the Artificial Intelligence debate.

We are left to wonder what Fort would have made of such things, just as we conjecture what he would have thought of the scientific scandals of the past forty years, including N-rays, polywater,[30] or C. G. Barkla's almost-recognised J phenomenon,[31] and in our own time, the equally almost-recognised phenomenon of cold fusion. Equally edifying is an Indiana University publication entitled *Dinosaur Flatulence as the Cause of Earth's Warming*, and a Washington State University Paper on *Cow Belching — How Much Methane in the Atmosphere?* We lack a present-day Charles Fort to comment on the activities of Philip Benson, a research psychologist of the University of St Andrews, who used computerised scanning techniques to graphically demonstrate how each of Elizabeth Taylor's eight husbands really had an identical face to hers. Yet another psychologist, Professor Victor Johnson at New Mexico State University, used massive funds to create the characteristics of what he termed the "ultimate beautiful face". Created by computers using millions of sample-simulations, the resulting image was unremarkable. As Fort might have said, considering the state of Mexico City, Professor Victor Johnson is just what the Mexicans need. We need not add further examples of a scrabble-game "science" descended to making better fly-sprays, improving dustbin handling, and faster rollerblades. All these things fit Fort's prophetic definition of scientific decay:

> The science of astronomy is going downward... attention is now minutely focused upon such technicalities as variations in shades of Jupiter's fourth satellite. I think that, in general acceptance, over-refinement indicates decadence.[32]

The scandals still abound. Hardly reported in Britain, the great Mirror Fusion project in America has been shut down, raising such a cloud of high-level scandal that charges of incest and cannibalism were just about the only accusations not being made. As Darwinian animals, the great national scientific corporate structures are now growing increasingly alert with regards to the next stage of the great Performance Game, abandoning responsible detachment and objectivity and scientific detachment for the new disciplines demanded by the support base of the now rapidly emerging supranational media and entertainment culture. A perfect example of the combining of "science" with these two sectors is provided by the work of Dr Gama Khan, of Tesco's Research Centre at Cheshunt. Dr Khan is tying to "design" the perfect cooked potato chip. He says:

> The perfect chip should spring open softly, similarly to the cushioned effect you find with the opening of glove boxes and cupholders in luxury cars.[33]

Over the past few years, many Fortean scientific episodes have included the closure by the House of Representatives of the $1.35 billion super-collidor. With a projected fifty-four-mile circumference, this monster had already flattened a town of 400 people, and was demanding a further $430 million for another year's continuous work. Its function (as advertised) was to "smash atoms together at speeds approaching that of light, recreating the immeasurably hot and dense conditions of the early universe." Perhaps future historians will regard such decayed and half-completed structures with the same awe as we regard the long neck of the giraffe, or the armoured weight of the rhinoceros, or the lintels of Stonehenge. The surrounding infrastructure of projects like the super-collider is reminiscent of the fractured planes of the perspectives of medieval maps. Perhaps, taking a hint from Fort, we should refer more to the warping of curves of meaning within strong scientific and techno-industrial perceptions. As well as usefully examining UFOs and inexplicable falls of tons of periwinkles, Fortean savants might like to look for example at the costs of the failed British Nimrod conversion, or the Pentagon's failed General York anti-aircraft tank, which must be the most expensive single project in military history, that is excepting the Rockwell B1 Lancer bomber, outdated by stealth technology, and hardly fully operational after many years of troubled development.

As record players, golf-ball typewriters, and still good 286/386 PCs now peer sadly from the tops of dustbins, a good consumer knows just exactly what Charles Fort means. What is unique about the systems that produce such loveable affectations is not their objective menace, such as communism or Nazism, but their equally dangerous and elusive promise of liberating both intellect and endeavour. This gradual breakdown of the best in us is far more tragic than the failure of the worst. If anything is to break the heart of our time, it is not the concentration camps and the atom bomb; it is that tragedy of great intellect[34] called science.

Charles Fort parodied scientists as Chaucer and Ben Jonson parodied alchemists, and Villon and Rabelais parodied Latinism. Like one of Solzhenitsyn's "voices from under the rubble", Fort wrote a *novum organum* of such a scientific fall, and predictably got little thanks for it. His own refusal to believe in anything that the great world told him is one of the great acts of liberating visionary courage of the twentieth-century. It is scandalously worse than even a refusal to buy, work, or view.

PART I

IMAGINATION WARS

A scientific priestcraft —

"Thou shalt not!" is crystallised in its frozen textbooks

I have data upon data of new lands that are not far away. I hold out expectations and the materials of new hopes and new despairs and new triumphs and new tragedies. I hold out my hands to point to the sky — there is a hierarchy that utters me manacles, I think — there is a dominant force that pronounces prisons that have dogmas for walls for such thoughts. It binds its formulas around all attempting extensions.

The Book of the Damned

1900 strange events

in

the bronx

There are few prizes in this world for penniless and starving men who sit in unheated rooms, surrounded by rejected manuscripts and the charred ruins of yet others, and yet still retain the strength of nerve to doubt if there is such a thing as a fact. But fortunately for the world, and unfortunately for facts, Charles Hoy Fort was such a man.

In the first years of our century, living in a run-down tenement room in the very poorest district of New York, Charles Fort sat surrounded by cardboard boxes full of over 40,000 notes of accounts of utterly fantastic events, culled from scientific journals and newspapers. Always near starvation and penury, Fort lived in constant danger of immediate eviction, but although surrounded by a similar noisy anarchic chaos to that which was in his boxes, he dedicated practically all his waking hours to flinging mud into the face of the scientific certainties of his time. The many anomalies which all his life he continued to find in the mechanistic and rational schemes of institutionalised belief were to form a terrifying vision of "reality" as far less stable than was ever thought. He spent practically all his life reading for many hours a day in libraries, museums, and archives, and he found and recorded thousands of anomalies as observed and reported throughout the world on land, sea, and in the air. He compiled observations of torpedo- and disc-shaped smoke-trailing objects in the skies throughout the nineteenth-century; of strange cattle injuries which looked more like extracted bio-samples than anything else; accounts of rains of frogs in Birmingham, on June 30, 1892; inscriptions on meteorites, black snow, blue moons, green suns, and showers of blood in the north-western part of Sienna on December 28, 1860.

Apart from numerous accounts of unidentified flying objects, mass panics, sightings of strange animals, winged beings, unaccountable explosions, and mysterious appearances and disappearances, he also dug out stories of both worms and stones falling from the skies of the world, together with sulphur, salt, coke, ashes, charcoal, various species of grain, combustible resinous substances, together with much material that quite defied analysis. Fort also gives us a few instances of reported ascents: two of washing from a line, one of sheets of paper, one of rubbish from a courtyard, two of stones from a field, and another of college students who clung to one of their friends to prevent him being taken upwards by some unknown force.

He called these recorded events "damned" in the sense that they did not seem to fit anywhere in the accepted universal scheme of things, and were therefore "rejected" by the scientific view. He was the first to take note of the singularity of the falls: things did not fall in a mix, as they would have to do to validate the frequently offered "whirlwind" explanation, but in *types*. Fort also found that such incidents frequently matched up with other strange phenomena experienced or observed at the same time, such as UFO sightings.

Tending these bizarre contradictions in the scheme of things rather like a zookeeper of fairy-forms, he referred to them as "little trollops and midgets, humpbacks and buffoons," and from his notes of such things in his many boxes, he claimed he could hear a "noisy silence" escaping. As Fort saw it, in its tragic need to over-simplify in order to try and understand phenomena, science blatantly ignored such deviant events, rather like a "watchman looking at half a dozen lanterns where a street's been torn up." This watchman, because of his chosen role and his closely defined system of reference, does not see "gas lights and kerosene lamps and electric lights in the neighbourhood: matches flaring, fires in stores, bonfires, house afire somewhere; lights of automobiles, illuminated signs"[1]. Louis Pauwels, the writer who translated Fort's first book, *The Book of the Damned*, into French, comments on the life of this eternal Faustian student:

> Principles, formulae, laws, phenomena of all kinds were devoured and digested at the New York Principal Library, at the British Museum, and also thanks to an enormous correspondence with all the biggest libraries and bookshops in the world. Result: forty thousand notes divided into thirteen hundred sections, written in pencil on minute scraps of paper in a stenographic language of his own invention. At the same time he resumes his enquiries into facts that have been rejected, but systematically this time, taking care to check and cross-check all his references. He plans his researches under headings covering astronomy, sociology, psychology, morphology, chemistry and magnetism...[2]

In his never-ending researches, Fort found an Aladdin's cave full of unexplained phenomena, some of which smacked of the very sinew of late Empire muscle. He discovered from all over the world reports of sky-falls of resin, amber, India rubber, various waxes and oils, butter, grease, woolly substances;

there was also material loosely identified in reports as nitric acid, turpentine, carbonate of soda; all appear to have fallen apparently from the sky at
various times, and some from quite fixed points in space. It is as if part of
the very heart of the nineteenth-century trade routes descended from the
heavens on occasion, for no rhyme or reason, and from nowhere in particular.
And there were considerable amounts of it: tons of dead fish, millions of
crabs, eels, shellfish, and minnows — all fall as if "the bottom of a super-
geographical pond had dropped out". In most cases Fort was able to record
the expert scientific reactions to such events, and found there, in the face of
this wonderfully unpredictable and theatrical display of amazing
impossibilities, a mundane and singular note that combined laughter, ridicule and denial.

Apart from his raging doubts about science, Fort's only other companions
were a few parakeets kept by Anna, his equally starving wife. Anna was an
Englishwoman from Sheffield, whom Fort married in 1896 when he was twenty-
two, and she was twenty-six. Fort was six feet tall and of a strong heavy build.
Anna, who at five-feet-four hardly came up to his shoulders, had known Fort
since she was thirteen. "I always loved him," she said to Dreiser, "but I never
thought I would marry him."

Tiffany Thayer gave Anna's maiden name as Filan, but on her marriage
certificate her name is Filing, and her parents are given as John Filing and
Catherine Haley of Sheffield. But as Damon Knight points out, "no record of
any Anna Filing or Filan born in those years can be found at Somerset House
or in the records of the Sheffield Borough Council."[3]

Anna's cooking was good, and Fort praised her home-brewed ale, but though
she was a kind and loving woman, she had little education and Fort's family
rather thought he married beneath him. She gave her middle-class husband mild
reproofs about his dress and his dislike of baths, and she beat him when
occasionally he squandered precious housekeeping money on getting drunk.
But nevertheless there was much love between them; Anna never chided her
husband for his complete lack of success in just about everything. Although
Tiffany Thayer, the founder of the Fortean Society, said that Anna "never read
his, or any other books," Damon Knight is of a different opinion. Referring to
the early years in London, he says, "In the evenings he read the latest chapters
of his books to Anna. They quarrelled sometimes over the marketing, about
which Fort was very particular."[4]

But at least the years in London after the Great War were better for the
Forts than the pre-1914 years in New York. In an interview with Theodore
Dreiser after the death of her husband, Anna said that there were times in those
days when they had to break up chairs for firewood, and Fort could not go out
looking for work in the rain, even to make one of his regular visits to the local
pawn-shop, because his shoes had practically no soles. Things improved somewhat for the couple when Fort's uncle Frank died in 1916 and the family estate
of Fort's grandfather Peter V. Fort passed to himself and two brothers, Raymond

1900
Strange
Events in
the Bronx

and Clarence. From this time Fort was just about financially independent. Things improved for him again when his brother Clarence died in 1917 and his share was divided between Charles and Raymond. Fort made wise investments in securities and real estate, though it is doubtful if he liked the title of this last entity.

Aaron Sussman,[5] who published *Lo!* in 1931, described Anna as "one of the most innocent innocents I have ever met". He visited Fort's apartment in the Bronx in 1930 and gave us a sketch of Anna just two years before her husband died. "She was a bustling, militant little hostess... she had a lovely way of speaking to you — she made you feel she was honoured and grateful that you had taken the time and trouble to come and see her."[6]

He recalls Fort himself as being "a very gentle man, inveterately polite, very tender towards Anna, most solicitous and concerned." Damon Knight confirms this general impression: "he had a deep voice and a booming laugh. He impressed Sussman as like Schweitzer or Einstein — withdrawn from the world, but enormously affectionate and interested in other people."

From 1905 to 1920 Fort did little else but sit in the New York Public Library gathering notes on unexplained phenomena. Between selling the occasional feature story to New York newspapers he worked intermittently in hotel kitchens, but as one of the great watchers of history, and even as a very resilient and extremely humorous man, he must have been depressed when on one occasion he was turned down as a night watchman by a local hotel. No doubt returning from many such disappointments to that "sanatorium of overworked coincidences" he called home, he would browse as he had browsed for years, through piles of journals and periodicals: *The American Almanac* of 1833; the *London Times* for the years 1880–93; the *Annual Record of Science*; twenty years' issues of the *Philosophical Magazine*; *Les Annales de la Societé Entomologique de France*, the *Monthly Weather Review*, *The Observatory* and the *Meteorological Journal*.

Throughout his four books we hear of poltergeist effects, of mysterious fires, and observations of airplanes before they were ever manufactured and flown. He is the very first serious reporter of unidentified undersea objects, and in forty years of collecting reports of such things he knew no rest. He gives reports of sightings of great extraplanetary geographies that disappear forever; we hear of stigmata, dowsing, fakirs, and comets that do not return as predicted. He tells us of cases of precognition, great strength, intuition, of knowledge of previous lives, mind-reading abilities, and the phenomenon of remote viewing. In our own time, we are only just beginning to take serious notice of such peculiar mental lop-sidedness in human beings, and to realise that Fort is also interesting because he is part of a fragmented, almost lost tradition. The writings of the Greek philosophers such as Pliny the Elder[7] all contain what could be call Forteana, as do the books of the traveller Marco Polo[8]. The bestiaries and natural histories of Edward Topsell[9] and Olaus Magnus[10] also contain much material that is "unexplained".

Professor Basil Willey[11] describes the seventeenth-century writer Sir Thomas Browne (1590–1645)[12] as living in an age "half scientific and half magical, looking back in one direction to Sir John Mandeville, and forward to Newton", adding that Browne talks of "unicorns and mermaids in a tone which implies that though part of him is incredulous, the world is still incalculable to contain such marvels."

Mandeville, author of a fourteenth-century book of travels, and who spoke of seeing the fountain of youth and anthills of gold dust, would certainly have warmed to read Fort comparing leading scientists such as Lord Kelvin to Chief Sitting Bull, or telling of worked iron implements found in lumps of coal; a bell-shaped vessel with floral designs on it made of an "unknown" metal, blasted from a bed of solid rock; a crystal lens found in the treasure-house at Nineveh; the discussion and listing of rains of almost every kind of substance; reports of the appearance of people from nowhere and the disappearance of people into nowhere; vitrified forts, and footprints found in Nicaragua under eleven strata of primordial rock; paranormal abilities, glimpses of unknown species of animals, teleportations, psychokinesis, miracles, levitations, and observations of both dark objects and semi-luminous objects, small and large, passing *slowly* in a controlled manner across the sun and moon.

Fort anticipated by over forty years the ideas of Desmond Leslie, Raymond Drake, Erich von Däniken, and George Hunt Williamson regarding "ancient astronauts", and from the 1960s onwards he was the influence on thousands of similar paperbacks in this area, many of which were mere paraphrases of Fort's then little-known pages, and frequently appeared without benefit of acknowledgement. Fort himself, as possibly the very first writer to consider seriously such fantastic claims outside the realms of entertaining fiction, knew from the start that the kind of opposition he would encounter would reach a religious level of fanatical opposition. He conceives of "materialistic science" as a "jealous god":

1900
Strange
Events in
the Bronx

> ... excluding, as works of the devil, all utterances against the seemingly uniform, regular, periodic; that to defy him would have brought on — withered by ridicule — shrinking away by publishers — contempt of friends and family — justifiable grounds for divorce — that one who would so defy would feel what unbelievers in relics of saints felt in an earlier age... quasi-existence strives for the positive state, aggregating, around a nucleus, or dominant, systemising members of a religion, a science, a society—[13]

Here, in plain form, is the first creation of the idea of a paradigm, which is that basic principle around which a culture or set of particular historical ideas forms itself. It later became the more familiar *programmatic* forms of our own time.

In between searching publications for choice telltale spores of the utterly fantastic, and taking his eternal notes, Fort would embalm butterflies and pickle grapes in whisky, but despite a popular view of him he was anything but a hermit. Before 1909, when he settled down to writing full-time, he had travelled widely in Britain, America and South Africa on a small income from a family-appointed guardian, Matthew Wallace. In his book *Prophet of the Unexplained*, Damon Knight gives a fascinating account of Fort's troubled relationship with his family, his early youth and education, and quotes from Fort's own account of his travels in the Albany *Argus*, of April 11, 1909:

> Southern Negroes, with the tatters and turbans; the white cabs of Cape Town, driven by coolies in white fezzes; the brown sails of vessels off the high, green-spread coast of Ireland; the pelicans of Tampa; a seal in the bay of Fundy; the glare of a steamer's wood fire on the banks of the Mississippi; going up the Firth of Clyde with a white village on one side and a red village on the other… All this, and never mind anything else, to fit myself for writing. Had a friend who was a prize-fighter; Jameson Raid; saw his belt brought back to Cape Town; bullet hole in it. The excitement of Cape Town, when the raid was on; factory whistles blowing at midnight.[14]

He knew every inch of New York, had friends in many of its tenements, docks, warehouses and saloons and, judging from some remarks to Theodore Dreiser, who managed to get *The Book of the Damned* published in the face of much opposition, Fort as a young man also knew plenty of what were then called houses of ill-fame.

In 1920, Fort (then forty-six years of age) came to live in London for six months with his wife. They lodged at 15 Marchmont Street, a short distance from the British Museum. Fort's mood at this time is best summed up by a letter written to Dreiser just before he left for Britain:

> Forces are moving me. I've cut ties with Albany, and published in the *Tribune* my dissatisfaction with the New York Public Library, so that I can't comfortably go back there, and have burned all my notes, 40,000 of them. Forces are moving me to London. Annie and I sail on the 27th. I have burned and destroyed and cut, but I have kept some letters — and may strange orthogenetic gods destroy me if I ever forget all that was done for me by Theodore Dreiser![15]

After returning to America for a few months to settle family business, the Forts were back in London by December 1921, lodging at 39 Marchmont Street, in rooms over a fruit shop. For the next eight years, Fort was to spend most of his time in the British Museum writing three other books that eventually appeared as *New Lands*, *Wild Talents* and *Lo!* He was a frequent visitor to Speaker's Corner, had many friends there, and is reported to have spoken himself on occasion. Damon Knight in an interview with Anna after Fort's death, describes their life at this time:

> Fort settled into a routine: up at eight, work on his notes till lunchtime; off

to the Museum at two, back at five. After supper, four or five times a week, he would take Anna to the movies; other evenings he went to Hyde Park, where he had found a congenial group of loungers to argue with. Said Anna, "Charlie left every night at nine when I came to meet him, after wandering around the park. The men used to make fun of him going home at nine, but he had had enough of it by this time. He liked solitude... He did not want anyone to come in, and he did not want to go out."[16]

But in those days, whether in New York or London, the conditions of what were called "lodgings" made it quite impossible to be a hermit. Universally in those days the sinks, lavatories and bathrooms were on a common staircase, and there was no limit to the number of people who could be accommodated in just one small sub let room, which was often sub let in turn by some other sub tenant. If he ever did wish to be left quite alone, perhaps Fort would invite baffled callers to play "super-checkers", this being a board game he had designed himself, with 1,600 squares. Any callers hardy enough to take up his offer were probably even more baffled when they were told that this game, rather like Fort's view of science, was a game in which anyone could cheat in any way they liked. In this atmosphere, it was only possible to be a hermit inside the self, and perhaps that is what Fort was. Paradoxically, despite his obvious enthusiasms about his travels, the very model of mind he was to go on to construct shows the outer shell of social consciousness as a dumb show, a complete falsehood. This became for him that unique twentieth-century institution called the Official Reality, that home of "Dogmatic Science" with its scarecrow head stuffed full of "scientific" straw:

1900
Strange
Events in
the Bronx

> So it is, that having attempted to systemise, by ignoring externality to the greatest possible degree, the notion of things dropping in upon this earth, from externality, is as unsettling and as unwelcome to science as — tin horns blowing in upon a musician's relatively symmetric composition — flies alighting upon a painter's attempted harmony, and tracking colours into another — a suffragist getting up and making a political speech at a prayer meeting.[17]

Damon Knight described the man who made such statements as "a sturdy young man, somewhat plump-faced, with curly hair and an absurd pince-nez, a little like Teddy Roosevelt". Louis Pauwels[18] sketched him in the late 1920s as looking like a "large shy seal". Wearing his green eye-shade, a fire-paranoid Fort would frequently follow his quite capable wife to the kitchen, apparently to make sure she did not set light to anything and thus create a danger to his boxes full of notes. Pauwels adds, "His hands were round and plump, his figure paunchy, and he had no neck, a big head growing bald, a large Asiatic nose, iron-rimmed spectacles, and moustaches *á la* Gurdjieff." Tiffany Thayer, in his Introduction to *The Books of Charles Fort*, is somewhat more complimentary. As Fort talked the night away

... it often occurred to me that his frame called for leather and buckles, that the board should have been bare and brown, washed by slops from heavy tankards and worn smooth by heavy sword-hands. The light should have been from flambeaux — to match our words — Faust and Villon should have stopped by in passing on their way to murder or conference with the devil.

These tenement scenes must have been like Alfred Jarry[19] producing Woody Allen in a kind of *Eraserhead* of the 1900s. We are back in the shaky, Chaplinesque black-and-white film frames of the period as we imagine the very walls of the Forts' sparsely furnished rented rooms lined with shoe-boxes full of tens of thousands of notes of strange happenings, such as a flying iceberg which fell in fragments on Rouen on July 5, 1853; winged beings observed at a height of 8,000 metres in the sky above Palermo on November 30; luminous wheels seen in the sea, remains of giants in Scotland, and coffins of little creatures seemingly from another world, found in cliffs at Edinburgh.

Tiffany Thayer describes the Forts' Bronx apartment at 2051 Ryer Avenue:

On the walls of the flat were framed specimens of giant spiders, butterflies, weird creatures adept at concealment, imitating the sticks and leaves to which they were affixed. There was also framed a photograph beside a hail-stone, both objects the same size, sent to Fort by a correspondent, and — under glass — a specimen of some stuff that looks dirty, shredded asbestos which had fallen from the sky in quantities covering several acres.[20]

Damon Knight completes the picture:

Fort worked in a small, dark room overlooking a courtyard; it contained an old oak desk, a typewriter, a bookcase, and a stack of cardboard boxes filled with notes. After a morning spent in the library, he usually worked here until five. Four or five times a week, he and Anna went to the movies after supper. His favourite actress was Lillian Gish.[21]

In these circumstances, if ever a wife engaged sympathy it was Anna Fort. Her husband, when he was not talking of such things, or writing short stories which were mostly rejected, would on occasion actively destroy not only his boxes of carefully collected notes, but also the vast novels he had written. One novel, *The Outcast Manufacturers*, was, however, published in 1909, and received good reviews. The book was said to be well ahead of its time and was favourably compared to the work of Ring Lardner and Sinclair Lewis, but alas, it brought him practically no income and went out of print rapidly.

When he was not writing, browsing, despairing, starving, or destroying his literary efforts, Fort spent most of his time in the reading rooms of public libraries, looking for even stranger things than he had found already. What his long-suffering wife said when her husband brought home stacks of tales about sea-monsters, mysterious fires and poltergeists on a winter's night in New York, instead of fuel, money or food, can only be guessed. Like the consump- tive Kafka, the tubercular D. H. Lawrence, and the almost-blind and anaemic James Joyce, Charles Fort definitely would not have been seen as eugenically fit for the burnished muscularity of the great new goal-directed, fact-driven, scientific society being built at a breakneck pace around him. If ever there was a candidate to be taken away at dawn for political re-education, it was Charles Fort. He not only refused to believe, he was further intent on deprogramming any "fact" virus that might have got into his system. Culturally isolated, he was surrounded by a world hostile to the realms of what he frequently called forbid- den knowledge — this being to him anything but "illusions," "fantasies," and "lies." These cat calls were undoubtedly screamed at him by a simple-minded and intellectually brutal world, convinced that science had the ultimate key to the interpretation of all phenomena, and all else had been swept aside. As history was bunk to Henry Ford, science to Charles Fort was as full of meta- physical rubbish, mystical nonsense and irrationality, as was all else in the cosmos. He could never see for the life of him why people used the phrase "it is in his imagination" when each and every thing existed in the imagination, including the blessed "facts" of scientists.

Fort's family, originally Dutch, had been in the United States for many genera- tions. His father was Charles Nelson Fort, the descendant of an old Dutch family, who were well-respected and prosperous merchants of Albany.[22] But though his family and national identity were firmly established, Charles Fort did not travel widely in America. He stayed in New York looking East to Europe, as if he had accepted that the mentality of an immigrant was to be with him forever. Though he wasn't Jewish, in the grainy black and white photographs of the period he looks like the classic Jewish intellectual of the time, fleeing from Warsaw or Moscow, bleeding with Dostoevskian wounds as he bled as a young boy from his father's beatings, and without any mother to run to.[23]

1900
Strange
Events in
the Bronx

   The shadow of father-denial was with Fort all his life. His male parent was to become Fact, the Official Reality, and Truth as received from all Established Authority. All these things became for him dread forms of an intellectual Satan. Thus Fort was a prototype early modern. He could be described as the Ameri- can Existential Hero Mk 1, with "exile" written on his brow as the mark of Cain. He had freed himself from the pre-industrial landscapes of Melville and Whitman, and had arrived at the very beginning of the twentieth-century with a head full of rejected wiring diagrams. He walked the streets of turn-of-the-century New York like the young Charles Chaplin, with a bundle of equally rejected manu- scripts under his arm. As Karl Marx had walked Paris and London generations before him, Fort was as near death and despair as a man can be, yet with a similar messianic soaring brain as Marx, and no soles on his battered shoes.

   In the pre-electric charcoal dark of the early nights of the twentieth-century, as gas lamps in New York or London were turned on one by one, he could have been mistaken for a figure from the stories of Kafka, Isaac Bashevis Singer, or indeed from Joyce's *Dubliners*. He lived his early life in New York also surrounded by the Irish, who at this time regarded themselves as a race as exiled as the Jews. Certainly Fort became the guardian of something both Catholic and indeed Talmudic in conception: *the questioning of the idea of the omnipotence and truth of fact and all materiality*. His work was also born of such a deep subjectivity: every second of his entire life was religiously dedicated to demonstrating that the world of objective social consciousness was a complete and blatant imposture.

If Jewishness did affect him, communism did not. For communists on the platforms in every great city of the world at this time, the enemy was the ruling class; but for Fort it was burgeoning science, that great fellow-travelling philosophy of "social-scientific" communism. Dying in 1932, he did not see his dread prophecies come to pass. The struggles, the counter-claims, the ideology, the murders and the many revolutions, all the screaming flood of nineteenth-century conflicts, were to finish in the burnt-out wiring-diagram worlds of Auschwitz and Hiroshima. There the nineteenth-century proper ended, and the last "committed writer" Arthur Miller jumped from the nineteenth-century into the twentieth and married Marilyn Monroe. In doing so, Miller saw the birth of an age that would have surprised both Marx and Fort: an age of media and entertainment in which both the old visible ruling class and the old industrial equations vanished into the powerful alchemy of corporate conspiracies with the entertainment/glamour complex as a controlling programme. Marx would have despaired, but Fort would have seen that his prophecies had been correct. Here indeed was an age ruled and controlled not by fact but by image and advertising, and the deep-laid plots of the military-technological-entertainment establishment.

But sitting half-starved in his tenement block in the year before WWI, Fort could only speculate on this coming world. He spent his time for the most part surrounded by boxes of what most people would have regarded as fairy stories. Attacked on all fronts by every kind of personal, social and financial instability, when considered by a good betting man, the battle between David and Goliath would be even odds compared with Charles Fort viewed as an enemy of say, the philosophy of Henry Ford. But according to accounts, for the most part Fort was anything but depressed, and a visitor would perhaps listen to him telling with glee of extraordinary things: the unbelievable strength of Betsy Ann Talks, who could easily lift a 500lb barrel high in the air; of fifteen-year-old Lulu Hurst, who threw 200lb men about without going near them; of Mary Richardson, who, sitting in a chair, defied the combined efforts of thirteen men who tried to move her; of Angelique Cottin, who could whirl about any object in a room without going near it; of Annie Abbot, who could be easily lifted by one man one moment, then not even by six men the next. Perhaps he would also read out some of his notes, telling of the spectacular healing powers of John Reese with his tens of thousands of cures, including his successful treatment of both Lloyd George and Winston Churchill. In between telling of his prophetic ideas about very early media-manipulation and mass mind-control, he might also have told of the Chinese seals or cubes of jade, each with an animal carved upon it, found over a wide area in Ireland, Roman coins in Indian burial mounds in North America, and even the strange appearances and disappearances of the Barbary apes of the Rock of Gibraltar.

Although most of Fort's references are to the nineteenth-century, he lived long enough to comment on Einstein, "moving-pictures," wireless, and quantum theory. Just before he died in 1932, his last book *Wild Talents* shows him to be aware of the discovery of the Appleton Layer, and also on the verge of grasping the principles of high-frequency radio direction finding, which later became "radar". He had a good grasp of basic calculus, and as *Lo!* and *New Lands* show in particular, he had a quite astonishing knowledge of the optical astronomy and celestial mechanics of his time. He was also fascinated by the wilder experiments of Marconi, Harry Hawker, Tesla, and Sir Oliver Lodge. He was also prophetically curious about Boolean algebra, which during the 1900s was an almost forgotten mathematical logic. Not all that long after Fort's death in 1932, this was to be picked up by Alan Turing and made the basis of that digital computing which was to crack the German Enigma code.

But these wide scientific and technological interests were not due to any positive enthusiasm on Fort's part. He saw all such theories and the burgeoning twentieth-century systems they were rapidly giving rise to, as outright oppression. The assumption of all "objective" thinking is that though it may indeed be difficult, finally it is possible to separate completely fact from fiction. Charles Fort simply did not believe that such a thing was possible. For him, all thinking is mythological, inescapably built of fantasy structures of varying degrees of "solidity." In this world model, a picture of Atlas bearing the globe of the Earth on his shoulders is as true a picture of "causation" as any creaking and anomaly-strewn apparatus of gravity mixed with electro magnetism mixed with orbit-wobbles, mixed with quantum-jumps and gravity-waves. His outrageous sense of humour might well have had him saying that the Atlas cosmos was also a damned sight more interesting, had glamour, mystery and elegance, and certainly far greater class than any gravity wave, big bang, or string theory.

1900 Strange Events in the Bronx

Fort is perhaps best known for his discovery of the falls of various substances from the sky. By relating the many falls of strange material to the differing spectrum of human reaction to them, he found that the degree of "exclusivity" (by that he meant the degree to which the significance of the strange is "vanished" or "managed" or "controlled" in the more modern social-psychological sense), varies directly according to the power of any vested interest of the observing group; he sees "wonder" itself become, therefore, a managed "commodity," as much as any other "consumer" supply. In this he can be seen as a most post-modern philosopher. As such, his ideas are applicable to our own consumer/entertainment society, and shows how all our thinking is pregnant with "advertising" of myriad forms, all advertising of course being essentially mythological in substance and form:

> The fall of sulphur from the sky has been especially repulsive to the modern orthodoxy — largely because of its associations with the superstitions or principles of the preceding orthodoxy — stories of devils: sulphurous exhalations. The power of the exclusionists lies in that in their stand are combined both modern and archaic systematists. Falls of sandstone and limestone are repulsive to both theologians and scientists. Sandstone and limestone suggest other worlds upon which occur processes like geological processes; but limestone, as a fossiliferous substance, is of course, especially of the unchosen.[24]

Thus in a Fortean world "objectivity" is revealed as the myth of *intellectuality* itself, producing its own highly specialised fables, which become cell-like worker-bee warriors in an imagination war. That we project ourselves into our knowledge systems, which in turn become mirrors of our ever-evolving selves, is well described by Barthes in his essay *The Brain of Einstein*,[25] written fifty years *after* Charles Fort's death:

> Einstein's brain is a mythical object... the product of his inventiveness came to acquire a magical dimension, and gave a new incarnation to the old esoteric image of a science entirely contained in a few letters. There is a single secret to the world, and this secret is held in one word; the universe is a safe of which humanity seeks the combination: Einstein almost found it, this is the myth of Einstein. In it, we find all the Gnostic themes: the unity of nature, the ideal possibility, the unfastening power of the world, the age-old struggle between a secret and an utterance, the idea that total knowledge can be discovered all at once, like a lock which suddenly opens after a thousand unsuccessful attempts.

This well describes the sense in which Fort saw, long before Barthes, that "certainties," "accuracies," "facts," and "rational truths," are projections of modern, updated mythologies. Fort even predicts that favourite creature of modern chaos theory, the butterfly, whose one wing-flutter can change the weather over the south of England: "Scientists are contractions of metaphysicians, in their local searches for completeness, and in their statements that, except for infinitesimal errors, plus or minus, completenesses have been found."[26]

This rounding off of the rough edges of observation and experience to fit generalised theories whilst chaos prowls around beyond the light of the cavemouth fires, reveals science as a most temporary refuge, whose mental barricades often consist of the equivalent kind of B-feature comic junk with which we usually fill mental vacancy. If we see this now, at the time Fort was writing there was little or no thinking about science being just as metaphysical-mythological as any other system of conceptual organisation. No wonder Fort was isolated and almost completely ignored, as was Barthes himself for nearly thirty years, *Mythologies*, written in the early 1950s, not being translated into English until 1972. Seeing purely intellectual constructions as highly wrought consumer products both in the early part of the century was a view too far in advance of its time. Fort shows that cultures, almost as live entities, require advertising to "sell" their products. Long before television, he showed that forces of mass persuasion such as science need advertising (just as do soap and shoes) in order to secure longevity as control mechanisms. As both Fort and Barthes show, in science as in showbusiness, glamour plays a part in the mythologising process that is the securing of "fact". In modern studies, "glamour" is only now being recognised as a socio-historical force just as valid as economics, geo-politics, or practical inventions. As glamour, fickle as always, declines, so does that mythologisng power which puts things on pedestals by means of a cultural hypnosis which is only just beginning to be understood, even in our own very much more glamour- and media-oriented entertainment state.

Fort's great example in support of this idea is the optical astronomy of the nineteenth-century. Although it managed to struggle on for many years, he is of the opinion that optical astronomy really died in the late nineteenth-century because these "scientists" really belonged to the sepia images of Lytton Strachey, rather than to the grease-smeared diagrams of well-thumbed electrical manuals. We can list a thousand mechanical forces, yet style exists in mythological time, and it will beat "fact" hands down in any Darwinian competition; not that "fact" will be dead, it will merely transform itself, hop to another branch, change its plumage, and even ask glamour for aid.

1900
Strange
Events in
the Bronx

In this sense, the Fortean view of nineteenth-century optical astronomy is not that what it "revealed" about nature was true or false, good, bad, or even indifferent, but that it became like all "objective" systems, a kind of intellectual rhino-horn: almost completely redundant, certainly beautiful and awe-inspiring, but a loser in ideological game-evolution.

the yarns
of
dickens and euclid

The twentieth-century in particular has always had a problem with the imagination. It somehow refuses to be safely corralled, distanced, conveniently half-castrated, and hung on a wall as a set of pretty colours. As if in fear of the mysterious and little-understood forces of imagination, all societies in their own way practice different kinds of fantasy limitation to try and maintain socio-psychological stability. In Fort's view, these limiting controls frequently take the form of explanations, these being in our own time increasingly "scientific" in nature. Such explanations form those great institutionalised systems of belief by means of which we control our causal relations, evaluate our moral life, and define our world-view. We equate these systems with solidity, with permanent worth, and we like to think that they enshrine some objective "factual" truths about our society, our culture, and ourselves.

But startlingly original ideas rarely present a complimentary and comforting picture of the human condition and its predicament. In a Fortean world, "facts" hardly exist: "the unadulterated, whether of the food we eat, or the air we breathe, or of idealism, or of villainy, is unfindable. Even adultery is adulterated."

Therefore, said he, his books were fictions in the sense that Dickens' *Pickwick Papers*, Swift's *Gulliver's Travels*, Newton's *Principia*, and Darwin's *Origin of Species* and every history of the United States and all other histories are fictions. In *Wild Talents* he continues:

> There is something about the yarns told by Dickens that sets them apart, as it were, from the yarns that were told by Euclid. There is much in Dickens' grotesqueries that has the correspondence with experience that is called

'truth,' whereas such Euclidean characters as 'mathematical points' are the vacancies that might be expected from a mind that has had scarcely any experience.[1]

Instead of "facts" as structural elements of consciousness, he prefers what might be termed a scale of experience along which an almost convincing permanence and "solidity" varies according to the character of cultural change, and the growth and decay of group interests, feelings, and relations.

> Though I have classed myself with some noted fictionists, I have to accept that the absolute fictionist never has existed. There is a fictional coloration to everybody's account of an 'actual occurrence,' and there is at least the lurk somewhere of what is called the 'actual' in everybody's yarns.

Such artificial distinctions, in Fortean terms, have to be continuously sustained in order for them to pose and remain as valid belief-scales at all. But within the terms of the ordering of this scale, the simple question of the "real" versus the "unreal" pales before the much more vital question of *exhaustion* within a kind of economy of belief. This can only be sustained in balance by practising a skilful game of not seeing as well as seeing. But historically, the energies and resources for such illusions, shot through with anomalies, runs out; as with nineteenth-century optical astronomy, the stage-fronts wear thin, and optical astronomy in turn joins the fascinating architectonics of the dead matter of Ptolemaic machinery, mediaeval heavens and hells, or the inadequacies of pre-quantum physics, before the next season of cultural games begins.

The yarns of Dickens and Euclid

Thus his "imp" notes in cardboard boxes represented to Fort much more than a mere catalogue of things science laughed at and rejected out of hand. These things (a large proportion culled from scientific journals, no less) were not "untrue" or "unreal", so much as they were (and still are)[2] parts of rejected design solutions, half-realised, undernourished systems-doodles, like the UFO, or even the ghost-figure with its head under its arm. Moreover, these bits and pieces of half-forms of mental driftwood have a dynamic relationship with the development of ideological systems. Putting together various and often hilarious, professorial encounters with strange substances (especially mushroom-like growths), Fort depicts scenes in which it looks as if the substances are finding the professors, and not vice versa. The substances seem to change their form in a kind of guessing game, particularly with the astute academic mind which demands categorisations, definitions, and what it calls "concrete evidence" — although when given such, Fort shows the evidence being frequently denied in order to fit preset criteria. What he criticises is not so much the inability to cope with anomalies, as the attempt to camouflage the inability, and also the complete failure to see the connections between particular incidents.[3]

Giving time, location, and reference, Fort shows a connection between meteorites and storms and the falls of what look like small artificially-shaped objects of various materials, some unidentified. He shows also that lights in the sky are accompanied frequently by the sighting of material falling from the sky. This is often "gelatinous or viscous matter", that is material which looks like frog-spawn; then there are jellyfish which fall from the sky, also "minute worms in filmy envelopes," precision-cut flakes of an unknown organic material, fibrous material, and most frequently material that is simply labelled as a "coniferous mass". Two-hundred square foot sheets of a substance similar to cotton-felt once descended in Siberia, and there are reports from all over the world of the fall of alkaline fibres, powders, grains, oily lumps of different colours, masses of cobwebs, masses of stinking stuff somewhat like "butter or grease", ashes, "carbonaceous matter," bituminous coal, and sulphur. There is also stuff identified as nitric acid and carbonate of soda; there are also turpentine, liquids that tasted like sugar, rosewater, slag, coke, and charcoal. And then there are the live things: frogs, fish, worms, snakes, eels, lizards, snails, and even on one occasion[4] a piece of alabaster accompanied by the fall of *a gopher turtle* from the skies above Vicksburg, Mississippi. In this instance, Fort shows himself as comically hesitant to mention what even *he* regards as "fantastic", because rumour had it that this turtle "hovered for six months or so over a small town".

Reports from all over the world showed that when fish fall they do so from a very specific limited area of the sky, and for the most part in straight lines. In most instances, the fish are alive and fresh, but sometimes they are "stinking and headless". Rather than "fall", some of these creatures just appear. In Memphis Tennessee, on January 15, 1877, thousands of snakes were found crawling "in a space of two blocks," but "none were found on roofs or any other elevation above ground," and "none were seen to fall."

Knowing that folk who report such things are often called liars, Fort comically defended himself by claiming that he himself was "outside the field of ordinary liars."[5] He relates a story from the *New York World* of July 29, 1908, saying that whilst detectives were investigating some street robberies in the neighbourhood of Lincoln Avenue, Pittsburgh on the 26th:

> ... a big, black dog sauntered past them. "Good morning!" said the dog. He disappeared in a thin, greenish vapour. There will be readers who will want to know what I mean by turning down this story, while accepting so many others in this book. It is because I never write about marvels. The wonderful, or the never-before-heard-of, I leave to whimsical, or radical, fellows. All books written by me are of quite ordinary occurrences.[6]

The nineteenth-century strove with might and main to excommunicate such anarchic events from its ordered consciousness, the professorial eyes of the time denying anything and everything just as their equivalents do today. Again in a similar fashion to our own time, the explanations produced were more fantastic than the phenomena themselves. Round about 1875 there was a fall of thousands of tons of ashes round about the Azores, and a Professor Daubree wrote in the 1875 issue of *Annual Record of Science* that these ashes had come from a huge fire which had ranged in the city of Chicago. However, even the nineteenth-century could protest on occasion at such preposterousness. The editor of the *Record* himself, in the issue of 1876, comments that it would be "in the highest degree improper to say that the ashes of Chicago were landed in the Azores".

The yarns
of Dickens
and Euclid

stories

about

stories

If, like most of his many imitators, Fort had given us merely lists of largely comic marvels, his work would have been no more important than say, such fascinating historical curiosities as Tottel's *Miscellany*, Froissart's *Chronicles* or Percy's *Reliques*. What he had thousands of examples of in the boxes stacked in his bare and threatened rooms is of course wonderfully inspiring nonsense, and no-one knew better than he that most of it was almost complete rubbish, the word "almost" in Fort's vocabulary being very important, for as he sees it, there are no absolute states of anything, since if there were, there could be no transference of one thing to another. But yes, in "scientific" terms there was certainly hardly any proper evidence for most of it; many of these tall tales at any time are without doubt founded on rumour, lies, insubstantial wish fulfilment and bar room jokes. But that only serves to make Fort's point. To him, these endlessly generated bastard spirals of ill-conceived and half-digested wasteful almost-stories were more accurate as maps of a live, active and endlessly creating consciousness than the over-simplified models of scientific inputs and outputs. Deceptions, frauds, mistakes *et al*, these represented a "reality" which is not objective in that they involve mind constantly losing, yet constantly rediscovering (often painfully) a vital dialogue with nature through a relationship which involves play, evasion, active deception, mimicking, acting, trying things out.

Fort drew a monumental picture of scientists almost squirming with panic and embarrassment before such an unstable state of affairs, desperately trying to snap-shoot some minute part of such process for just one fleeting out-of-focus picture. From the Fortean point of view, such a camera is one of those "clocks" and "measuring-rods" both Einstein and Eddington used demonstratively in their arguments to give the idea of "pointer readings" as descriptions of experience. But from the post-modern point of view, the camera itself consists equally of waste, fantasy, dead-ends, decayed illusory certainties, tempting accuracies, structures from other lives, half-glimpses of future almost-lives, as both consciousness, experience, technological product, and measuring-systems themselves move sideways, backwards, and up and down at the same time. Fort had what we now call a post-modern view of instrumentation: any camera is hence deep historical background in which "fact" and "fiction", technology, action and intent, merge into complete symbiosis in Fort's view of mind. This mind-stuff he pictures as being rather like "A super-sea of Sargasso," full of "derelicts, rubbish, old cargoes from interplanetary wrecks", and "things from the time of the Alexanders, Caesars, and Napoleons of Mars, or Jupiter, or Neptune". To point out that such a level of highly-wrought imaginative complexity may work with inefficiency, a certain level of anarchy, positively evil motivations, and even downright charlatanism, to often play a part in deciding what is "real", was to strike a blow against the materialistic science of Fort's day in its grossly over-simplified view of human mentality. That what we so glibly call "the higher reasoning" may have to work its way through "things raised by this Earth's cyclones: horses and barns and elephants and flies, and dodos, pterodactyls and moas; leaves from modern trees and leaves from the carboniferous era, accumulations of centuries, cyclones of Egypt, Greece, and Assyria", and may have to use these things somehow as vital elements of complex reasoning, can hardly be considered by AI programmers today, because it is impossible to create even fuzzy, or neural (still less binary) paradigms for such disparate levels of mental entropy.

Stories about Stories

In any case, there would be no prizes for the programmer who created something which wastes as much time and plays as many doubtful tricks as does the human brain and the changing levels of its never-ending story-machine, both conscious and unconscious. Were artificial intelligence ever to approach even a reasonable approximation to human intelligence, the industrialists who inevitably finance such projects would be very disappointed. Such a level of AI would want to play, take time off, smash things, tell tall stories, indulge in libellous prattle, fail completely or say to itself as Oscar Wilde did, that "nothing is of the slightest importance".

Far worse than all of these things put together, such a mind might even withdraw its labour indefinitely. It might even reveal people telling quarter-truths like the scientists, half-truths like Charles Fort, and three-quarter-truths like some of the great heroes of humanity, and that would not do at all: "I do not know how to find out anything new without being offensive." As intelligence approaches anything like an approximation to "reality" (and to Fort "reality" was always an approximation) it approached trouble: "Every science is a mutilated octopus. If its tentacles were not clipped to stumps, it would feel its way into disturbing contacts."

Fort's view of mental activity is therefore of anything but a singular, tidy, operation: he opposes behaviourism, finite Pavlovian action-reactions, any kind of functioning seen as an isolation, and is in direct opposition to the depressing pathologies of the prevailing Freudian school. Of what, Fort asks, do "thinking" and "reality" consist, when certain imbalanced superfluities occur whose very blatancy causes us to ignore, even deny them? With regard to the many accounts of tons of what looked like furnace slag washed up on the sea shore of Slaines, Scotland during May of 1862, he speculates upon a passing extraterrestrial source:

> Slag washed up on the Scottish coast — to have produced so much of it would have required the united output of all the smelting works in the world… my notion is that of an island near an oceanic trade-route: it might receive debris from passing vessels.[1]

Why not indeed? But an important political battle emerges with that question — Fort's thinking is not so simple as to be merely a plea to replace one theory with another, as much as a general plea to try to see both mind and world in all their wondrous and very often subversive and paradoxical complexity, rather than seeing the cosmos as essentially mundane. For space ships, read angels; it really doesn't matter. In a Fortean universe, what is *thought* will in some form appear, though in an absurd, partial, unexpected, and frequently comic form: like the absurd strength of the women performers previously mentioned, or the idea that Kaspar Hauser was an impostor when, Fort says, there can be no such thing as a *complete* impostor: "I believe nothing of my own that I have ever written. I cannot accept that the products of minds are subject-matter for beliefs."

Such a world model which recognises only degrees of tragi-comic *fictions* within imaginative projections, rather than "objectivities" is disturbing of course to those of sober mien and rational disposition. Science is a reflection of that human view which would valiantly wish nature into being a completely serious, coherent, well-directed, fair-playing entity that has a clearly definable direction and purpose. The idea of *play* and even active *deception* as being essential components in the relationship between mind and nature is more or less ruled out as philosophically absurd; scientific methods, since they are essentially locked into paradigms of work, worth, and conscious studied application, can never analyse the psychological function of a complete waste of time. As yet (with possibly the exception of Bergson's essay, *Le Rire*, and some rather loose and hesitant chapters of Koestler), there is no psychology of laughter. Neither is there a psychology that sees deviance and fantasy as being anything but positively pathological: that is, as things we must "cure" ourselves of in order to regain the "health" of "factual truth".

Within such a system of intellectual eugenics, neither science nor religion could ever possibly conceive of truth as being comic. Yet Fort's scientists are wonderfully comic figures. They come on stage like old music hall comedians to reveal their beloved "breakthroughs", "advances," and "important dis-coveries" most of which poison land, sea, air, and earth. More often than not, their equally beloved statistics are concerned with row upon row of the unburied victims of the "conquest of nature".

In this, it seems that wonder, play, and laughter are always political dyna-mite. Not only are they largely inaccessible to science, but they also signify freedom, whereas the mundane and the "factual" offers only psychological enslavement in terms of mass guilt. In Samuel Beckett's play *Endgame*, a character describes visiting a friend in a mental home. He takes his friend to a window that looks out to sea, and shows him the herring fleet coming in from the sea at sunset. The patient then turns from the window. All he had seen were ashes. In a sense both Beckett and Fort here are talking about guilt so deep that even if their particular versions of Plato's cave walls were to melt away, humanity would reinvent them as *controls*.

Science, that "accumulated lunacy of fifty centuries", is *political* control over the world of appearances. In Fort's terms, science secured such control by being essentially the supreme art of beautifully structured mundane things; some of these he pictures frequently as works of art in themselves, being incredible structures of not-seeing, rather like the searched-for box of matches which is not seen although right before the eyes, because the mind is mo-mentarily elsewhere. If, says Fort, "a monster from somewhere else should arrive upon the land of this earth, and perhaps being out of adaptation, should die upon land, it would not be seen."

Stories about Stories

In his mighty blasts at rationalism, common sense, and reason, Fort por-trays science and objectivity as monstrous conspiracies against wonder, inno-cence, love, and all imaginative transcendence. In this, he regarded science as a kind of emerging dialectical Newspeak of his time. He wanted to show its dogmatic puritanism which, even in those early days before the Great War, was emerging as the mental equivalent to a kind of brainwashing semi-commu-nist Christianity, complete with politically correct explanations: such things being regarded by Fort as the modern equivalent to forced religious confes-sions of the past. He also takes good care to temper his own anti-scientific puritanism with good humour:

> If a red-hot stove should drop from a cloud into Broadway, someone would find that at the time of the occurrence, a moving van had passed, and that the moving men had tired of the stove, or something — that it had not been really red-hot, but had been rouged instead of blacked, by some absent-minded housekeeper. Compared with some of the scientific explanations that we have encountered, there's considerable restraint, I think, in that one.[2]

As for any extraterrestrial visitors, they would, in a typical Fortean progress, decline by going up in the world:

Throw-backs, translated to this earth, would not, unless intensely atavistic, take to what we regard as vices, but to what their own far-advanced people regard as perhaps unmentionable, or anyway, unprintable, degradations. They would join our churches, and wallow in pews. They'd lose all sense of decency and become college professors. Let a fall start, and the decline is swift. They'd end up as members of Congress.

enter

sonnabend

Just as reports of most peculiar events fled to Fort's shabby rooms for seeming refuge, early twentieth-century writers fled to the ghettos in droves. Indeed many such still dwell therein. They pulled the disturbed night over themselves before sleep as some magical cloak of protection against the best and the worst intentions of plan, philosophy, and rationale beginning to be sold by the first flickering screens around them.

But at the turn of the nineteenth-century everything, everybody, was fleeing: the old world had fled, the populations were fleeing, and would continue to flee for three decades after Fort's death; ideas, art and literature were also on the move; what were they all running from? They were running from science and the first embryo forms of two other monsters: socialism, national and international. Now the second pair are both dead, and the first, like many a nineteenth-century clergyman, is having doubts. This mass evacuation of bodies and souls can now be seen as an expanded metaphor describing a battle against the armoured ranks of the gathering forces of twentieth-century mass persuasion.

Fort spent his time not in the America of golden legend, but virtually in the midst of fleeing Europe, seeing Europe's destitute mass arrive practically on his equally destitute doorstep. He might well have been living not in New York, but on the quayside of one of the great European embarkation ports, thronged with hundreds of thousands of the fleeing European peasantry, ready to sail to the promised land with one bag, half a hope, and sometimes no shoes.

Fort's New York was also the world of the young Henry Miller, another great outsider, and in both writers there can be felt a similar intensity of anarchic, ghetto-like excitements from this period, and also a feeling of existential separateness from the simple-minded Henry Ford world, where everything just ate everything else. Both in his atmospheric short stories, and in the novel, *The Outcast Manufacturers*, Fort wrote of the poor, the exiled, and the thoughtful, who had absolutely no choice but to grovel in the dust, and go out into the soulless commercial and industrial materialistic society that was being built rapidly around them. With a very unhappy childhood behind him, Fort can be seen as he sits in his sparsely furnished rooms as rather like Dostoevsky's character in *The Strange Fellow*; though smiling perhaps, he is virtually alone, and most times near starvation, almost with a pistol on a nearby table, with only his intellectual disgust to feed upon. And, just like the countless penniless refugees around him, Fort had only his imagination as a resource to plot a new world.

What we know about this figure at the table in the years immediately before the Great War is that he is a very good writer, and yet his fiction is either unpublished, or largely unsuccessful, for any reason other than its quality. This is a pretty good picture of the mood and condition at this time of a lot of men who, many years later, were to become some of the illustrious names of our century. Damon Knight, quoting from Fort's diary of December 1907, shows his position to be very similar to that of D. H. Lawrence or James Joyce in this same period, and will sound more than familiar bells to many present-day mute inglorious Miltons:

> Have not been paid for one story since May. Have two dollars left. Watson [the family solicitor] has cheated me out of $155. Dreiser has sent back two stories he told me he would buy, one even advertised to appear in his next number. There will be no money from the house next month. I owe fifteen dollars since July on the mortgage. Everything is pawned. W. has led me to believe he would buy the house and now backs out. I am unable to write. I can do nothing else for a living. My mind is filled with pictures of myself cutting my throat or leaping out of the window, head first.[1]

Commenting on the position writers found themselves in at this time, Frederick Karl and Leo Hamalian, in their introduction to *The Existential Imagination*, observe:

> … man's alienation from himself is the very problem with which Tolstoy later concerned himself: to examine situations in which man is estranged from himself because he is trapped by a society that cannot fulfil his deepest needs… in his despair, he faces the possibility of suicide, the complete nulli-fication of his self. Tolstoy suggests that the individual may need to face death before he can make the decision that will change his life.[2]

Like any guerrilla fighter, Fort had very few things going for him, probably only two in number. First, he had an idea that science was not all that it made itself out to be; its definitions had too much of a cocksure air about them, and its over-simplified arguments were often quite circular. For the most part, he saw scientific practitioners as being essentially social conformists, drawn from a fairly narrow lower-middle-class base, the system-drones of the burgeoning techno-industrial society of his day. In the broadest sense, we now see that he was correct in his view; quite unlike the arts, science has few bohemians, it is largely the activity of faceless corporate drones, and as such cannot help but align itself with massive institutionalised authority. The patronising social policies of science (essentially about stability, rule, formula, good behaviour, and predictability), are reflected completely in its essentially lower-middle-class practitioners.

Even in the early 1900s, science had already begun to take decisions over parliament, society's sanction, law, democratic principles, and established constitutions — all decisions based on its renowned "facts". But what, Fort must have asked himself at some time before the First World War, looking at his strange collection of boxed anomalies, were "facts"? As Damon Knight points out, "the man who begins by questioning Euclid, Newton and Darwin, has set his foot on a dangerous path."[3]

The second thing he had going for him was his dissatisfaction with his own fiction. He gives the impression that the results, though more than highly satisfactory, were never anything like what he wanted. Theodore Dreiser said that Fort gave him some of the "best humorous short stories that I have seen produced in America... they were realistic, ironic, wise, and in a way, beautiful. I think I published six or seven. And other editors did the same."[4] If he had persisted, Fort might have given us a Bronx *Dubliners*; certainly his scenes of tenement life have a similar feel, but at some time or other he must have decided that his true strength of mind lay elsewhere. Just as James Joyce took a momentous decision after he finished *A Portrait of the Artist*, Fort must have decided that he was one of those writers who must go on to create their own quite unique form. Prevailing language and forms being unsatisfactory to him, he must have asked himself why should he continue with pure invention, when he could, being Charles Fort, take any piece of so-called "reality," and produce from it as many fantasies as he needed? Instead of battering "reality" to death with literary artifice, he could release its potential, coax out its secrets, let it speak naturally, even show that it was not "real" in any case. The result would be revolutionary in literary terms: showing verifiable "facts" to contain much more "strangeness" than had ever been realised. In doing this, he was to extend ideas of what *fiction* was capable of, other than that facetious and ephemeral entertainment it frequently descends to, in our own time.

He wrote to Maynard Shipley on March 1, 1931:

Something that you see in *Lo!* is that it is a kind of non-fictional fiction, or that, though concerned with entomological and astronomical matters, and so on, it is "thrilling" and "melodramatic." I have a theory that the moving pictures will pretty near drive out the novel, as they have very much reduced the importance of the stage — but that there will arise writing that will

Enter Sonnabend

retain the principles of dramatic structure of the novel, but, not having human beings for its characters, will not be producible in the pictures, and will survive independently. Maybe I am a pioneer in a new writing that instead of old-fashioned heroes and villains, will have floods and bugs and stars and earthquakes for its characters and motifs."[5]

As soon as he was convinced that he could combine his separate strengths, namely his undoubted literary talents and his hatred of science (even his biographer names science as his "enemy"), he embarked on a quite original form of what might be termed discursive fiction.

The first thing that is obvious in *The Book of the Damned* is that Fort has got rid of himself as a *persona* and is using a narrating voice. This is a powerful technique that solved the problem he had encountered in his conventional fiction. With this voice, he was now free to do what we suppose he always wanted to do, that is combine externally observed reports of all kinds of anomalies, culled from years of study of generations of printed matter ranging across a wide field of human interest, with a vast interior monologue in which Fort reinvents both his fiction and himself.

Lawrence Weschler[6] wrote a wonderfully rhapsodic novel about Fort's life and views, entitled *Mr Wilson's Cabinet of Wonder*,[7] and he gave Fort a name: Geoffrey Sonnabend. The narrator of Fort's four books shall hereafter be referred to as Sonnabend, if only because Fort is the spiritual father of Weschler's character.

Of course as Fort's "I", Sonnabend is not there merely to present information. Fort runs him as a complete character. He can involve Sonnabend himself with the drama of his own opinions, he can fail, succeed, be full of contradictions and often unjustified spleen. He can be unfair, waste time and be all the things that human beings are in their failure and despair, their hopes and dreams.

Few writers if any on Fort have noticed this character. They assume the books were written as a kind of extended notebook by Fort himself, who merely strung them together into four major theme blocks. The truth is that Fort never gave up his fiction, and Sonnabend is a character in a novel searching the infinitely smooth surface of the world of appearances to try to find that haircrack that means escape is perhaps possible. In his search he discovers a massive conspiracy. Map all the concealments he finds, and the plot is revealed as that map of fractured intellect which (though his author was never to know it) led to Auschwitz and Hiroshima. He finds indeed a spectre haunting science. It is the spectre of shameful denial. Other characters such as George Orwell's Winston Smith were to find the monstrous impostures of communism and Nazism, but Fort's Sonnabend finds the biggest lie of all: the scientific method.

It is this deep political message within Fort's work that has saved him from the terrible fate of being regarded as a provider of rattling good after-dinner frog-fall tales for ageing hippies and fallen bohemians of a certain age. The concealments and denials found by Sonnabend are the outline of a holocaust of the imagination. What he finds in his endless searches are not the mistakes of folk as fallible as he, they are not those understandable human concealments, those follies of ego, memory and desire that make life comically worthwhile. What he uncovers is a picture of science as a map of terror, concealment, disguises; removing a cover of massively engineered cultural advertising, Sonnabend, through his view of science as a "headless and limbless stomach, an amoeba-like gut that maintains itself by incorporating the assimilable and rejecting the indigestible"[8] reveals socially applied scientific method as a tale of torture, horror, destruction, corporate manipulation and betrayal. In other words Fort's character discovers early on what Robert Oppenheimer rediscovered for himself at Los Alamos in 1945: a sense of sin, which is a metaphysical thing of infinite age.

In this, Fort is the American ancestor of all conspiracy writers: from the 1953 *Flying Saucers Have Landed* by Desmond Leslie[9] and George Adamski,[10] to books of our own time such as *The Gemstone File*,[11] *Mind Control, World Control*,[12] and the Apocalypse Culture series published by Adam Parfrey's Feral House. Such important books would not have been possible without Fort's thinking. Like no other author, he ferreted out the pattern of reasoning inside the brain of that nation which, a few years after his death, was to become the most powerful in the world. Though he certainly looked east and not west, nevertheless Fort was an American who lived at the dawn of the modern American world. The power of the United States is a strength destined to last for hundreds of years, and for better or for worse it is a power founded on the mysteries and intrigues of science and capitalism. American culture runs through the body and soul of everyone on planet Earth like a new tree grows through an old house. It is impossible not to be an American to some significant degree.

Enter Sonnabend

In this important sense, to follow Fort's thinking through the varying moods of Sonnabend (sullen, excited, depressing, sneering and despairing in turn as they often are), is to start on a path which provides an entry to that structure of denials constituting the modern military-industrial-mythological complex. Once on that path, once into that structure (the veins of an eye, the memory pathways of a carp), we take a journey where we can see that the Warren JFK Investigation Commission of 1967 is essentially the same entity as the Condon Committee report on UFOs of 1969. Though every single individual has been changed like a worn component, and Fort is long dead, both the medium and the message are unchanged.

religio americana:

systems

analysis

Fort's Sonnabend is the first truly modern American head. Though he hates the Henry Ford world, he is knows he is inextricably involved with its plugs and wires, its sockets and connectors, its first hot radio valves and its burgeoning screen images and electronic pulsations. Essentially America had freed itself from the ancient, decrepit and intellectually bankrupt European religions that had caused so much damage to societies and cultures, and wrought nothing but suffering upon mankind. Now those mysteries were dead, were sterile, and metaphysics had found a new refuge in the corporate software of glamour and mass entertainments. Even in Fort's time of early media innocence, the mass of American folk had more knowledge of early film stars such as Lillian Gish than God. This had not happened before. The performer was rapidly replacing the priest, and Fort might have added that the performer did humanity a whole lot more good than the pre-industrial language of the gaitered parson, who in this vastly accelerated new industrial time was a threadbare figure mumbling in a eighteenth-century twilight. He had been upstaged, and the star had freed the new consumer from a sterile sexless cave-mouth time. Christ was being out-advertised, and his poor suffering figure stood no chance against glamorous mysteries of machines, products and new techno-adventures supported by the cultural mystique of science.

The foremost American writers of the time such as Theodore Dreiser and Ben Hecht detected this in Fort's work: he was the future. Nearer our own time, that great futurologist Buckminster Fuller found tremendous significance in his work. "Fort was in love with the world that jilted him," Fuller says in his introduction to Damon Knight's biography of Fort.

With that remark, all of a sudden we have the key to Sonnabend's constantly changing mood: it is unrequited love.

This one theme unites the Fort quartet: *The Book of the Damned*, *New Lands*, *Wild Talents* and *Lo!* As one, they make up an experimental novel that certainly compares well with James Joyce's *Ulysses*. Sonnabend's fractured relationship with the outer world is as tragically unsatisfactory as Bloom's relationship with his wife Molly. In Joyce's novel Bloom is a somewhat passive creature, and he is anything but political. Lacking almost all exterior, he becomes lost in a vast interior of memories and sensations. He is shipwrecked and exiled in a culture that is not his own.

Admittedly Fort's books lack the physical atmosphere and vast inspirations present in *Ulysses*, but they have a certain great strength that makes them comparable with Joyce's novel. Though Sonnabend has reached the same conclusion as Bloom, that the world is complex imposture, Bloom has given up, content to observe and be borne onwards by a stream of infinite poetry. But if Bloom is a passive aesthete, Sonnabend is on the attack. For him, there is much to be done. For Bloom, each changing mood, each and every sensation, is satisfaction in itself. For Sonnabend, each move in the world of affairs and intellect, each knuckle and joint of mechanical consciousness, is a system of denial and deception that must be attacked and exposed.

But if the world is pure imposture, then both characters know that somehow the concrete world can be subverted. If it can be subverted, then escape from Plato's cave is possible.

Religio Americana: Systems Analysis

In this, Sonnabend is Bloom doing everything that Bloom does not do. Sonnabend, in tracing the impostures of consciousness, rediscovers the outer world of science and technology, of politics and affairs, of cultural ideologies, and examines the shadow-impostures they are all based upon. Joyce's magical invocation of provincial Ireland at the turn of the century was nonetheless that of a country cut off almost absolutely from everything that could be called "modern" in this respect. If the world of *Ulysses* is a dying world seen in the last gleams of the pre-industrial Celtic twilight, Sonnabend's world is full of the bangs and clashes and sparks and test tubes of the new-born techno-scientific Leviathan. His book can be seen as the plots and scripts of young America, as distinct from the swansong of Yeats' Celtic twilight.

Therefore, unlike James Joyce, and again quite unlike any writer in English, Fort was not interested in literature for its own aesthetic sake. He wanted to develop his new technique into a devastating weapon against what he viewed as rationalist oppression in general and scientific oppression in particular. In doing so, he was to give literary expression back some political and discursive power, some "real thinking" — T. S. Eliot referred to that literature that not only had intellectual backbone, but took the risk of immersing itself in the blood and bones of an age, rather than retreating into that camp neo-Edwardian chintz with which we in our time are only too familiar.

Why, one asks, a *weapon*?

In the days long before novels were written mainly by camp show business and media personalities, there was something called literary commitment. When many men and women, some brilliant and thoughtful, some
resentful, and some positively evil, sit almost starving and alone in shabby
rooms vowing vengeance against the world, more than mere individual mis-
fortunes or bad strokes of fate are involved. There has been a breakdown of
all that is best in the relationship between the individual and society, and in
the early years of the twentieth-century, there were many such men and
women, and many such breakdowns. That part of the structure of European
society which had previously given the writer and thinker a proper place had
broken down, and was being pushed off the roadside of history, overwhelmed
by the streams of refugees of all political colours, going they knew not where.
It was as if literature itself was on the move: characters appeared from the
pages of Dostoevsky, such as Lenin and Adolf Hitler; from the pages of
Proust, such as Eliot and Pound. These early twentieth-century writers (and
unfortunately Adolf Hitler must be included amongst them) were fundamentally disturbed, restless, full of spleen and political fire from many of the
most extreme directions of the political compass. All were almost overwhelmed
by the breathless pace of the social, intellectual, and moral changes brought
about in a short historical time by science and communism. When affluence
and mass media in our own time have made the protesting political writer
almost as obsolete as Chaucer's rusty-armoured Knight, it is often difficult to
get an idea of the nuclear forces that were building up in Fort's formative
years. He grew up in a world where Freud had changed the idea of the nature
of the mind, Einstein had changed the idea of the space and time in which
that mind existed, and Marx had changed forever the idea of the social
relations between such minds. All three thinkers had employed scientific, or
semi-scientific, techniques to form their separate visions, and tragically had
contributed to an explosive anti-Semitic reaction radiating from all points of
the intellectual compass.

Fort gives the impression time and again of seeing humanity as a kind of
more-than-willing plankton for such powerful belief-systems, and he was probably the first to use the word "system" in the full modern sense, indicating a
political-industrial-military-*mythological* complex. In his terms, many of these
"systems", both left and right, middle, and religion, act as a powerful narcotic
in that some (but not all), are produced by great geniuses. Fort regarded elaborate thought structures, such as the body of astronomical knowledge, as almost-live entities in themselves, being so many *forms* of doped information.
Such things might be termed Fortean animals: that is, creatures sculptured of
pure information arrays that graze on human minds, taking them over, possess-
ing them so that when a particular information virus gets a grip, everything is
seen and interpreted through it. Many times he expresses strongly the eerie
idea that systems choose vulnerable human beings and social groups, live off
them as prey, and not vice versa. When he says "I think we are property," he

does not necessarily mean that little green men from UFOs farm us like ani-mals, but rather that prowling ideas do, ideas from which indeed little green men (and many other things, including little white women[1]) may indeed emerge, or partly emerge.

Often thought of as a completely isolated writer, Fort's ideas connect him with the generally disturbed influences of his time, inspiring and depressing by turn, with very little in between. Changing social forces are sharply focused in such individuals, and Fort is only just beginning to be being seen as part of the existentialist avant-garde of the formative years of this century. Thirty years after the publication of *The Book of the Damned*, Sartre was to put forward the view that a new basis for humanism was to be found in an intense subjectivity. But Fort actually provided the solution to the problem of existential alienation long before writers such as Camus and Sartre had stated it, and this solution was to counter-attack. The enemy (identified as the way the world would like itself to be seen) *must* have weak points, and Fort found them. As a thinker, his character Sonnabend would not be content to be compared to Pierre, Sartre's madman in a darkened room, or even later, as Beckett's Vladimir or Estragon. Almost all historians are agreed that science, technology and the Industrial Revolution they created had, by and large, destroyed at least the overt political power of Christianity. Science was very much the new power in the land, but as Fort points out, its weakest philosophical point was that it defined things in terms of other things that could not be defined! Since no one knows what magnetism, electricity and gravity are, he points out, with immaculate logic, then our culture is founded on countless acts of mythological faith, quite equal to spoon bending, the Resurrection, or the powers of sacred tree-kangaroos of north Borneo.

Religio Americana: Systems Analysis

But despite the power of his counter-attack, Fort's disadvantage as a writer was that, rather like his theories of embryo-phenomenon, and era-intelligence, he said too much too soon. As always, the reading public preferred a more whimsical literature, and in any case he was writing long before any real doubts about science had formed. In the 1900s, the new view was overwhelming ill-educated politicians, sending writers into the escapism of pure aesthetics and baffling philosophers such as Jaspers and Heidegger.

The only people who had a smile on their face during Fort's lifetime were the left-wing sociologists such as Beatrice Webb, and agitating communists like Lenin and Trotsky. But their over-neat cultural welding of "fact" and "fiction", new and old, into the seamless fronts of new kinds of reforming (and often opposed) crusades was the kind of fusion that Fort warred against, and this gives his theory of implicitly manufactured fictions much political and social relevance. He could never see why, against the monstrous pretensions of such clashing claims to "reality" as the views of the left-wingers, the vision of the "Angels of Mons" over the Western Front, with all its undoubted absurdity, could not be seen to have an equal claim to be "real," at least politically: "let anybody who does not like the idea that his mind may be most subtly control-

● ●

led, without his knowledge of it, think back to what propagandists did with his beliefs in the years 1914–18."[2]

Fort's idea of mass mind-control by media manipulation was probably the very first warning of its kind, in the terms that we understand it. Fort sees a clash, not between the classes or between the rich and the poor as did Marx and the Webbs, but between their *imaginations*, both. Peering over the immediate horizon, he hints that the new technology (in his case films and radio) would not be used to search for objective truth, but rather for imagination control.

For Fort, systems act as almost disembodied information-animals. In other words, in the full sense meant much later by Marshall McLuhan, science is a full-fledged conceptual *medium.* In Fort's time, neither the Webbs nor indeed the Curies or even H. G. Wells realised that science was quite out of control in this way. Like the later electronic visual *medium*, science was a tidal wave that swamped every aspect of culture, and human beings contributed little other than technical work, as regards controlling its shape, growth, and the changes it would bring about. The much-vaunted "discoveries" of science are in Fortean terms as largely irrelevant as, say, seeing television in terms of a single "good" programme. Just like the actual act of *viewing*, it is more the systematic *method* of scientific thinking that has taken human beings over. "Discoveries" in this sense merely change the product, not the store; they are mere channel-surfing in a kind of cyberspace of intellectual consumerism. Fort's thinking, we must remember, was many years before Marshall "media" McLuhan, Thomas "paradigm" Khun, and indeed Andy "fifteen minutes of fame" Warhol. Given this kind of evolution of the scientific method of thinking and the development of its attendant sets of exclusivity paradigms, in Fort's view different *kinds* of discovery are almost completely determined within the paradigm-key that has been set. Diametrically opposed to the uniqueness of artistic works, C. P. Snow points out that the death of a single scientist hardly matters scientifically; sooner or later someone else will come along and solve the problem.[3] In this sense, there are no "real" discoveries, just a series of closed product-loops that Fort called "Dominants".

As far as such scientific absolutism is concerned, Sonnabend is a very angry young man:

> So now, in the twentieth century, with a change of terms, and a change in underlying consciousness, our attitude towards the New Dominant is the attitude of the scientists of the nineteenth century to the Old Dominant. We do not insist that our data and interpretations shall be as shocking, grotesque, evil, ridiculous, childish, insincere, laughable, ignorant to nineteenth-centuryites as were their data and interpretations to the mediaeval-minded. We ask only whether data and interpretations correlate. If they do, they are acceptable only for a short time, or as nuclei, or scaffolding, or preliminary sketches, or as gropings or tentativenesses. Later, of course, when we cool off and harden and radiate into space most of our present mobility, which

expresses in modesty and stability, we shall acknowledge no scaffoldings, gropings, or tentativenesses, but think we utter absolute facts.[4]

During Fort's formative youth, the entire nineteenth-century was coming apart at the seams and many weird and wonderful design-solutions were trying to sell themselves in order to get into the vacuum created by the century's death. Apart from the communists, the Webbs, Shaw, Wells, and even the young Adolf Hitler stood on opposed soapboxes — all had "solutions" to a new age which was a surreal maze of bewildering social change and intellectual uncertainty. Around the core of Fort's almost inconceivable anti-science quest, there gathers therefore the shadow-energies of the more obvious struggles of class war versus right-wing mysticism, of economic theory versus racial eugenics, of industrialisation versus older, traditional patterns of life. Fort was not in the least directly concerned with any of these dynamics, but like any disturbed neighbourhood, when the culture is in a frenzy there is no "off" switch, and many doomed explanations abound. Sonnabend comments on vast amounts of furnace slag deposited in Scotland, and attributed to a volcanic eruption thousands of miles away:

> The fate of all explanations is to close one door only to have another fly open. I should say that my own notions upon this subject will be considered irrational, but at least my gregariousness is satisfied in associating here with the preposterous — or this writer, and those who think in his rut, have to say that they can think of four discharges from one far-distant volcano, passing over a greater part of Europe, precipitating nowhere else, discharging precisely over one small northern parish—
> But also of three other discharges, from another far-distant volcano, showing the same precise preference, if not marksmanship, for one small parish in Scotland.[5]

Religio Americana: Systems Analysis

Here we imagine Sonnabend on the kind of soapbox Fort himself stood in London at Hyde Park Corner in the 1920s. There is a detectable energetic intellectual rabble-rousing element in this kind of talk. Something in it smacks of the immediate pre-1917 era, trailing back through 1870, to the disturbances of '48, '32, and even back to the drums, flags, trumpets and rolling heads of 1792. Our own more affluent age has somewhat soft-focused the edges of this kind of emotion, but there is still no mistaking the urgent voice here warning about the many new explanations that were already on offer in the cultural supermarkets in the early years of the century, all causing much soapbox frenzy in the world.

We can imagine that Fort, whilst on his Hyde Park soapbox, was violently opposed by followers of Marx and the British left-wing social democrats of the period. There must have been some explosive reactions to a man who talked not of wages, living conditions, class war, or the evils of top-hatted capitalism, but of showers of countless tons of "furnace slag" in Slaines, Scotland, during

May, 1862!

The style might have been appreciated, but the content — well, Fort would certainly have found himself out on a limb. Hearing what appeared to be the bogus talk of a complete madman might well have balked any of his audience who remained after the first few minutes. They might well have gone off to listen to more plausible madmen who talked of much more likely and sensible things, such as revolution, poverty and strikes.

Fort practised this kind of activist-agitator pressure almost as a way of life, just as he also inherited a childhood as unhappy and uncertain as his Age. He was only really pleased when he found anomalies to throw in the face of authoritarian science, and the search for such things, like the search by Lenin for supposed class and economic crimes, or the search by Hitler for equally supposed Jewish crimes, was a visionary grail-quest. Damon Knight has written very eloquently about Fort's troubled youth and his bad relationship with his cruel and domineering father. These tensions were combined in Fort with an almost Proust-like burden of the knowledge of several rapidly changing worlds, and at times Sonnabend is discernibly exhausted by his vision, which begins to dilate and pulse like the new heart, eyes, and crude artificial brains of the first electro-robotic age.

Sonnabend looks back over the entire nineteenth-century, yet is able to grasp the implications of the impact of electronics, nuclear physics and mass advertising. Just before he died in 1932, in his last book, *Wild Talents*, Fort is already responding to such things as the high-frequency atmospheric radio-propagation experiments of Appleton, so that by this time Sonnabend is truly Charlie Chaplin trapped in the gears, wheels and electrics of the film *Modern Times*. Though he struggles to free himself from the emerging systems of the modern Leviathan, nevertheless he is fascinated by it all. Throughout the four books, although he damns systems technology there is also a detectable fascination, and he looks upon scientific complexity as others gazed upon cathedrals and pyramids. He is frightened, but in awe. The sheer tragic cleverness of it all intrigues him. He stares wild-eyed at the glamour and intrigue and intellectual eroticism within what was the *artificial* construction of a new pantheon. He talks almost enthusiastically of the stranger experiments of Marconi, Tesla, and Harry Hawker, all of whom at various times declared that they had detected "signals from Mars" on their early experimental electronic apparatus.[6] Fort was also reaching out almost unconsciously for space: he gives many examples[7] of balloon experiments recording temperature and density of air in the upper atmosphere. In this, he appears to sense (like a quite few other thinkers of his time) that space is some future scientific frontier.

This voracious intellectual appetite worked well with his media-conscious mind, one of the very first of its type. In this, he was one of the first electric citizens: he sees the beginning of our own wired society, when the "strange", transforming its paradigms in turn, changed from being something hoisted from the holds of the last wooden ships into electromechanical constructs with their associated metaphors. The old world stuff of relatively primitive mercantile technologies involved in rubber, canvas, lens, canal and rail changed, in Fort's time, to pulse, particle and signal, and also into the entirely new dimension of the air. Fort was fortunate enough to be in the position to bridge the historical gap and see the new explanations born out of the old: not as that dignified weathering of natural change beloved by conventional historians, but as quick-fix ideological sales campaigns. Cultural time was accelerating, and he was the first (accompanied by the far happier and far more successful Wells)[8] to detect the beginning of that rapid-frame presentation of paraphrased "information" involved in new methods of social control and persuasion, and to realise that the idea of free "choice" in old-fashioned terms of careful judgement and evaluation was becoming quite meaningless. This view is based on Fort's assumption that each and every person, each and every form of social organisation is based on manipulative mythological engineering.

Viewing our own entertainment state in 2002, we can see how prophetic was his view.

Apart from natural catastrophes and wars, great physical changes within the lifetime of a citizen of the Ancient World were rare. Even for Hardy's very last generation of native and barely literate English peasants, there were few changes in one lifetime. But by 1910 when Fort finally began to get what he really wanted down on paper, strange new shapes were moving through the clouds, the air was starting to crackle with signals, and the artistic and intellectual worlds were in as equal a ferment as the scientific and technological spheres. We can imagine one of Hardy's characters getting up one day, to see a no doubt baffled and disapproving Egdon Heath crowned with a high aerial, and suddenly knowing that the world himself and his family had inhabited since the days of the Conquest had died overnight, to the accompaniment of a barely audible "new foxtrot from the Savoy Hotel, London".

Religio Americana: Systems Analysis

the

damned

imagination

The Book of the Damned opens with a dramatised demonology of things imagined, which are cursed, rejected and cast out of mind. But when compared with
politics and religion proper, both dedicated to different kinds of thought control in their own way, the opening of this book gives a strange picture of
sinners. We cannot see any miserable faces; there are no lines of shuffling
prisoners, penitents, or cries for forgiveness; there are no show-trials, inquisi-
tions, torturing of heretics, or labour camps. Neither do we encounter broken
moral principles, vile oaths, tears, grief, terrible crimes, lists of evil doings, or
the curses of the wronged. There are no screams of the tortured, howls of the
vengeful, moans of the utterly lost. In Fort's vision, burning lakes of sulphur
and pits of hellfire are places of *ideological* damnation. They display Milton's
misshapen forms and Dante's grotesque shades as cast-out anomalous thoughts,
events, and experiences, part-blending with personalities, groups, ideas and
individual and collective destinies. From what heaven has this rejected host
been cast out? From the narrow heaven of institutionalised science, and what
better picture is there of Europe's political prisoners of the twentieth-century
than the following?

> Some of them are corpses, skeletons, mummies, twitching, tottering, ani-
> mated by companions that have been damned alive. There are giants that
> will walk by, though sound asleep. There are things that are theorems and
> things that are rags; they'll go by like Euclid arm in arm with the spirit of
> anarchy. Here and there will flit little harlots. Many are clowns. But many
> are of the highest respectability. Some are assassins. There are pale stenches
> and gaunt superstitions and mere shadows and lively malices: whims and

amiabilities. The naive and the pedantic and the bizarre and the grotesque and the sincere and the insincere, the profound and the puerile.

The power that has said to all these things that they are damned, is Dogmatic Science.

But they'll march.

The little harlots will caper, the freaks will distract attention. and the clowns will break the rhythm of the whole with their buffooneries...[1]

But this essentially Christian metaphor with which *The Book of the Damned* opens, is hardly completed. Christianity does not see evil as functional, as assisting any process at all; it sees it as something totally destructive, something to be got rid off, therefore envisaging a great end of all days, a supreme triumph of good, when the "noise" of evil exists no longer. Fort's devil-events are not evil or destructive in this absolute sense; yes, they tip the applecart over, but it is only to stop systems of belief decaying into atrophy, which is really Fort's definition of the function of anomalies. He is thus more tragedian than Christian. His deviant events have more of the pagan imp in them than the Satan of Genesis. Within institutionalised frameworks of human thinking, frequently he describes anomalies as behaving like some classical tragicomic element, not only eventually bringing systems into chaos, but revealing the hilarious chicanery upon which many of our basic ideas and cultural assumptions are constructed. As he points out frequently, more often than not his disturbance is healthy. Mental stage-fronts have to be torn down one way or another, for mental freedom, just as political barriers have to be destroyed for physical and ideological freedom. In this sense, the world seen from a Fortean point of view is not an uncaring world, but a world of extraordinary human possibilities, a resurrection of the human imagination as uniquely connected to nature in a way that we have almost forgotten.

The Damned Imagination

History in general, and the twentieth-century in particular, has had a great deal of trouble with the idea of the imagination as such an active psychological element. Although now fallen from its historically high cerebral throne to some faculty belonging to what are essentially non-cerebral systems, such as television, nevertheless the word imagination still smacks of mysticism, of dangerous primitivism, indeed of the occult.[2] The intellect can make convincing things, the emotions can give deep human moral understanding, but though the imagination is an element in all this activity, pure imagining for its own sake is far less understood, and has always been a most curious and awesome element of the human personality. In its purest form it appears to have no directly worthy social role, other than as a casual inspiration for mere entertainments. The imagination therefore, appears to be a great anarchic loose cannon of the mind which knows hardly a difference between the sleeping and waking life; its many busy simultaneous levels are still psychologically baffling, and its penchant for making endless patterns which are quite independent of personal needs or directed collective goals is as disturbing to us as it was to

Antiquity. More often than not, the imagination lacks all efficiency and focus, and quite unlike the intellect and the emotions, with which it has an endlessly troubled relationship, the singular form of imagination more often than not refuses to be tasked, tamed, directed, or even communicated with.

Shakespeare speaks of the imagination only with awe; Yeats, de Quincey and Shelley were terrified by its power; Coleridge, Pound and Dylan Thomas were almost destroyed by it as it raged out of control within them. Dictators try to annihilate the imagination, religions try to control it, politicians censor it, left-wingers hate it, psychologists try to change it, science mistrusts it almost completely, and in popular usage, the imagination is equated almost completely with that thing which is most difficult to define called "unreality". Only the mass media of our own time uses the imagination in any way creatively, but is very careful to confine Coleridge's "shaping spirit" to the anodyne and narrow confines of electronic media and its ephemeral low culture diversions.

Thus for a phenomenon which is said to lack the physical transforming power of other elements of mind, and which takes scant interest[3] in the immediate needs and circumstances of any other parts of the finite self, the very idea of imagining arouses antagonisms in inverse proportion to its seemingly almost passive function. Traditionally, this paradox appears to be due to the universal suspicion that the imagination has some hidden secret energy far greater than even the intellect or the emotions. Although in operation, inner visualisations would appear to change nothing, they are still, nevertheless, inextricably associated with all kinds of magical ideas, and are often seen as having an elemental quality far more anarchic, subversive and dangerous than any gross physical act. The outlines of such a physical act are known, recognised and assimilated very quickly, but the outlines of an imagined threat are not so easily dealt with,[4] and illnesses and even deaths purely caused by fear and various forms of self-suggestion alone are not uncommon. We like to think of our own time as more enlightened than others in this respect, but autoeroticism for instance, despite modern sexual sophistication and openness, is still the target of universal ridicule. Few admit to the practice, lest like all dreamers they are seen as strange, weak, different, momentarily sundered from the tribe, and thus for a short time, out of group-control. Erotic imagining in particular still contains the secrets of an intensely private pact between the raised images and an inviolate element of self, any finite physical act of self-stimulation falling away in importance as timbers fall away from the hull of a launched ship. Such a state still smacks somehow of the primal, and whether achieved by perfectly conventional sex, drugs, or plain meditation, there is an innate feeling that it might just be possible to forget what the "reality" rules are. This eerie feeling is often aroused by the stories that Fort's tireless Sonnabend culls from thousands of magazines, newspapers, and journals, a "normality" every aspect of which smacks of the imagination; there is a feeling that in some of the stories he describes, a curtain has lifted to reveal a drama of which we are totally unaware.

Eroticism is of course usually equated with sex, just as "digital" is mistakenly equated with everything electronic. But there is such a thing as intellectual eroticism, quite parallel to feelings of physical arousal. Louis Pauwels and Jacques Bergier, authors of *The Morning of the Magicians*, a legendary book much influenced by Fortean ideas, comment on Charles Fort and what we might term the Walter Mitty syndrome:

> The truth is that the slightest allusion to the fact that the Universe may contain vast areas of the Great Unknown has a disturbing effect and disagreeable effect on men's minds. Mr Charles Fort, in fact, was behaving like an erotomaniac: let us keep our vices secret so that society shall not be furious at discovering that it has been allowing large tracts in the field of sexuality to lie fallow. The next stage was to advance from indulgence in a crazy hobby to a declaration of principles, and from being a crank to becoming a prophet. From now on there was real work to be done — revolutionary work.[5]

Thus in this sense pure thought is still dynamite: the inward-looking and the highly imaginative are often still looked upon with the same kind of suspicion as any lone and independent woman was regarded in medieval Europe, or any lone man in Mao's China or Stalin's Russia. G. N. M. Tyrrell, in a classic work on psychology, comments that "to many, the contemplative is an abnormal person",[6] and goes on to quote William James' criticism of the "medical mind" for regarding intuitive or mystical states as "intellectual superstition", often accompanied by bodily "degeneration and hysteria".[7] Reinforced by burgeoning communist belief, early science perpetuated the idea of "fantasy" as intellectual contamination. In this sense, such things as perpetual motion machines are heavily propagandised as elements of pretty and amusing noise, irrelevant as Walter Mitty's daydreams.

The Damned Imagination

But Fort gives us an entirely different view. In *Wild Talents* he discusses the perpetual motion machines of Lester J. Hendershot and John Worrell Keely, and puts forward the idea of the quasi-discovery, or the almost-event, of which in our own time the "virtual reality" of the discovery of cold fusion is a good example.[8] This kind of almost-event, or Fortean part-form, appears to occupy a position within a kind of octave of appearances. In Fort's view, at times such things work or are solid, at other times they do not work at all or vanish beyond recall. In this they are unstable states or what might be called knife-edge systems. If we subtract from one person's doubt about the existence of fairies, another person's positive belief in such things, the outline of what remains forms a classic Fortean locus describing an ideo-material space. The dimensions of this locus, as an information vector, have largely been lost to the modern mind. Science is hence in the philosophically ludicrous position of being incapable of dealing with short-run, or unstable macrocosmic events that occur within this kind of Fortean space and time. However, science more than willingly recognises such instability either in the microcosmic world or in the super macrocosmos, both of which we note, with political suspicion, are quite unreachable by persons on the Clapham omnibus. By means of science's implicit wonder-management, such persons are reassured that both their kitchen and the sky immediately above it are quite free from anomalistic effects!

But Fort does not provide such convenient no-go areas for his collection of anomalies. Most of his evidence is drawn from what is essentially the localised kitchen-world. As such, more often than we would like to believe, some of the contents of a boiling pot of changing reality options invades the general spectrum of cognition — then we may witness a peculiar bite in a sheep's neck from a savage something which has no likelihood of ever being found, simply because it was such a snowflake event that no system based on industrially repeatable demands could recognise or manage it. Such knife-edge events as he describes are built not from matter, but from bubbles of pure information, and within a Fortean space, they are weak information forms at first, "pale things" quite exhausted after the run up from the beach, or their raid on a farm. A lot of these part-forms die almost as they are born, like the many strange shapes of winged and propeller-driven airborne forms seen in the skies of the early part of the twentieth-century that could not be accounted for.[9] In Fort's space of pure mind-stuff, still other similar hybrid forms get the drag coefficients and the power/weight ratio right, gather strength, and disappear inland to wreak havoc with the cities of the interior. Science still has difficulty in recognising that the forms of irrational fears and equally irrational loves may actively help shape the macrocosmos, down to the last rivet head: in this, Fort has helped to rediscover the third grid, the hinterland between idea and matter that the Western world might well have lost completely without writers such as he.

Against these guerrilla bands of half-forms in this hinterland, the armoured phalanx of a singular and discursive science (which has replaced an equally oppressive religion) can do little but suffer a million mysterious cuts when night falls. The great wounded beast knows that it is being assaulted by whole dimensions of missing causality involving clumsy, doll-like figures and cartoon actions such as those created by Thurber's character, Walter Mitty, and those strange figures described by John Keel in *The Mothman Prophecies*. Such cartoons are like the patently misbehaving structures of observations so well described by Fort. Nevertheless, many marvellously professional and extremely well informed searchlight eyes still look for formal, conscious, and integral patterns. But perhaps, like Hendershot's "miracle" motor, Emma Piggot's fire-raising, Keely's perpetual motion machine, and even Lee Harvey Oswald's mail-order Mannlicher-Carcano rifle, these cartoon entities worked for a short time as, in Oswald's case, no gun has ever worked before or since. Perhaps — and here is the real Fortean point — Oswald, Hendershot and Keely didn't quite know how or why the devices they created worked so erratically.

But many dare not speak of such unstable events, just as many communists dared not speak of the gaping faults within some monstrous industrial plan, or a Second World War Polish farmer dared not speak of the many trains which passed in the night, all going to one place.

Fort is amongst the most rare category of writers who are "political" because they make us aware of what is happening to us in the deepest sense. He points to a rediscovery of the way that fantasy-processes determine the perception of time, change, and indeed the creation and growth of fact and product in themselves. Thus he demonstrates the workings of that operational cargo cult which is modern techno-capitalism, and whose fuel is engineered mystique. The belief that the new experiments in the new laboratories will be an improvement on the old experiments in the old laboratories is a millennial promise worthy of any island cult of New Guinea, worshipping, as many there do, the skeletal rusting parts of the corpse of the American military machine of over fifty years ago. In this sense, Fort cautions us about scientific promises and expectations. No matter how hard the islanders try visualising the world that manufactured their "magical" bits of B-29 wings, they cannot visualise technological time and its cost/resources spectrum. For them, any day scores of B-29s will land on the long-overgrown strip with tins of hamburgers for free. But the apple pie America that made the B-29 is gone with Glenn Miller's orchestra, the Marshall Plan, and General McArthur's return to Bataan, while the far fewer (and much more expensive) B-52s of our own day are only seen as sky-trails in the high Pacific blue. In any case, landing on a grass strip in a B-52 would be suicide for the crew, and certain death also for many fundamentalist believers. If such a thing did happen, it would seem to be a wounded bird in great trouble, and if the watchers below were saying their prayers as it approached, so too would be the captain and his crew. As for the hamburgers, well, there might be some scorched USAF lunch-tins available after the crash, and when they were found, whole cycles of belief could be rejuvenated: McDonald's USAF compo-packs might become a techno-industrial packaged sacrament, indicating that whilst times might be hard, at least the gods were trying. Little do the natives know that some members of the crews of the godlike silver vehicles wonder what transformation mysteries the natives are guarding in their turn. The crews have some knowledge that is thousands of years ahead of the natives, yet the primitives probably have some knowledge that the crews have lost thousands of years ago, and they might wonder why these gods need any radio apparatus to communicate over great distances. Both animals, in their dreaming, are searching for one another.

This tale is told to illustrate a situation where the "facts" give us practically no information at all. All the "facts" will tell us is that there is a "successful" being up in the sky with his "successful" product, being watched by backward primitives who have not even yet made a wheel, never mind their first TV documentary. Similarly, all the "facts" will tell us is that Charles Fort, in terms of book sales, was an all-time loser.

This is a useful Fortean view of the way that cultural perspectives work. Peter Worsley in *The Trumpet Shall Sound* (1957), says that "Marx once de-

The
Damned
Imagination

scribed the agrarian history of the Roman Empire as its 'secret history'; the secret history of the Middle Ages is the history of millenarian and allied sects, a history which is only now being written."[10] Part of such a secret history of our own time are the dimensions of the Oswald investigation and the UFO. They are both elements in authentic modern mystery-plays, part of a cycle of Western techno-shamanism (no need to travel to exotic realms!), which indicates that both mind and the physical world follow ritualised sequences which we have part-forgotten; and they show that the worship of "facts" is often as useful as bowing before a scorched tin of standard issue 1944 USAF compo-sausages. But Fortean thinking is not exclusive of anything: even "facts" might, on occasion, just work.

The result of this downright mass politicisation of wonder is that by and large, our society does not recognise the state of matter implied by the Fortean view, and neither does it see that matter and belief are connected in such an intimate way. The fundamental Fortean equation can be derived from these conditions of denial versus acceptance. Fort's basic paradigm is that nothing is "real" or "unreal" in the absolute sense. Along the locus of belief, the archetypal mysteries of science (such as electricity, magnetism, and gravitation!) are greater in manifest *frequency* than, say, the "mysteries" of the wretched "paranormal" or alchemical practices. Science has become undeniably predominant, but like the religion it replaced, it has merely won the advertising battle between a complex of weak and strong imaginations.

There are of course denials that the imagination has any kind of power at all, other than to paint pretty pictures. Even in the post-communist hangover, people who are highly imaginative are often accused of social and personal failure, of lacking all sense of group adjustment. There are certainly some people in our more enlightened times who would say that Walter Mitty, for example, should have therapy to have all his mind projections "outed;" he should be "fanshened" in the old Chinese communist sense, or "deprogrammed" in the New Christian sense, or worse, be subjected to the far deeper rituals of social democracy.

This suspicion of the lone condition reaches back, of course, far beyond communism to the Old Testament tents of Shem, and is because it is a psychological state that most effectively resists any kind of cultural brainwashing. Though almost all group activity is a form of brainwashing, much of this is fortunately healthy, creative and necessary, such as sports, schooling, the military and scholastics. But control of any developing inwardness in communist societies in particular was achieved by making every single moment of privacy into the equivalent to a mortal sin in the essentially religio-dialectical terms of the communist view of life. Internal model making is still, it seems, cultural dynamite. Fort himself comments on such sinful intellectual temptation,[11] quoting the editorial of the *New York Sun* of September 3, 1930, which in turn quotes Professor Henry E. Armstrong of the Department of Chemistry at City and Guilds College, South Kensington, London:

The public is being played upon and utterly misled by the dreamery of the rival mathematical astronomers and physicists — not to mention the clerics — who are raising the game of notoriety to a fine art; in rivalry to religious mysticism, a scientific pornography is being developed, and attracts the more because it is mysterious.[12]

From Trotsky to Marcuse, back to the Surrealists, returning again through the Situationists to Punk, the connection between revolutionary movements and changes in sexual attitudes has been well analysed.[13] In his ensuing comment on the above, Fort draws a picture of the anomaly as indicating a kind of often criminally savage relationship, a kind of Dionysiac coupling within the intellect: "our quasi-existence proceeds from rape to the crooning of lullabies" where "bold, bad, intruders of theories"; all represent "revolt inside," which then "develops into revolution." Fort comments on the above:

Prof. Armstrong's accusation of pornography may seem unduly stimulating: but, judging by their lecheries in other respects, one sees that all the astronomers have to do is to discover that stars have sex, and they'll have us sneaking to bookstores, for salacious "pronouncements" and "determinations" upon the latest celestial scandals. This would popularise them. And after anything becomes popular — then what?

His anomalies vary from "little harlots", and "ruffians with dishonourable intentions", to "wandering comedians that were hated, or scorned, pitied, embraced, conventionalised":

But my interest is… in bringing together seeming incongruities, and finding that they have affinity. I am very much aware of the invigoration of products of ideas that are foreign to each other, if they mate. This is exogamy, practised with thoughts — to fertilise a volcanic eruption with a storm of frogs — or to mingle the fall of an edible substance from the sky with the unexplained appearance of Cagliostro. But I am a pioneer and no purist, and some of these stud-stunts of introducing vagabond ideas to each other may have about the eugenic value of some of the romances in houses of ill fame. I cannot expect to be both promiscuous and respectable. Later, most likely, some of these unions will be properly licensed.[14]

The
Damned
Imagination

We still care to keep, even our own cynical time, certain examples of powerful intellectual eroticism that are pure cultural bedrock. These are with us forever, as if their power to overwhelm fact is still awe-inspiring, reminding us of an almost forgotten power, the centre of mind/nature magical transformation wrought by an unshackled and supremely individual private imagination. These remind us of unredeemed nature, of the passion unto death described by Goethe's *The Sorrows of Young Werther*, and the hallucinatory horror of Coleridge's *The Rime of the Ancient Mariner*. Hamlet's limitless imaginings nearly drive him mad; Chaucer's Troilus, in the intensity of his love, transforms an oncoming farm-cart into an image of the returning Cressyde, and Don Quixote sees the enchanted Dulcinea everywhere and in anything. But these are the tales of the deep past, and though it is a long journey from Prospero to Walter Mitty, James Thurber shows in his celebrated short story (published in 1932, the year of Fort's death), how far the imagination has fallen from Prospero's idea of it as a magical transforming faculty, to a mere Pavlovian function which dances to the flip of a penny like a strung marionette, providing a momentary gratification; it is the imagination reduced to instant consumer product-pornography.

walter mitty
strikes
back

Perhaps Laurence Sterne's Uncle Toby and Thurber's Walter Mitty are the two most likely characters in English literature to have a broken perpetual motion machine secreted away somewhere in an attic. For Mitty, as for Uncle Toby (and indeed for T. S. Eliot's J. Alfred Prufrock), letting the thoughts merely roam has become essentially a compensatory action, a palliative; imagination has lost its transforming power:

> I have heard the mermaids singing, each to each.
> I do not think they will sing to me.[1]

For Prufrock, as for Sonnabend in his lowest moments, the concrete world is almost completely omnipotent; fragile thought structures with their dreams of love, power, and ambition are easily smashed to pieces in a world that contains nothing but ugliness, the mundane, and the objective brutalism of the system-machine. Like Shakespeare's "mechanicals" (meaning the almost dead), and like Kafka's eternal exiles (of which Charles Fort was certainly one), Mitty, Sonnabend, and Prufrock are effectively concentration camp prisoners, wandering through a world of null possibilities in the *Leidstadt*, or city of sorrows predicted by Goethe. That these wastelands, whose names are legion, came into being between 1939 and 1945, one wasteland indeed not far from Goethe's beloved Weimar, is a kind of Fortean warning about the danger of a culture losing the connection between politics, literature, imagination, and what we far too easily term reality. At Nuremberg in 1945, in the absence of the faintest clue of just exactly what to put on trial, we tried Nazi leaders as we would try horse thieves. If Charles Fort's ideas mean anything,

they mean just that: truth is on trial when a UFO sighting becomes trans-
formed into a tractor's headlights, a supersonic pelican, or that most de-
lightfully British UFO explanation, the "earthlight".

Thurber's *The Secret Life of Walter Mitty* rapidly became one of the most celebrated short stories of the century, and although it was immensely more
popular than Fort's *Wild Talents*, published in the same year, the critical reaction
to these two works was essentially the same. They were both treated as purely
lightweight comic tales, just as Orwell's *Animal Farm* was at first treated by a
British publisher as a child's story about country life. These works were not
seen (and indeed on the whole, are still not seen) as descriptions of some
appalling disaster of mind, spirit and imagination.

Like K and Josef K, the two central characters of *The Castle* and *The Trial*,
both Walter Mitty and Sonnabend have been effectively silenced by a psychosocial immensity whose bland enormity reminds us of our own media-soaked
society. The difference is that over Kafka's work there is the shadow of the
coming Jewish Holocaust, whilst Sonnabend and Mitty relate much more to
modern conditions in that they are both prisoners of early intellectual consumerism and image manipulation. These are things that the sick Franz Kafka,
slowly dying in a starving Prague amidst fragments of the wrecked "fossil
monarchies" of the old Austro-Hungarian empire, could hardly have been expected to have experienced or understood.

Life for the characters of both Fort and Thurber has become a continuously
run consumerist show-trial, an endless mini-series superfluity, rather like the
half-starved bones of Kafka's landscapes of body, state and soul. In this
sense both Fort and Thurber, being far more aware of radio, films and the
sugar-dreams of young and lusty capitalism than Kafka, announce the birth of
entertainment state. In their "brave new world," well-fed purchasers (who have
largely replaced workers, and party members) are supposing to be enjoying
themselves in their new warm homes, any labour or concentration camp being
quite unnecessary. Thus Fort and Thurber announce the birth of "cool" control,
and the first diseases of force-fed image happiness, which, being (as distinct
from concentration camps) without antidote, were extremely virulent. Unlike
the troubled Sonnabend, Mitty has accepted his lot almost completely; the
thread between imagination and realisation lies broken in the consumer dust.
Like Orwell's equally broken Winston Smith,[2] Mitty can be released to his
respectable suburban ghetto to live a "normal life" — that is, to practice salivat-
ing consumer dialectics with the rest of society; he has accepted that the things
he imagines could never be.

Unlike Sonnabend, Mitty's alienation is complete in that he does not recognise the strengths that he sees in his imagination as his own lost strengths;
these are parts of him which have been forgotten because the vital connection
between imagination, time, and being has been destroyed. There is all that raw
power loose in his head and Mitty simply does not know what to do with it. He
has been deprived of the very idea that he is connected to these images in a

much more vital sense than just as a passive observer. Science, as "objec-tive" belief[3] has made his imagined world into passive entertainment only; it therefore can no longer be used to synthesise, to discover, to create power-transformations between the real and the unreal. Mitty lacks that Fortean sliding scale of being that enables Sonnabend to make adjustments. Mitty's last hopes of magical transformation have become jammed in the rut of the so-called concrete, with its catastrophically absolute distinctions.

Occasionally, this ancient faculty kick-starts a noisy connection almost by accident. *Ha'penny* (1947) is a short story by Alan Paton showing that when stage-fronts are penetrated, there is a psycho-physical crisis. A homeless boy constructs an imaginary family, and when he is told that this family does not really exist, the boy dies. Thus is induced a loss of confidence, and an inability to deal with invasive "objective" ideologies. As any good witch doctor knows, most illnesses are rooted in the inability of the self to defeat invasive doubts about itself. Sonnabend, unlike Walter Mitty, may smile and laugh, he may think he is being very smart; but Sonnabend, like Mitty again, and also like poor Ha'penny, has lost his strength, too; he is sitting starving in a garret, almost unemployable — the world has almost wiped him out.

Yet unlike Mitty and Ha'penny, Sonnabend is bringing his tactical concen-tration out of shock: slowly and carefully he is building a system of intellectual subversion. Out of sight and sound of the marching ranks of glittering mass persuasion, within Sonnabend clear orders are being issued and centres of resistance established. Why does Sonnabend write at all? Because writing alone remains unassailably the highest tradition. It is the only weapon against the big world, which as usual, is telling lies. Everywhere Sonnabend digs up bits of broken imaginations that appear like the bones of a long-buried massacre. In this, the terror of Fort's discoveries is often equal to that in Kafka's work.

Thurber's story is particularly apt here because Fort lived indeed like a Walter Mitty all his life, dedicating his entire existence to attacking what he considered to be the complete imposture of all rational thinking. Like Mitty and Josef K again (and indeed Beckett's Vladimir and Estragon long after them), such an activity to Sonnabend is a battle against infinity *par excellence*, the ultimate intellectual *kamikaze*:

Walter Mitty Strikes Back

> In *The Earth and the Stars*, p. 211, Abbot tells of the spectroscopic determinations, by which the new star in Perseus (Feb. 22, 1901) was found to be at a distance of 300 light years from this earth. The news was pub-lished in the newspapers. A new star had appeared, about the year 1600, and its light was not seen upon this earth until Feb. 22nd, 1901. And the astronomers were able to tell this — that way back, at a moment when Queen Elizabeth — well, whatever she was doing, maybe it wouldn't be too discreet to inquire into just what she was doing — but the astronomers told that just when Queen Elizabeth was doing whatever she was doing, the heavens were doing a new star. And where am I, comparatively? Where are my poor, little yarns of flows of methylated spirits from ceilings, and 'myste-

rious strangers', and bodies on railway lines, compared with a yarn of the new star and Queen Elizabeth?[4]

But almost like a finally triumphant Walter Mitty reaching out to touch one of his creations, Sonnabend, continuing, finds a fault-line:

> But the good little star restores my conceit. In the face of all spectroscopes in all observatories, it shot out nebulous rings that moved at a rate of two or three seconds of arc a day. If they were 300 light years away, this was a velocity far greater than that of light is said to be. If they were 300 light years away, it was motion at the rate of 220,000 miles a second. There were dogmas that could not stand this, and spectroscopic determinations, which were in agreement, were another case of agreements working out, as they shouldn't have worked out. The astronomers had to cut down one of their beloved immensities.

Abbot explained this inconsistency by attributing the first "pronouncements" to "the roughness of the observations." But about twenty years later this situation, essentially the same in all particulars, was repeated. On May 27, 1925 a new star was discovered in the southern constellation, Pictor. By spectroscopic determination, Harvard Observatory announced in November 1927 that the distance of this new star was "determined" to be 540 light years, but some months later, the astronomers hit trouble, for upon March 27, 1928 the new star *split*:

> When the split was seen, astronomers of the South African observatory repudiated the gospel of their spectroscopes of three years before. There must have been much roughness, even though there had been three years in which to plane down the splinters. They cut the distance from 540 to forty light years. If there should be any more reductions like this, there may start a slump of immensities down towards a conception of a thinkable-sized formation of stars. A distance cut down $60 \times 60 \times 24 \times 365 \times 500 \times 186,000$ is a good start.[5]

Such comedy, counterpointed by verifiable quotations from the outer world, is a powerful satirical technique. Throughout Fort's four books, there is a motif of an anti-gravity argument: that is, his collected examples of objects which appear to go *up* instead of down. Corpses from graves, stones, and even on one occasion a horse and a barn, all were observed to go up! In the case of the former, "several hundred feet into the air," in the case of the latter, there is no evidence that they ever came down again at all.

But there are times when Sonnabend is not so jubilant. These are times when he seems defeated and exhausted, as if the weight of the opposition were too much for him. He then appears to doubt himself, momentarily; he falls into cliché, loses himself in a fractured grammar and becomes defensive and rather lame. Part of his problem is that he is using language to investigate language, whereas most writers take the far less risky path of working things out in their head, using the language as merely a tool for expression of the idea. But Sonnabend, like Leopold Bloom, is trying to get at something in the corner of the conscious "I", for which a semi-passive language would not be suitable. Like any good reconnaissance force, he fights his way into trouble in order to fight his way out again and get back with vital information, rather breathless, with coinages of his own like "frogeity" and "intermediatism", although there are other casualties, such as a lightly wounded syntax.

Part of the comic irony is that Sonnabend fully recognises that the structures of science are as much within him as without. In any cultural fluid, the "off" switch is often extremely difficult to find. In fracturing grammar, he is trying to break the semantic and verbal assumptions that two hundred years of semi-rationalised specialisations and developments have laid upon the language and concepts that he has inherited as natural processes. Given this, following Sonnabend's thought processes is often rather like debugging a hacking operation. One follows it by the spore of omissions rather than paths. He cannot for example, say "the fact is", "in reality," "speaking objectively," or "impartially weighing the evidence", when he has had to demolish most of those immensely powerful clichés in order to develop his own particular form of attack. He realises this is hopeless of course, and is content to criticise science at the same time as he uses mathematical concepts to describe a whirlwind's progress as "axial", yet it discharging its picked-up waste "tangentially".

Walter Mitty Strikes Back

More often than not, however, he manages to disentangle all this dialectically colonising apparatus, and the effect is rather like lifting a stone from full frontal consciousness and seeing what wonders are underneath. It enables him to show us how illusory is that overlay of historical assumptions which govern the seeing of the rationalist fallacies, that pretend to demolish all other fallacies which have gone before. What is revealed when he has successfully penetrated the system camouflage? The mythopoaeic world. He develops an affection for the rediscovered heretical thoughts of this old-new world, and mimics his own grammatical "unintelligibility" as well as that of the heretical seeing:

> But I like best the super-wolves that were seen to cross the sun during the earthquake at Palermo.
> They howled.
> Or the loves of the worlds. The call they feel for one another. They try to move closer and howl when they get there.
> The howls of the planets.
> I have discovered a new unintelligibility.

But Fort's theory was much more important than merely proving a right (science) against a wrong (usually called the "paranormal"), or vice versa; his basic idea is that all conscious structures (and that includes science of course) work to a certain degree of allowance.

> I do not know that telepathy exists. I think so, according to many notes that I have taken upon vagrant impressions that come and go, when my mind is upon something else. I have often experimented. When I incline to think that there is telepathy, the experiments are convincing that there is. When I think over the same experiments, and incline against, they indicate that there isn't.[6]

The result of realising that nothing is quite real or unreal, true or untrue is surprisingly mentally therapeutic. Sonnabend says that there are so many heresies within him that he has freed his mind of all concrete beliefs, "heresies" he defines as "incredible credulities — or pseudo credulities". He says, "I cannot trace my infidelities, or my enlightenments, back to their sources," and thus he avoids getting involved in the trap of limitless "solution" games:

> It is my method not to try and solve problems — so far as the solubility-insolubility of problems permits — in whatever narrow specialisations of thought I find them stated: but, if, for instance, I come across a mystery that the spiritualists have taken over, to have an eye for data that may have bearing upon, from chemical, zoological, meteorological, sociological, or entomological sources — being unable to fail, of course, because the analogue of anything electrical, or planetary, is findable in biological, ethical, or political phenomena.[7]

Somewhere within these switching analogues that are constantly evolving is the self. Certainly the things we make come from our thoughts, and therefore our thoughts are still present in the very nature of the things we make. We ourselves, as parts of these ideas, are also therefore *within* the things we make. Basically this is Berkeley's position,[8] but Fort extends it to build a system of access points through which is allowed an unconsciously controlled action at a distance *outside* the self. He gives the examples (slightly different versions of which are still to be seen every week in the popular press) of prenatal markings and definite letters and pictures naturally forming upon bodies of humans and animals. The implication is that since this occurs all the time, somewhere there is a roaring billion channel traffic surge between matter and spirit and idea and designs of which (perhaps thankfully) we can only see a very small part. Therefore perhaps understandably to calm ourselves, we call it an "accident" when a spoon bends, a cup flies, or voices are heard in the head that lead to a rescue. That many of these occurrences are not repeatable is a channel restriction upon which much sanity (and also tribal power) depends. Many times in the Pacific area in the late nineteenth-century, men and women, whose ancestors had made nothing but mud huts and stone axes for countless thousands of years, must have parted the bush and glimpsed the lights of a big sailing cutter or even a first steam vessel. Many times in Charles Fort's work do we come across this deep cultural fear; we feel that Sonnabend is knocking on the doors of the almost-inconceivable, and the reader is peeping through his own particular foliage with as much fear and trembling as any maker of stone axes seeing smoke from a funnel.

The result of such a view is to push aside all "factual" statements about both self and society, and all clean, separable definitions. It takes a lot of intellectual courage to confront a painful and messy chaos, as distinct from trusting to formula, finite destiny, and fixed definable deterministic purpose. Most people of course prefer to live in a universe in which things are as they appear to be. This is a world in which doctors cure people, policemen arrest criminals, scientists discover harmonious "universal" laws through their "cleverness", and governments tell the truth. But throughout the great anti-science debate in the work of Charles Fort, we have a journey of the modern soul attempting to rid itself of such simplistic and witless "objective" contaminations.

It is likely that few natives cared to think that there were things beyond even the steamship-master's understanding. Against such fear, natives like ourselves in turn understandably manufacture certainties, if only to get some sleep when night falls. This is Fort's view of the function of scepticism as a control, not as a separator of "fact" from "fiction".

Walter
Mitty
Strikes
Back

holy
war

The right to reject systems of rational thought on principle alone was for Fort as important as the right to withdraw labour was for other, very different, think-ers of his particular epoch. In the twentienth-century, taking the German exam-ple alone, the Anglo-Saxon mind always seems to have a great deal of intellec-tual difficulty in conceiving of the idea of ideological non-conformity, and un-fortunately for Fort the world preferred more obvious and more easily digested meats than his. This meant that he remained perhaps the most obscure of all published writers in English until the 1960s, when "alternative" movements of all kinds started taking notice of him.

For the rejected, poverty-stricken and often bitter Sonnabend, the attack on fact is a holy war within the collective imagination itself, as if that imagination is always trying desperately to understand its own inner transforming nature. Despite his often curious grammar, Sonnabend shows an outsider sentiment that could be from any page of Dostoevsky's *Notes from the Underground*, with a touch of Céline's *Journey to the End of Night*:

> Once upon a time, when mine was an undeveloped suspiciousness, and I'd
> let dogmatists pull their pedantries over my perceptions, I nevertheless col-
> lected occasional notes upon what seemed to be unexplained phenomena. I
> don't do things mildly, and at the same time enjoy myself in different ways:
> I act as if trying to make allness out of something. A search for the unex-
> plained became an obsession. I undertook the job of going through all the
> scientific periodicals, at least by way of indexes, published in English and
> French, from the year 1800, available in the libraries of New York and Lon-
> don. As I went along, with my little suspicions in their infancies, new sub-

jects appeared to me — something queer about some hailstones — the odd and the unexplained in archaeological discoveries, and in Arctic explorations. By the time I got through with the 'grand tour', as I called this search of all available periodicals, to distinguish it from special investigations, I was interested in so many subjects that cropped up later, or that I had missed much earlier, that I made the tour all over again — and then again had the same experience, and had to go touring again — and so on — until now it is my recognition that in every field of phenomena — and in later years I have multiplied my subjects by very much shifting to the newspapers — is somewhere the unexplained, or the irreconcilable, or the mysterious — in the unformable motions of all planets; volcanic eruptions, murders, hailstorms, protective colorations of insects, chemical reactions, disappearances of human beings, stars, comets, juries, diseases, cats, lampposts, newly married couples, cathode rays, hoaxes, impostures, wars, births, deaths.

Everywhere is the tabooed, or the disregarded. The monks of science dwell in smuggeries that are walled away from the event-jungles. Or some of them do. Nowadays a good many of them are going native. There are scientific dervishes who whirl amok, brandishing startling statements; but mostly they whirl not far from their origins, and their excitements are exaggerations of old-fashioned complacencies.[1]

Holy War

This is as good a declaration of total war against all received experience as will be found in the far better known works of later writers such as Sartre, Camus or Beckett. But although in contrast to most antiheroes Sonnabend exercises the right to thoroughly enjoy himself, he is as ghetto-isolated as Kafka's Josef K or Orwell's Winston Smith. Like Sonnabend, such characters may whistle in the dark since for such, the imagination is always the problem: they desire, but the concrete will not yield. Godot, as it were, is always just around the corner, like a Five Year Plan, a political promise, or a scientific "cure for cancer". Though Sonnabend as outsider is not broken, like T. S. Eliot's Prufrock he nevertheless cannot join the herd, put his shoulder to the wheel or carry a party card, just as he cannot accept the so-called concrete; both smother his besieged individuality, force it into ghettos, perhaps to prepare it for far worse, such as the coming of media and television. In this respect it is possible to take a Fortean view of Kafka's castle as being the body of both burgeoning science and communism and their associated bureaucracies spinning their quite endless "factual" systems which claim to push aside all other forms of valuation and experience, pretending to "liberate" the mind from any and every kind of metaphysical, religious, and mystical "nonsense". In their way, both Fort and Kafka were sounding very early warnings that such factual systems are labyrinths in themselves, ghetto alley death traps in which all proper identity is exterminated by being cut off from all sources of magical transformations.

Just as with Josef K again, the massive resources of the conscious world may whisper to Fort's introspective Sonnabend, marooned in his garret, that he is not special, he is not chosen, and he cannot escape. Yet still there is the search in the impossible dark of the prison cell floor of the cold water pad, squat, or embankment box (yes, it all still goes on!), the knowledge that somewhere there must be a fault-line that will show the much-vaunted absoluteness of the propagandised scientific "reality" to be as vulnerable a stage-front as all mythological constructs.

In this sense Sonnabend's relations with science are rather like Winston Smith's relations with his interrogator, O'Brien. In the fiction of our own consumer-society, the interrogator[2] appears to have disappeared, along with the gulag victim and the working class hero, but the interrogator was very much a figure of Fort's milieu, as he was for Orwell, Kafka and Arthur Koestler[3]. Fort sees science as such a cultural interrogator; in his view, institutionally it forces experience into saying yes because it cannot comprehend refusal on principle alone in the face of overwhelming "evidence." Today, the interrogator has received a totally new image: he is liberal, informative; now "hot" methods of social-control are as obsolete as a Maoist commune, an East German steelworks, BBC Radio Four, or writing to an MP or Congressman in order to "change" something. The new interrogator is "cool" in the McLuhan sense. No longer is a definite yes or no needed, all that is required is a purchase, and all that is needed for that transaction is to stop thinking and look at the coloured lights on the screen. No wonder many folk think that aliens have abducted them.

PART 2

FACTS AS ART FORM

In days of yore, when I was an especially bad young one, punishment was having to go to the store, Saturdays, and work. I had to scrape off labels of other dealers' canned goods, and paste on my parents' label. One time I had pyramids of canned goods, containing a variety of fruits and vegetables. But I had used all except peach labels. I pasted the peach labels on peach cans, and then came to apricots. Well, aren't apricots peaches? And there are plums that are virtually apricots. I went on, either mischievously, or scientifically, pasting the peach labels on cans of plums, cherries, string beans, succotash. I can't quite define my motive, because to this day it has not been decided whether I am a humorist or a scientist. I think that it was mischief, but, as we go along, there will come a more respectful recognition that also it was a scientific procedure.

Wild Talents

A perfectly smooth and round nutshell would be the most probable history of the bubble in imaginary time. On the other hand, imaginary time histories that are not perfectly smooth and round could correspond to the formation of galaxies and the development of intelligent life. Thus it is only the slightly "hairy" nutshells which will be observed by beings like us who are intelligent enough to ask why they have to be hairy.

Stephen Hawking, *The Universe in a Nutshell*

I could be bounded in a nutshell, and count myself a king of infinite space, were it not that I have bad dreams.

Hamlet, II. ii

gas lamp
theatre

Gas
Lamp
Theatre

In Fort's time, quite distinct from our own, any writer worth his salt was brought up in a climate of resistance to just about everything. The whole world was in ferment, and the atmosphere in New York must have been at times like that in St Petersburg in the 1890s, or indeed the northern manufacturing districts of Britain at this same time. The troubled birth of modern American capitalism had anarchists and communists threatening bombs, and not the terrorists of almost exactly 100 years later. The scene is well described by Isaac Bashevis Singer in *Property*, his story about New York at the turn of the century:

> When I came to America in the early nineties, in the Yiddish neighbourhood on the Lower East Side, anarchism still flourished. Not all of us wanted to wait until capital was concentrated and Kautsky or De Leon gave the signal that the hour of revolution had arrived... guests used to come from Russia and Germany — sometimes even from Spain. Our meetings were always crowded. Most of the delegates from Russia spoke Yiddish. We were vain enough to believe that if a couple of bombs were thrown the masses would rise up like one man and abolish all governments.[1]

In the midst of this disturbed atmosphere, Fort collected events which no one else had time to notice, still less examine. These things fled to him like animals from a forest fire. In the early 1900s, the rate of change in all major cultural directions, both in Europe and America, was almost vertical. The old world's traditional intellectual and philosophical matter was collapsing as quickly as was the old Austro-Hungarian empire; one month brought more changes to cities and seas (and skies indeed), than the last nineteenth-century generation saw in a lifetime. Many of the last of those who had seen the face of William Gladstone and Abraham Lincoln gathered in town squares by duck pond and saloon bar to listen to a horn speaker crackle of "dance music, songs, and vaudeville". The first high aerials could be seen on the village skylines, and full-blown electronic media just only a few historical hours away was pushing the last serpents from the last haunted maps.

Only one thing was certain about this new world — it did not look like it was going to be a good place for the independent thinker, unless he was a capitalist/mechanist, such as Edison, Ford, or Marconi, three of the new masters of this new universe. Practical geniuses they might be, but philosophers they were not, and if the great new society was going to be about anything, it was going to be about their kind of grand causation and all its ramifications: conquest of nature, accretion of property, the ruthless getting of wealth and power, the quest for the acquisition of image and social status.

The newly emerging technologies of Fort's time were of course recognised immediately as a powerful means of helping all these many and varied processes to mount their own mythological engineering projects. Many times Fort made the point that as new technology became available it would be taken over rapidly by different interest sectors, all of whom had their own separate mythological agendas in addition to that of straight science. H. G. Wells and Jules Verne were of course the best known writers of this period who warned of such things, but there were others less well known. For example, there was the manipulative techno-Pope in the 1904 novel *Hadrian VII* by "Frederick Baron Corvo"[2] whose brilliantly comic character George Arthur Rose predicted certainly the Vatican world wide web site. Another writer of a similar ilk was Joris-Karl Huysmans, in whose 1884 novel *Against Nature* appears the aristocrat Duc Jean des Esseintes who would surely have loved to get his decadent hands on a modern video or film studio.

Hence even as early as the turn of the nineteenth-century, techno-mysticism was already become a new spiritual thirst. The cultural advertising of social-democratic "factually objective" conventional experimental science was no more than a juvenile excuse, tossed like a sprat to the naïve, just as all conquering explorers tell the natives that they are there for their "benefit". Even during Fort's lifetime, the excuses of science were become supports falling away under a newly launched ship full of corruption and tragic devastation. By 2001, some sixty-nine years after his death, Fort's prophetic view of the activities of corporate science are evident. There is the spoiling of earth, sea, sky and water; there is radiation and pollution, and we witness the mass destruction of the rain forests. We see in applied technologies that corruption, conspiracy and exploitative greed many now associate with scientific advance. We also see the mass "experimental" torture of countless millions of animals and indeed hundreds of human beings in the name of the "cause".

Sonnabend sees this as much more than a plain and simple political accusation, however. He sees science emerging as a kind of colonising spore secreted from networks of ideological deception, a form of live ideological protein that acts almost like an alien invasion. Moreover, he knows that institutions, cultures, and indeed religions whole and entire are going to be based on these misconceptions, the follies of certainty and claimed "objective" truths. He sees therefore a human tragedy rather than simple-minded rights and wrongs. We do what we do because we are built that way. The angry young man Sonnabend has refused to be bludgeoned into accepting the crude and brutal Marxist machinery of explanation of his time. He has replaced it with advanced ideas about the interaction of thought and media in which for the first time in history, the idea of *advertisements* instead of *facts* is considered. Prophetically for this time, Sonnabend reaches right into the heart of our own web-gaming world and even goes so far as to suggest the virtual event, such as Y2K:

> It does not matter how preposterous some of my own notions are going to seem. They cannot be more out of accordance with events upon this earth than is such an attribution of the blazing sky of a nation to searchlights or to lamps in tram cars. If I should write that the stars are probably between forty and fifty miles away, I'd be not much more a trimmer than is such a barber, whose clips are said to be scientific. Maybe they are scientific. Though, mostly, barbers are artists, some of them do consider themselves scientific.[3]

Gas Lamp Theatre

This most comical view of mass self-deception was advanced for Fort's time, and his ideas here make him the first post-modern philosopher. In the first decade of the twentieth-century, mental operations were conceived of as things somewhat mechanical and finite; they had very simple Pavlovian inputs and outputs, and clanked and squeaked rather like steam-driven artificial limbs. Freud's discovery of the unconscious and the implications of his book *The Interpretation of Dreams* had been very slow in making an impression upon the thinking world. Fort's idea of hidden agendas being the deceptive plots of the unconscious took very much longer again to be recognised.

Such original thinking as this of course always causes trouble. Henry Ford, rather like Plato, never ceased pointing out that artists, writers and philosophers were dangerous: they always asked too many questions, and the new American machine, rather like its opposed communist machine, dealt with individuality, uniqueness, eccentricity and all deviations from any norm in the manner of all such mass social "solutions": it ate them up and it spat out the pieces. It turned the originators of such things into witless losers, cracks, oddballs and eccentrics; it saw people as being of no account whatsoever. In Russia, such misfits as Charles Fort disappeared overnight, thrown into the backs of open trucks, never to be seen again. In America, they were privileged to starve to death quite visibly. Much later in Europe, the Nazis gassed all such oddballs as they could lay hands on.

The twentieth-century in particular has not, therefore, been a very easy patch for the idiosyncratic thinker such as Charles Fort, who did not have a collective atom or industrially responsive muscle in his entire being. Like Henry Miller, or Allen Ginsberg, Fort could not knock in a nail, and like Dickens' Mr Micawber, he was always waiting for something to turn up. For a poor man in the New York of that time, what usually turned up was a fate worse than death. Lulla Rosenfeld in *Bright Star of Exile*, tells of what tended to happen to many of the kind of people Fort must have lived with and known:

> The wheel of fortune turned sharply in America. Education and learning counted for nothing here. Tradesmen and labourers went into the savage pushcart life of Hester Street, fought their way up, became contractors, shop owners, great manufacturers. Intellectuals and professionals preferred the factories, certain they would soon get out again. Most of these men were lost forever in the sweatshops.[4]

Like many a good mind, Fort's attitude to this kind of situation was not of the best. In 1915, he wrote to Theodore Dreiser:

> One time when I was down worst I ever have been, I was studying the infinitesimal calculus. Every morning I'd try to write something that would bring in some money; every morning, by ten o'clock, I was back studying transcendental functions and things. It's utterly past my power to do things I feel I ought to do.[5]

He may have been down, but Fort was perhaps the very first thinker and writer to see that media and the performer would emerge from the system-soup to be somewhat surprising historical victors. As we now know, they helped demolish monolithic scientific communism, but kept certain scientific elements for their own illimitable purpose. It is as if Fort had this kind of twinkling doll's house horizon in mind when he makes Sonnabend employ a variety of what might be called anti-cultural sales techniques, or consumer resistance to science. It must be borne in mind his kind of "post-modern" thinking was, of course, non-existent in the early 1900s.

Fort claimed that goody-two-shoes rationalism was about performance style, just as was anything else. Part of his technique in constructing the character of Sonnabend, is, on the one hand, to make him appear to keep his discovery of anomalistic wonders well under a kind of dour Johnsonian lock and key, then allowing him to reveal wonders rather like casually loosing hungry ferrets from a sack at a sedate dinner party of well-heeled "experts" who have dined far too well for far too long:

> There's not a notion in this book that has a more frightful, or ridiculous, mien than had the notion of human footprints in rocks, when that now respectabilised ruffian, or clown, was first heard from. It seems bewildering to one whose interests are not scientific that such rows should be raised over such trifles: but the feeling of a systematist towards such an intruder

is just about what anyone's would be if a tramp from the street should come in, sit at one's dinner table, and say he belonged there. We know what hypnosis can do: let him insist with all his might that he does belong there, and one begins to suspect that he may be right; that he may have higher perceptions of what's right. The prohibitionists had this worked out very skilfully.[6]

At most times, Sonnabend appears to be passively collecting his contradictions and anomalies as Darwin collected specimens. That is, he starts passively, and then gradually reveals his amazing collection until the wonders become vast, engulfing all else, so turning the world of experience on its head. This action affects the entire cultural performance game such that it appears that rationalisations (as well as fantasies) have in turn become cast-out anomalies in a world become pure performance:

Water falls on a tree, in Oklahoma. It is told of in an entomological magazine. Water falls in a house in Eccleston. I read that in a spiritualist's periodical, though I went to a newspaper for the data. These are the isolations, or the specialisations, of conventional treatments. I tell of water falling upon a tree, in Oklahoma, and of water falling in a house, in Eccleston, and think that both phenomena are manifestations of one force. It is my attempt to smash false demarcations: to take data away from the narrow and exclusive treatments by spiritualists, astronomers, meteorologists, entomologists: also denying the validity of usurpations of words and ideas by metaphysicians and theologians.[7]

Gas
Lamp
Theatre

All these techniques give Sonnabend's comic ironies great strength. As master of ceremonies, he is a great actor and raconteur; imitating the typically "exact" tone of voice of individual rationalist enemies. He then expands his range to mimic the whole style of nineteenth-century constituted authority, complete with its pompous announcements of "accurate" and "factual" truths delivered from on high. He is at his best when he mock-reasons from "evidence" by mock-demonstration and analogy. In many of these performances, he reasons dramatically, his images operating like an early electronic village lantern slide.

In a telling example, three philological "experts" begin to "translate" engraved alphabetic characters found on a small, flat, oval stone disk in an excavated mound at Grave Creek, West Virginia, in 1838 — and we have an early impression of the first gas-lamp soundbites, the beginning of that electric age flicker which now poses as "information":

Translation by M. Jombard:
"Thy orders are laws: thou shinest in impetuous elan and rapid chamois."

M. Maurice Schwab:
"The chief of Emigration who reached these places (or this island) has

fixed these characters forever."

M. Oppert:
"The grave of one who was assassinated here. May God, to revenge him, strike his murderer, cutting off the hand of his existence."[8]

In this sense, Fort's quartet of the damned belongs to a tradition which connects Dan Leno to Max Wall, the difference being that Sonnabend has a rather wider range of targets, and as the world's first existential comedian, he frequently drops all stage technique and goes for the throat:

> If Life cannot be positively differentiated from anything else, the appearance of life is deception. If, in mentality, there is no absolute dividing line between intellectuality and imbecility, all wisdom is partly idiocy. The seeker of wisdom departs more and more from the state of the idiot, only to find that he is returning. Belief after belief fades from his mind: so his goal is the juncture of two obliterations. One is of knowing nothing, and the other is of knowing that there is nothing to know.[9]

It is this variety of Sonnabend's dramatic performance that gives the fabric of the four-book argument its great strength. As a change from working himself into such nihilistic corners as above, he peoples the cosmic vacancy he has momentarily created by building "alternative" theories to science, only to knock them down again as entertaining illusions. It appears that the gurus, shamans and witch doctors tell the same lies as the nice reasonable men in white coats with the plausible smiles. This reminds us of the words of Swedenborg: "When the angels begin to speak to a man, he must beware, for they will tell him more outrageous lies than he could ever believe."[10]

What Sonnabend really means to demonstrate by all this switching around of focus is his view of Mind as kind of Legoland, infinite in extension, containing as many kinds of cellular systems game, of which science is but a singular variety. He sees the mind as a massive bullshit machine whose mental video frames can be slowed or speeded at will, and whose fuzziness can be of any degree.

The one object of Sonnabend's stage technique is to stop any view falling into stasis; patterns of ideological formations to him are regions of conceptual pixels whose potentials, when organised, may reveal Donald Duck, or the face of Dante dying in Ravenna. Any terror, ancient or modern, any beauty, silly or profound, may emerge from the dark, according to the state of the game. It all depends on how hard is the focus, how urgent is the need, how powerful is the agenda. If we choose, we can have the destructive military game, the intellectual games of science, the gnome games of the arts, or the non-cerebral games of sports and media. All these systems are tripped into further extensions by developing different kinds of anomalies within themselves. The function of the anomaly becomes therefore clear: it serves to trip any system into the next stage of its larval development.

Here is the very first nucleus of the idea of mind as a being full of computer programs or menus. Since a lot of these ideas were formed round about 1910, even to approximate to the modern idea of Internet "cyberspace" is quite an astonishing achievement. In this sense Fort does not see science so much as lies, but as a series of game possibilities subject to varying degrees of exhaustion, obsolescence, and downright decay.

Thus the technique is identical with the purpose: like Harlequin or Pierrot, master of ceremonies or clubbable raconteur, Sonnabend changes his mood, experiments with his own views, questions them, even rejects his own opinions, is angry at vivisection, politicians, conscription and the enormities of the Great War. The events he describes are made more eerie by the continuously unfolding framework of very careful factual proceeding, which at times is played like a ghost scientist dissecting a dead body of dead facts. Sonnabend frequently laughs at this ironic concreteness within himself, but he knows it gives his ideas great strength. Were he to rave, were he to become enthusiastic (even less, as he notes tongue-in-cheek, *imaginative*), the strangeness would rapidly compound itself, and he also knows he would be lost, become another hole-in-the-corner eccentric with tales of things which go bump in the night. In *Wild Talents* he says that he has not yet come across a report of a character in a "moving-picture" jumping out and assaulting a member of the audience; he dare not imagine such a thing very intensely, because he knows that (a not-uncommon experience) it is likely that such a visualisation would increase the possibility of him coming across a report of just such a thing, within a very short time!

Gas
Lamp
Theatre

Of course Sonnabend's technique of constantly feeding us external reference enables him to underline and reinforce absurdities that otherwise would be ignored. He quotes the journal *Comptes Rendus* (24–812) of October 16 and 17, 1846,[11] regarding a heavy and extensive "red rain" falling in France. This rain was so vividly blood-red, that it quite terrified many people. One chemist noted thirty-five percent of organic corpuscles in this semi-liquid material, and it was noted "larks, quail, ducks, and water hens, some of them alive, fell at Lyon and Grenoble and other places."

Laurence Sterne's novel *Tristram Shandy*, published in 1760, is reckoned to be the first novel written in the broken stream-of-consciousness style that was developed by James Joyce in his novel *Ulysses*, published in 1922. Here is a fragment of the infinite monologue of Sterne's character, Uncle Toby, who speaks for an entire lifetime of how he got his wound at the battle of Namur:

> ... my uncle Toby was generally more eloquent and particular in his account of it; and the many perplexities he was in, arose out of the almost insurmountable difficulties he found in telling his story intelligibly, and giving such clear ideas of the differences and distinction between the scarp and the counter-scarp, — the glacis and covered-way, — the half-moon and ravelin, as to make his company fully comprehend where and what he was about.[12]

Here is Joyce, mimicking in a similar way, the polite verbosity of his day:

—Of course, Mr Bloom proceeded to stipulate, you must look at both sides of the question. It is hard to lay down any hard and fast rules as to right and wrong but room for improvement all round there certainly is though every country, they say, our own distressful included, has the government it deserves. But with a little goodwill all round. It's all very fine to boast of mutual superiority but what about mutual equality? I resent violence or intolerance in any shape or form. It never reaches anything or stops anything. A revolution must come on the due instalments plan. It's a patent absurdity on the face of it to hate people because they live round the corner and speak another vernacular, so to speak.[13]

And here is Charles Fort, doing exactly the same thing:

Our expression is that there is an association between reported objects, like extra-mundane visitors, and the nearest approaches by the planet Venus to this earth. Perhaps unfortunately this is our expression, because it makes for more restriction than we intend. The objects, or the voyagers, have often been seen during the few hours of the visibility of Venus, when the planet is nearest. 'Then such an object is Venus,' say the astronomers. If anybody wonders why, if these seeming navigators can come close to this earth — as they do approach, if they appear only in a local sky — they do not then come all the way to this earth, let him as a sea captain ask why said captain never purposely descends to the bottom of the ocean, though travelling not far away. However, I conceive of a great variety of extra-mundanians, and I am now collecting data for a future expression — that some kinds of beings from outer space can adapt to our conditions, which may be like the bottom of a sea, and have been seen, but have supposed to be psychic phenomena.[14]

Certainly this style has something of the wit and courage in experimentation of both Joyce and Sterne. *The Book of the Damned* appeared some three years before Joyce's *Ulysses*, and it is interesting to compare features of the two works. Fort's Sonnabend is Joyce's Leopold Bloom with a difference. Joyce describes just one day (from dawn to dusk) of Bloom's life: June 6, 1904. This day of course proves to be infinite, as are all other days. Infinity is portrayed as a limitless unfolding of intense subjectivities, physically rather like the modern idea of a chaos fractal. The external events of this one day are but a backdrop to the infinities that make up Bloom's identity.[15] Within each moment of his existence, both time and death become meaningless before this unfolding of the infinities of experience in terms of the purest of poetic textures. Though he was perhaps the greatest novelist of the twentieth-century, Joyce shows a typical fault of most writers of his time: he ignores science and technology almost completely.

But for Sonnabend the external world is a problem. It lies to him, and the lie grows and prospers in the form of science. Since science still flourishes as such, this means that the modern reader of Fort may look out of his window at some scientific construct and see it through Fortean eyes. Such an extra-literary dimension is unusual, to say the least; it means that as well as creating a landmark in the literature of existential resistance, Fort has created a form which can be constantly updated. Sonnabend also offers a system of analysis sorely needed by a media-soaked scientific age in which "information" has become largely a Fortean stage-construct where the changed hemline of a famous actress could easily annihilate an alien invasion, or even the threat of nuclear war.

This is a most peculiar literary achievement. It constructs a new literary/artistic dimension. Humanity has in general lacked a sophisticated tool to attack scientific statements, which stalk the planet as if they were the lords and masters of all history, in many cases getting away with murder, and often not metaphorically. Moreover Fort's method involves no shaking of goat's feet, no dancing naked round midwinter fires, pissing on church altars, or any such blushing hokum, but instead is a system of effective philosophical attack.

In this external dimension, "facts" play a part in a kind of subplot of myth. In the examples Sonnabend gives of strange substances which have fallen from the sky, he shows that there is always an understandable human attempt to define such substances in terms of something that is known that is much more familiar. Referring to very large flakes of a "coal-black leafy mass" which fell during a snow storm at Memel in 1646, and which was described as tearing fibrously like paper and smelling like seaweed, Sonnabend notes the ensuing discussion of the *Proceedings of the Royal Irish Academy*:

Gas Lamp Theatre

> ... it was brought out that there is a substance, of rather rare occurrence, that has been known to form in thin sheets upon marsh land.
> It looks like greenish felt.
> The substance of Memel:
> Damp, coal-black, leafy mass.
> But, if broken up, the marsh-substance is flake-like, and it tears fibrously.
> An elephant can be identified as a sunflower — both have long stems. A camel is indistinguishable from a peanut — if only their humps be considered.[16]

Sonnabend now does a quick costume-change, appearing as vaudeville master of ceremonies, and again he gives the gas-lamp soundbites, but this time lighting up a long-forgotten snow storm in the seventeenth-century, no less:

> ... now we have an all-star cast: and they're not only Irish; they're royal Irish. The royal Irishmen excluded "coal blackness" and included fibrousness: so then that this substance was "marsh paper", which "had been raised into the air by storms of wind, and had again fallen".

> Second act:
> It was said that, according to M. Ehrenberg, "the meteor-paper was found to consist partly of vegetable matter, chiefly of conifervae."

Third act:
Meeting of Royal Irishmen: chairs, tables, Irishmen:
Some flakes of marsh-paper were exhibited.
Their composition was chiefly of conifervae.[17]

Adding that there is also another similarity between a peanut and a camel, namely that both can go without water for a long time, Sonnabend the master of ceremonies continues:

Now it's not so very unreasonable, at least to the free and easy vaudeville standards that, throughout this book, we are considering, to think that a green substance could be snatched up from one place in a whirlwind and fall as a black substance somewhere else: but the royal Irishmen excluded something else, and it is a datum that was accessible to them as it is to me: That, according to Chladni,[18] this was no little, local deposition that was seen to occur by some definite person living near a pond somewhere.
It was tremendous fall from a vast sky-area.
Likely enough all the marsh-paper in the world could not have supplied it.
At the same time, this substance was falling in 'great quantities', in Norway and Pomerania. Or see Kirkwood, Meteoric Astronomy, p.66:
Substance like charred paper fell in Norway and other parts of northern Europe, Jan. 31, 1686.[19]

Thus "facts" are seen through a music hall focus in which time is become performance theatre: intellectual, scientific, mythological, apocryphal shells of disintegrating ego-projections. Sonnabend sees nothing more or less than the stage-fronts of literature in which his own work (for yes, Sonnabend knows he is writing a novel, though sometimes he tries to conceal it from us; note the "this book" above), as orchestrated mass of activity in which all things are possible. Take the minuscule obscurity, open it like a fractal, and there, there is not only the experiential universe, but the self, the same self which was the same self way back in Memel in 1646. For Sonnabend there appears to be no difference between what he is writing and anything else, given the double-form he has created for himself. His mind is his book, and is the world of all experience. In this sense one always gets the unmistakable impression from Charles Fort that learning is *remembering*. He finds pieces of himself in the deep past, blinding recognitions in the part-dismembered debates of long ago; they are echoes of a lost family, a whole vessel once he knew: the truth is he clings to anomalies like the lost children of a forgotten tribe.

History for Sonnabend thus becomes a kind of rabbit hole composed of inspirations threading through reasonably objective reports and descriptions, then through personality and time itself. He sees a living drama with a complete script of characters, whose destinies network into an ever-widening penumbra of the uncertain definitions, and the endless discussions of the great human "evidence" game. The effect is as if a dark cold universe of mentality were suddenly alive with numberless alien signals. Sonnabend has switched the galactic lights on, and his great anti-science crusade becomes almost unnecessary; he used it as a route to come to know and come near to that chaotic absurdity within both the cosmos and *himself*:

> So many of our data are upon a godness that so much resembles idiocy that to attribute intelligence to it may even be even blasphemous. Early in this theological treatise we noted a widespread feeling that there is something of the divine in imbecility.[20]

And just when we are completely within Sonnabend's theatre of inspirations, and enjoying a rattling good tale of the sane turning into the insane and vice versa, frequently we have to drag ourselves back from the brink just like a deliberate Brechtian alienation, as we realise that such unbelievable things as revealed happened *external* to the text, yet still remain thinned-out versions of the text.

Sonnabend's often unusual grammar well represents the splintered dialectics of the interface between literary expression and direct physical and emotional experience. Like the grammar of *Ulysses*, it is a grammar of those regions in which the edges of perception are always nattering at one another, pushing and pulling one another into almost battling frames of reference, just as do the strange events Sonnabend pulls out from his cuttings boxes. The difficulties of descriptions of high strangeness are like the typical difficulties of translation of one form to another: nothing is one hundred per cent, indeed, everything is half-real, almost-real, nearly false, a quarter-true, or almost-true; nothing quite fits. Like the limit in the calculus, we never get to what Fort called "absolute positiveness," otherwise the cosmos would lock itself up, unable to change, and Achilles would, as it were, have finally caught up with the tortoise. The Fortean element in a scene is therefore the element of destabilisation in that scene, forcing our assumptions about anything and everything to be constantly on the move. The incidents selected by Fort for his books are therefore those which appear most of all to subvert their own tendency to solidify into "correct interpretations;" in this sense, we do not have "accuracy" so much as we have endless streams of broken bitmapped approximations to that complete we call the "absolute". This, of course, is rather like reinventing Plato's cave-shadows as transient and imperfect copies of "reality".

Gas Lamp Theatre

By means of this grammatical drama, we follow Sonnabend rather as we follow Joyce's Leopold Bloom in *nightown*. When we enter the dimensions of a Fortean event, the fractured planes of the scene afford syntax suitable to them. Sonnabend deliberately fractures the grammar not because he does not want us to see things clearly, but because no event in his view is absolutely clear in itself. Constructing a suitable grammatical form was Joyce's problem, too, and it is amazing how both Joyce and Fort, writing at almost exactly at the same time, have on many occasions a very similar style. Both would have agreed that the corner of the eye defeats us if we do not develop a language for it, and the strange, by definition, is always in the corner

of the mental eye. In this sense we can forgive Sonnabend for his broken
clauses, his riotous use of semi and full colons, his typography which frequently
hangs in mid-air, an often baffling paragraph juxtaposition, and a reversed
subject/object relationship in sentences which frequently fall apart grammati-
cally like a clown's ladder upon which is balanced a tub of wallpaper paste. To
these we must add also the coining, the suspended hyphens, and the over-
extended reasoning which seems to mock its own ironies within ironies. Fort's
style certainly gives the phrase "Latin American" a new meaning.

The anomaly of course demands a new anomalistic tense, and when Fort
forms such a tense, momentarily he often loses a reader deliberately to demonstrate how patently false is an "event" such as he describes. He also wishes to
show how just as false is the stream of phoney information describing the
event, interpreting it, defining it, not only trying to vanish an event, but often
trying to manufacture one.

From the Fortean view therefore, what little "information" may be available
about anything (and that is precious little), reaches us in a form which is fragmentary, full of cross-traffic noises, streams of poses, vanishing stage-sets,
systems of pseudo-facts, junk-science, kiss-me-quick cosmology, convenience-
food profundities, wash'n'go truths, all the sales paraphernalia of the very early
electronic village, in which the performer was beginning to feel his strength.
But just as we think that reader, author, and verifiable external event are lost
together, vanished like Florida votes, Sonnabend reappears like the demon
king. He bears unforgettable anomalistic nuggets, culled from the four corners
of the "scientific" culture of the late Victorian age. Knowing the modern equivalents to the following, any troubled reader's sanity recovers in the face of
seeing both knowledge and creation not as orders of facts, or even angels, but
as orders of mercifully comic headlines announcing such wonders that quite
put in the shade any fat lady, unicorn or three-headed penis floating in a bottle
of formaldehyde.

Consider that like the Y2K phenomenon, an entire planet named Vulcan
once made such a virtual appearance:

The disregarded:
Observation, of July 26, 1819, by Gruthinson — but that was of two bodies
that crossed the sun together—

Nature, 14–469:
That, according to the astronomer, J. R. Hind, Benjamin Scott, City Cham-
berlain of London, and a Mr Wray, had, in 1847, seen a body similar to
"Vulcan" cross the sun.

Similar observation by Hind and Lowe, March 12, 1849 (*L'Annee
Scientifique*, 1876–9).

Nature, 14–505:

Body the apparent size of Mercury, seen, Jan. 29, 1860, by F. A. R. Russell and four other observers, crossing the sun.

De Vico's observation of July 12, 1837 (*Observatory*, 2–424).

L'Annee Scientifique, 1865–16:
That another amateur astronomer, M. Coumbray, of Constantinople, had written to Leverrier,[21] that, upon the March 8, 1865, he had seen a black point, sharply outlined, traverse the disk of the sun. It detached itself from a group of sun spots near the limb of the sun, and took 48 minutes to reach the other limb. Figuring upon the diagram sent by M. Coumbray, a central passage would have taken a little more than an hour. This observation was disregarded by Leverrier, because his formula required about four times that velocity. The point here is that these other observations are as authentic as those that Leverrier included; that, then, upon data as good as the data of "Vulcan", there must be other "Vulcans" — the heroic and defiant disregard, then, of trying to formulate one, omitting the others, which, by orthodox doctrine, must have influenced it greatly, if all were in the relatively narrow space between Mercury and the sun.[22]

This kind of thing, whilst it may not quite put us on our feet again completely, perhaps makes us think in a way we have not thought before, as good a justification for being a writer as any. It is a hard way of doing it, but strangeness being what it is, there is perhaps no other way. Shelves are lined with countless volumes which attempt conscious intellectual formulation of the strange, but the strange often appears behind the back of these authors waggling its thumb at them. In trying to find the location of the strange, they look anywhere but where Fort looked: that is, into the conceptual architectures within the descriptive language that governs our reasoning. The wit and the delightful juxtapositions alone are worth a million pages of statistics about Zener card scores that try to demonstrate (or "disprove") the existence of the wretched "paranormal". There is even enough "objective evidence" to satisfy those troubled souls who require the plainer fare demanded by cultural fear, and for sheer fun, there are also some telling cameos of Fort's era:

Gas
Lamp
Theatre

If we weren't so accustomed to Science in its essential aspect of Disregard, we'd be mystified and impressed, like the editor of *Nature*, with the formulation of these data: agreement of so many instances would seem incredible as a coincidence: but our acceptance is that, with just enough disregard, astronomers, and fortune-tellers can formulate anything — or we'd engage, ourselves, to formulate periodicities in the crowds in Broadway — say that every Wednesday morning, a tall man, with one leg and a black eye, carrying a rubber plant, passes the Singer Building at quarter past ten o'clock. Of course it couldn't really be done, unless such a man did have such periodicity, but if some Wednesday mornings it should be a small child lugging a

barrel, or a fat negress with a week's wash, by ordinary disregard that would be prediction good enough for the kind of quasi-existence we're in. So whether we accuse, or whether we think that the word "accuse" over-dignifies an attitude toward a quasi-astronomer, or mere figment in a super-dream, our acceptance is that Leverrier never did formulate observations—
That he picked out observations that could be formulated—
That of this type are all formulas—
That, if Leverrier had not been himself helplessly hypnotised, or if he had in him more than a tincture of realness, never could have been beguiled by such a quasi-process, but that he was hypnotised, and so extended, or transferred, his condition to others, that upon March 22, 1877, he had this earth bristling with telescopes, with the rigid and almost inanimate forms of astronomers behind them.
— And not a blessed thing of any unusuality was seen upon that day or succeeding days.
But that the science of Astronomy suffered the slightest in prestige?
It couldn't. The spirit of 1877 was behind it. If, in an embryo, some cells should not live up to the phenomenon of the era, the others will sustain the scheduled appearances. Not until an embryo enters the mammalian stage are cells of the reptilian stage false cells.[23]

In this respect, it is rather a pity that Fort does not seem to have known of Karl Schwarzschild's[24] experiments in 1916. The quite definite anomalies in Mercury's orbit upon which Leverrier based his idea of the motions of the planet Vulcan were used to confirm Einstein's general theory of relativity, which predicted such an advance of Mercury's perihelion. This would no doubt have provided Fort with a unique example of how anomalies quantum-jump from one orbit of reference to quite another, rather like a self-sustaining intellectual virus. It seems that the only thing in a Fortean world-model that can be accurately predicted is that all new theories will be full of anomalies, of which certainly both relativity and quantum theory are prime examples. Here is a modern description of quantum theory that is the equivalent to anything in Joyce, Sterne, or Fort:

... objects exist in a twilight state of all positions and velocities; particles of matter are waves of energy; and one particle can, indeed, exert a ghostly influence on another at the other side of the universe.[25]

Such confidence of the establishment certainly rivals the confidence of those cast out. It was with similar "scientific" enthusiasm that on May 15, 1932, the year of Fort's death, Wilbert C. Cunningham wrote from the Raleigh Hotel, Stout Street, Denver to "The Observers At Mount Wilson", claiming confidently:

... the planets, and the sun itself actually grew from the fundamental crystal structures naturally developed in the solar primary cubic crystalli-

sation system. In this system of natural creation the atom has no functional existence, practical use, or place in the sun, therefore the typical
solar atom, which seems quite chaotic, is entirely neglected.

But ten days later, Cunningham's description of himself has changed. He
is now a "Physico-Spiritual Writer Medium", but in his letter to Professor
Hubble (he of the much-abused telescope), Cunningham shows that his cosmic view has not changed:

> ... crystalline chemical elements of the air, will become more tangible when
> the natural (electric) law accountable for this state of being, mode of
> passing on, perpetuity, etc., is made known to the people thru [*sic*] the
> work of the Spirit World.

We might compare, without comment, the following thought from physicist
"proper" George Smoot, author of *Wrinkles in Time:*

> At a ten-millionth of a trillionth of a millionth of a second after the big bang
> — the earliest moment about which we can sensibly talk, and then only with
> some suspension of disbelief — all the universe we can observe today was
> the tiniest fraction of the size of a proton. Space and time had only just
> begun. Remember, the universe did not expand into existing space after the
> big bang; it expanded as it went.

Gas
Lamp
Theatre

And bearing the idea of "as it went" in mind, we might consider an offering from *X Factor* magazine:

> Under the right conditions, for the briefest moment (around one billionth of
> a second), the collision liberates the quarks and gluons that make up the
> protons and neutrons of the ions.

After that, let there be no more accusations of eccentricity against Wilbert
C. Cunningham or anyone else.

Sonnabend uses the cut and thrust of such typical arguments to create
fictitious planets (Monstrator and Elvera and Azuria), which, like Leverrier's
Vulcan, cannot be seen because they should not be seen, but are almost real
because they are almost seen. Such a war between emerging paradigms
reveals deep cultural conflicts between fact and metaphysics, time and idea.
As the belief systems fight it out, we are reminded of the recent mass suicide related to sightings of the Hale-Bopp comet. Sonnabend continues:

> I think it would be credible enough to say that many times have Monstrator
> and Elvera and Azuria crossed telescopic fields of vision, and were not even
> seen — because it wouldn't be proper to see them; it wouldn't be respect-
> able, it wouldn't be respectful: it would be insulting to old bones to see them:

it would bring on evil influences from the relics of St. Isaac to see them... [26]

We note that Fort did not pick opponents of average ability. Leverrier was a great astronomer, and undoubtedly had some element of genius — but that is largely the point Fort wishes to make. Just as Arthur Koestler was later to demonstrate in *The Sleepwalkers*, Fort wished to show that genius crashes through and leaves dense anomalous dust behind for lesser minds to ponder over. He also wanted to demonstrate how utterly fantastic preoccupations work extraordinarily well with superbly tuned rationalism in the process of scientific discovery. Just like digital and analogue procedures, the two faculties quite readily interface, and are really scaled symbiotic versions of one another.

When the mathematics has been nicely worked out (frequently in reverse) after the event, and when what was originally a disordered and frequently fantasy-inspired procedure has been edited in "presentable" logical sequence, it all looks as if the mind in its highest manifestations works like a well-oiled fully conscious logical machine, which starts at some beginning and proceeds to some end by means of a clear procedure. Many are then baffled when they happily commence such a procedure and get absolutely nowhere, whereas any good street-salesman could have told them that sensible, common-sense approaches form a very small minority of stories, some of which are hardly worth the telling. In this sense, a West End theatre entrepreneur who knows that the very best formulas may not work in terms of bottoms on seats (as an index of belief-quotas) is nearer the truth than any scientist.

It is difficult to avoid the conclusion that in Fortean terms, Leverrier's "Vulcan" was *almost* created, but was edited out of a "proper", that is an "allowed", realisation frame by a natural process of psychological weathering. Rather than simply shouting "madman" or "impostor" in such cases, it is far better to view such a thing as casting light on many such mysteries in other areas — if we assume that an almost material thing such as Vulcan was acting as a catalyst, a half-formed helper who disappeared into the mist after the job was done, leaving behind the discovery of Neptune, that is a "decent and respectable" piece of "acceptable" solidity. In Fortean terms, "Vulcan" was waiting in the wings in case anything went wrong with Neptune. Now that *is* relativistic, as Fort would say; just as relativistic as was the thing seen by a Dr Harris upon the evening of January 27, 1912, as communicated to *Popular Astronomy*, 20–398:

> Dr Harris saw, upon the moon, "an intensely black object." He estimated it to be 250 miles long and fifty miles wide. "The object resembled a crow poised, as near as anything." Clouds then cut off observation.
> Dr Harris writes: "I cannot but think that a very interesting and curious phenomenon happened."[27]

Or, as Fort would say, all factual discoveries are a reworking of myth, and all religion is a politicisation of mysticism.

mountains,
trials
and laboratories

The Book of the Damned was written under the threatening atmosphere of the years just before the First World War. This book is almost exactly contemporaneous with Thomas Mann's *The Magic Mountain* (1924), and also with Kafka's *The Trial* (published in 1924 after Kafka's death). There is detectable a similarly desperate Manichean struggle for Mind hanging over this first published book, the writing of which focused Fort's life and energies as his "pure" fiction had not done. A wartime sense of urgency also supplies its non-stop energies; this was to be a book with an almost military mission, and a definite objective. Fort's sometimes difficult, original and complex vision was at last coming together; the book was to be his masterpiece. As such, *The Book of the Damned* must have been written while American youth, singing "The Yanks Are Coming", were crammed piecemeal into their rusty, coal-burning (and largely unescorted) Atlantic transports, with their zigzag camouflaged grey and black hulls facing storms, mines, submarines, and surface raiders. These raw, semi-educated and half-trained recruits had no idea of what they were eventually to face in the trenches, and they were probably not encouraged when General Pershing, their commander-in-chief, told them that they were going to France "to die", scores of thousands of them, of course, doing exactly that. It is likely that Fort saw lots of these embarkations, and also he must have seen the activity in the recruiting offices, the never-ending arrival of troop trains, and the dense smoke of massed shipping from the harbour. He must also have seen the flags, the patriotic posters, the weeping families, the uniforms and the everlasting farewells. As a newspaper man, he must have been deeply affected by hearing of the monstrous slaughter in France. He must also have been angry that the casualty lists did not tell of the unbelievable military incompetence that caused them. Fort could not have read Wilfred Owen's *Anthem For Doomed Youth*, or come across the work of Isaac Rosenberg, Siegfried Sassoon, or Robert Graves, because their war poetry was, by and large, only available in America after the Great War, and then only read by a very few.

One has the undeniable feeling that Fort, Kafka and Mann, writing at exactly the same time as these poets were suffering in the trenches, were all trying to tear down an equally monstrous lie. They were certainly under the same kind of psychic pressure — although Mann's fame, wealth and social background contrasts strongly with that of the impoverished and unpublished Charles Fort, and the half-starved, desperately ill, and equally unpublished Franz Kafka, whose disappearing giant mole, in his short story *The Giant Mole*, is the perfect Fortean animal. In Kafka's story, the "scholar", sounding rather like Orwell's O'Brien in a relaxed mood, explains what happens to over-curious witnesses of anomalous high strangeness, and is a wonderful example of the Fortean mechanics of cultural banishment, with any discovery of a break in the universal rules almost equated to sin:

> Your discovery, of course, would be carried further, for it is not so trifling that, once having achieved recognition, it could be forgotten again. But you would not hear much more about it, and what you heard you would scarcely understand. Every new discovery is assumed at once into the sum-total of knowledge, and with that ceases in a sense to be a discovery; it dissolves into the whole and disappears, and one must have a trained scientific eye even to recognise it after that. For it is related to fundamental axioms of whose existence we don't even know, and in the debates of science it is raised on these axioms into the very clouds. How can we be expected to understand such things?[1]

In Thomas Mann's novel *The Magic Mountain*, it is as if the quite well-educated, rich, and reasonably intelligent patients of the International Sanatorium Berghof have collapsed under the pressures of that last question. All they can do is dress up and perform a kind of grotesque cabaret, almost it seems for Hans Castorp alone, who sits almost petrified at a table, rather like Gustave Aschenbach as he faces the sinister "baritone buffo" street player guitarist in Mann's *Death in Venice* (1912).

Fort's Sonnabend is an inmate of Mann's sanatorium. He is surrounded by disintegrating geographies of intellect that appear and reappear as equally grotesque and intimidating cultural masks. For all three authors these masks are factual systems of reference that, like all such systems, pose as "reality." Sonnabend and the leading characters in both *The Magic Mountain* and Kafka's *The Trial* are all pictured as if they have become tangled inexorably in those systems of complex and arbitrary reference which are the faces of a newly emerging world, quite unlike anything they have ever experienced. They have almost collapsed under the shock and weight of the deluge that the new scientifically oriented world has released upon them; consequently, the world as they see it has been fragmented, reduced to irrelevancies and trivia, and they have been left isolated, with only their own inturned egos for company. Kafka's "teacher" continues:

> Often as we listen to some learned discussion, we may be under the impression that it is about your discovery, when it is about something different, and the next time, when we think it is about something else, and not about your discovery at all, it may turn out to be about that and that alone.

This is the very essence of the language of twentieth-century bureaucracy. At the cool end, it is the language of the social worker, the town councillor, the civil servant; at the hot end, it is the language of the communist interrogator. In the face of such blandness and utterly "socialised" mediocrity, Sonnabend is as physically and spiritually isolated as any character of Mann or Kafka. But he is not despairing. He is not to die like Aschenbach in *Death in Venice*, full of diseased and corrupt thoughts, or like Josef K of *The Trial*, who is eventually shot "like a dog" on the edge of that twilight land which was to become so familiar to millions of Kafka's Jewish race. Though sometimes despairing, Sonnabend is still something of a free and energetic American as he yet clowns with scientific systems of his day, as if frolicking in a sea of that highly entertaining and brilliantly structured junk heap called Hollywood, America's "magic mountain".

Mountains, Trials and Laboratories

In this sense Fort's resistance to mass persuasion, compared to Mann's and Kafka's, is completely original: more often than not, he collapses the scientific house of cards by laughing at it. For the most part he refuses to be either depressed, intimidated, or even awe-struck by what he sees as science's posturing high seriousness and mock profundity, seeing these things as masks of cultural advertising from different interest-groups, and hence preceding post-modern thought by nearly seventy years.

the
kaiser's
disc jockey

Both Fort and Mann criticise responsible, educated people in particular because of what they feel is the failure of such people to see that their tactical
intellect is in shock: the intelligent stand before "big science" like a rabbit
before headlights, and are ready to be sold anything from National Socialism
to international socialism, with science serving both sides with equal enthusiasm. Many such folk were busy taking up the new careers offered by science
and technology and for both authors, twentieth-century intellectual consumerism has arrived, so that traditional concentration has been shattered by countless ideological feeding frenzies, some of which both Mann and Kafka guessed
would lead Germany on to yet a second great catastrophe.

   To use Orwell's phrase, for these two early twentieth-century authors "the
proles are free", and they describe a tragedy not of the mass, but of the well-
educated and intelligent, which of course is what most doctors and scientists
are or certainly should be. They see therefore, a failing of the most innovative,
intelligent sections of mankind, and that makes the disaster they describe
more profound, in that it is a failing of that very middle class which had achieved
social-scientific change almost of its own accord. Both authors see the amass-
ing of infinite realms of schemes of useless "factual" knowledge by this social
group as a positive affliction. This class is not criticised in terms of its being a
social class as such, but in terms of what is happening to its intellect — that
faculty which brought it into existence as a class in the first place. For Mann's
Hans Castorp, just some of these lemming-like urges are fashion, social ca-
chet, the preoccupation with food, and that endless ephemeral chat of the rich
bourgeoisie which is a kind of timeless universal white noise in every chatter-
ing class culture. The characters in *The Magic Mountain* are ill primarily because

they have lost their concentration. They have nothing to do; they have lost all sense of mission, national commitment, cultural function and personal intellectual focus. Militant Zionism at this time was hated not only on racial grounds, but because it offered exactly the opposite view.

In the modern world, Mann's type is not unfamiliar to us; *The Magic Mountain* shows mental decadence perfectly as Hans Castorp, for a short time, reigns supreme as the Kaiser's first disc jockey (it must be remembered that this was a long time before intellectuals spoke like disc jockeys). This representative picture of decay is more than familiar to us in our own time as we see Castorp faced with the problems of categorising, interpreting, and presenting his precious 78rpm "gramophone records", and considering how best to give short talks, comments and bits of equally useless information in between. Thus was born an early and quite original idea of media "presentation" as a burgeoning mental and social affliction with which science (and just about everything else) was to become tragically involved. This "presentation" of information (with suitable entertainment in between) was quite foreign to the fastidious, aloof and dignified nineteenth-century, and is very much how Fort saw the progress of scientifically generated "knowledge": as a continuous and increasing vulgarisation of all intellectual response that we recognise more acutely today in terms of the descent of science into developing better fly-sprays and cornflakes whose edges are less sharp. Even before 1923, in those crystal set days when *The Magic Mountain* was being written, Entertainment State was well on its way to dominance, prepared if necessary to arrange a suitable commercial break between Moses and God, with Hollywood doing the catering. Fort was the first to prophecy that profundity would have an Equity card, and high seriousness a contract, and plenty of rehearsal time.

The Kaiser's Disc Jockey

Mann also sees the sanatorium doctor's "scientific" knowledge, compiled by "facts", as a part of intellectual decadence. For Kafka too, the lawyer's endless reams of statutes in *The Trial* are a kind of counting disease, his lawyers being quite interchangeable with scientists in that the reality carve-up becomes a Fortean deal between performance presentations. The numbers of lawyers are the numbers of facts; they only stop multiplying when the two interfacing physical and mental Turing machines manufacturing them both come to a halt.[1] Our three authors are thus united in that they see the modern brain being turned into endless corridors lined with filing cabinets brimming over with full stops, the kind of thing well described by Fort:

> The only seemingly conclusive utterance, or seemingly substantial thing to cling to, is a product of dishonesty, ignorance, or fatigue. All sciences go back and back, until they're worn out with the process, or until mechanical reaction occurs: then they move forward — as it were. Then they become dogmatic, and take for bases, positions that were only points of exhaustion. So chemistry divided and sub-divided down to atoms; then, in the essential insecurity of all quasi-constructions, it built up a system, which, to anyone so obsessed by his own hypnoses that he is exempt to the chemist's

hypnoses, is perceptibly enough an intellectual anaemia built upon infinitesimal debilities.[2]

In other words, the trouble with facts has always been the same: if they exist at all, a single instant contains an infinite number of them. What one does to relate any second instant to this first instant is therefore difficult to see. Facts also suffer from the constant changing of the goalposts that define their fundamental nature. Then, to make matters even worse, these troublesome little monads can on occasion appear to be hardly "facts" in any proper sense at all, merely hopeful extensions of the fictions of a pragmatic innocence. Erich Heller, in his essay *Goethe and the Idea of Scientific Truth*, comments:

> One knows, of course, how many scientific theories have, for very long periods of time, stood the test of experience until they had to be discarded owing to man's decision, not merely to make other experiments, but to have different experiences; one also knows how often, after having lain for whole epochs in the cosmic dustbin of untruth, a theory, in one form or another, has been fetched back in triumph. For more unsophisticated aesthetic demands the game of musical chairs in which, ever since Newton and Huygens, the corpuscles and waves of light have found themselves involved — until, by a blatant breach of the rules of the game, they simply sat down together in one seat — may be as entertaining as the outdated but certainly loftier idea of musical spheres.[3]

Charles Fort would probably say that if there is something called a fact, he has not yet come across one. Not that this matters in Kafka's particular universe however, because for Josef K these "facts" are almost identical, just as are the faces of the lawyers and the officials around him. For Mann, Fort and Kafka, the world has started to put far too much early trust into these burgeoning "factual" systems as a totally new mythology, and Sonnabend gives dread warning that the search for a single "fact" as an absolute "standard" is doomed:

> There is something of ultra-pathos — of cosmic sadness — in this universal search for a standard, and in belief that one has been revealed by either inspiration or analysis, then the dogged clinging to a poor sham of a thing long after its insufficiency has been shown — or renewed hope and search for the special that can be true, or for something local that could be universal. It's as if "true meteoritic material" were a "rock of ages" to some scientific men. They cling. But clingers cannot hold out welcoming arms.[4]

Mann shows a mistrust of science quite equal to that of Fort by his description of the ludicrous medical arrangements at the extremely expensive sanatorium. The technical procedures, the crude apparatus, the transparent opinions of the doctors, the intimidating air of "professional" authority, all are shown as being as useless as their much later equivalents in Solzhenitsyn's *Cancer Ward*.

But if Mann's Hans Castorp and Solzhenitsyn's Oleg Kostoglotov think they get little information from their doctors, they are lucky compared with Kafka's K as far as lack of information is concerned. Throughout *The Castle*, after all his entreaties and communications, K gets one message only from the authorities in the castle, and that tells him to shut his mouth and "stay at his post". This of course, in early (and perhaps even late) twentieth-century language, meant stay at the new much-vaunted production lines, take your money, and don't ask questions. In the terms of both Mann and Solzhenitsyn, this means listen to the doctors and the communists respectively, hand yourself over to them completely, and don't bother trying to do any independent thinking yourself. In Fort's terms, it means trust the scientists. In this respect it seems that twentieth-century authority (and that means essentially twentieth-century science) is always asking us to wait for the new experiments in the new laboratories, which of course will be much better than the old experiments in the old laboratories. Fort's reply would probably be that if we believe that, we'd believe anything.

The analogy here with universal "planning," that great ark of the communist covenant, is unmistakable. Thirty years on, as Kostoglotov of *Cancer Ward* looks back, he sees that these scientific promises were the direct equivalent to the old communist sequential Five Year Plans, which as we now know, produced nothing for nobody — as distinct from its opposed capitalist equivalent, the instalment plan, which produced an equivalent nothing for everybody. Mann's sanatorium contains whole structures of those same pseudo-scientific designer reassurances, such as the "Gaffky number", determined from analysis of the sputum, and about as useful as a clout round a patient's ear. The sick Hans Castorp is x-rayed in an atmosphere and with an apparatus made of up all kinds of ritualised mythologies of the new age, the kind of awe-inspiring ideological induction well described by thousands of cases of medically hypnotised UFO abductees; in the dim light of a pre-1914 X-ray room, Hans Castorp sniffs "stale ozone", and a shiver runs down his back as he sees:

The Kaiser's Disc Jockey

> Lenses, switch-boards, towering measuring instruments, a box like a camera on a rolling stand, glass diapositives in rows set in the walls. Hard to say whether this was a photographic studio, a dark room, or an inventor's workshop and a technological witches' kitchen.[5]

Massive switches are thrown, releasing thousands of volts, and there follows a scene from a later Flash Gordon movie:

> ... there were explosions like pistol-shots, blue sparks on the measuring apparatus; long lightnings crackled along the walls. Somewhere in the room appeared a red light, like a threatening eye, and a phial in Joachim's rear filled with green.

Thirty years later, the thrill has gone. The voltages are the same, but they are under far better control, and poor Joachim's rear is in far less danger. Such light and sound shows as that above have been toned down; as media, they have become far more "cool," only the names (Siemens, I. G. Farben, Telfunken, Krupp), have been changed to protect the orders of demonology. The dirty benches, wire tangles, the lone eccentrics and the ivory tower built of class gulfs are gone. The scientists like the Mafia are becoming respectable, democratised, and like some fallen aristocracy, they ride bicycles and even come to live next door. This much improved presentation made no difference to the devastating radiation sickness that came from the much earlier constructions of enlightened and benevolent reason. To get some idea of what this means in terms of the magnitudes of raw exposure involved, Marie Curie's notebooks are still intensely radioactive, and her undoubted genius was tragically stifled by radiation-induced cancer. What it did to the rest of the world is still largely unrecorded.

A few seconds of historical time on from poor Joachim's exposure, Marie Curie takes such a radiological contraption to the Western Front, probably causing more long-term damage to her grateful patients than the shrapnel and bullets that her equipment located. Yet more historical seconds on, and the demons emerge from yet other lakes of burning sulphur: ICI, EMI, IBM, whatever. But now the voltages are under even better control, the shielding of the X-rays is "improved", or so say the cultural advertisements. Just how "improved" it is was revealed only recently by Dr Alice Stewart's research on the damage done by x-rays on foetuses, work that was "reluctantly acknowledged".[6] Similarly, Solzhenitsyn's descriptions of early "hormone therapy", and injections of "Sinestrol", are summed up by Shulubin's remark to Oleg in *Cancer Ward*: "Another idol of the theatre is our over-willingness to agree with the arguments of science." The X-ray treatments in the Soviet Union of the 1940s and 1950s are good examples of such mass applications of the "scientific method", applied to humanity just like the equivalent mass applications of simple-minded half-educated formulae, born like grail cups from Marxist-Leninist night schools:

> But then, ten, fifteen, or eighteen years ago when the term radiation sickness did not exist, x-ray radiation had seemed such a straightforward, reliable, and foolproof method, such a magnificent achievement of modern medical technique, that it was considered retrograde, almost sabotage of public health, to refuse to use it and to look out for other, parallel, or round-about methods. They were afraid only of acute, immediate damage to tissue and bone, but even in those days they rapidly learnt to avoid that. So — they irradiated! They irradiated with wild enthusiasm! Even benign tumours. Even small children.
>
> And these children had grown up. Young men and young women, sometimes even married, were coming in with irreversible mutilations of those parts of the body which had been so zealously irradiated.[7]

At times, both Oleg and Hans Castorp sound rather like Sonnabend in a particular mood, as all three characters examine mental, physical, and ideological afflictions as reflections of one another. Time, inspiration, and literary character flash back and forth over personal, political, and social geographies of mind: Solzhenitsyn is still a questioning boy as thousands of miles away, a middle-aged Charles Fort works in his sparsely furnished rented rooms, surrounded by boxes full of tall tales; at almost precisely the same stroke of the historical clock, the sick Kafka is confined to a thin mattress in Prague; for many such European Jews in the years to come, such a mattress would have been an inconceivable bonus. Meantime, for Mann's pure creation Herr Castorp, as consumptive as Kafka, the clock moves steadily on to August, 1914, a title Solzhenitsyn was later to make his own:

> But then, arrived at the molecule, one stood on the brink of another abyss, which yawned yet mysteriously than that between organic and inorganic nature: the gulf between the material and the immaterial. For the molecule was composed of atoms, and the atom was nowhere near large enough even to be spoken of as extraordinarily small. It was so small, such a tiny, early, transitional mass, a coagulation of the insubstantial, of the not-yet-substantial, and yet substance-like, of energy, that it was scarcely possible yet — or, it if had been, was now no longer possible — to think of it as material, but rather as mean and border-line between material and immaterial... the abyss between the material and the immaterial yawned as widely, pressed more opportunately — yes, more opportunately — to be closed, as that between organic and inorganic nature. There must be a chemistry of the immaterial, there must be combinations of the insubstantial, out of which sprang the material — the atoms might represent protozoa of material, by their nature substance, and still not quite yet substance.[8]

The Kaiser's Disc Jockey

This idea of the "not quite yet substance", this "border-line between material and immaterial", unites Fort and Mann, Kafka's K and Sonnabend, in the resistance of authors and characters both to "factual" authority. It is as if in the face of what was obviously going to be the first war of the newly born military-industrial complex, there was a search underway both in literature and life for a fault in the theoretical base of this all-consuming monster. The first attack is the refusal to believe in its omnipotence, its invasive power to dominate and kill. Fort, Mann, and Kafka found the Achilles heel of science in terms of the anomaly, defined as that single hair-out-of-place which, when found, means that the system is doomed in ideological time. Finally, K makes the castle answer. This, in its admittance of recognition, is an important victory over the castle; if it has a voice, it suffers. If the beast suffers, somehow it must love. Now can K die; the castle is, after all, vulnerable. Recognition, though passive, means that he has managed to enter the system. Entering the system means that he has tricked the castle, like a counter-virus. Yes, he has been located, and therefore he is certain to die, but at least he has been given a kind of identity, he is no longer *nothing:* that is, two cents' worth of salt and water. The castle has made its first mistake. Before he dies, he will scar its rockface with his name. Given that, was he ever a "land surveyor" in the first place? Perhaps, in the end, it is only an identity card which dies, and not K. Just as Fort knows that science will survive, K knows the castle will still be there long after he is dead, but that is of no matter; in making both castle and science speak, as it were, both writers have helped collapse a monstrous imposture posing as an aloof, objective disinterestedness. In this, both writers have cracked their interrogators. In a typical early twentieth-century life, that was often more than sufficient to sustain half-starved and utterly ignored visionaries like Fort and Kafka, to convince them that like many other political prisoners after them such as Solzhenitsyn's Ivan Denisovitch, that they could make it to the next day, and perhaps even the day after that. Perhaps that is all a true twentieth-century hero expected, or indeed ever could expect.

In this war against that forced interrogation which he too, sees as science, Fort also manages to collapse the stage-fronts of a whole series of similar castles of his own, and they are full of things just as interesting as faceless officials, depressed doctors, or the lost bourgeoisie of old Europe:

> My own pseudo-conclusion: that we've been damned by giants sound asleep, or by great scientific principles and abstractions that cannot realise themselves: that little harlots have visited their caprices upon us; that clowns, with buckets of water from which they pretend to cast thousands of good-sized fishes have anathematised us for laughing disrespectfully, because, as with all clowns, underlying buffoonery is the desire to be taken seriously; that pale ignorances, presiding over microscopes by which they cannot distinguish flesh from nostoc or fishes' spawn or frogs' spawn, have visited upon us their wan solemnities. We've been damned by corpses and skeletons and mummies, which twitch and totter with pseudo-life derived from conveniences.[9]

These are what could easily be imagined as the last thoughts of Mann's Hans Castorp, as with his "burning face and stiffening fingers", and wrapped against the cold on the balcony of the hospital, he gazes down in the night at the glittering valley below the sanatorium. He knows he is at the mercy of those forces that are soon to pluck him from his isolation, and thrust him, as a no doubt doomed infantryman, into the first battle darkness of the Great War, yet still the inexorable process of thought continues:

> Yet arrived at the "not even small", the measure slipped out of the hands; for "not even small" meant the same as "enormously large"; and the step to the atom proved to be without exaggeration portentous in the highest degree, For at the very moment when one had assisted at the final division of matter, when one had divided it into the impossibly small, at that moment there suddenly appeared upon the horizon the astronomical cosmos![10]

If the following passage by Fort is compared to this, we can see how many of the scientific and indeed mathematical ideas of their time had penetrated the thoughts of both men. In other words, the "system" they recognise is deep within them. Both struggle somewhat unsuccessfully to cast off powerful scientific analogues from their moral view as they would cast off a positively demonological affliction:

> We have complained a great deal. At least we are not so dull as to have the delusion that we know just exactly what it is that we are complaining about. We speak seemingly definitely enough of "the System", but we're building upon observations by members of that very system. Or what we are doing — gathering up the loose heresies of the orthodox. Of course "the System" fringes and ravels away, having no real outline. A Swift will antagonise "the System", a Lockyer will call him back; but then a Lockyer will vary with a "meteoric hypothesis", and a Swift, will in return, represent "the System". This state is to us typical of all intermediatist phenomena; or that conceivably is anything really anything, if its parts are likely to be their own opposites at any time. We speak of astronomers — as if there were real astronomers — but who have lost their identity in a System — as if it were a real System — but behind that System is plainly a rapport, or loss of identity in the Spirit of an Era.[11]

The
Kaiser's
Disc Jockey

marketing

belief

For both Fort and Mann, "media" is raw systems-anthropology. Due to a vast increase in the suggestive power of modern information and entertainment systems, the early predictions of both men as regards the manipulation of the real/unreal mythological interface have largely come about. Recently, stress-counsellors were on call for viewers who were about to experience the death of a favourite character in a soap series. This incident was well advertised before-hand, complete with pictures of the pseudo-death (and also the pseudo-grief) before it was broadcast. It was also said that such counselling would be available for viewers who did not have the opportunity to see the programme, because of the "general anxiety" caused. We thus have a "general anxiety" caused by something which may or may not have been directly witnessed or experienced by the populace, and which was artificially created in the first place. This idea comes accompanied by tabloid suggestions that all author-ity (scientists, the royal family, presidents) could be replaced by actors; this of course would make the circle of belief-into-substance quite complete, reducing technology to being merely an ancillary factor in the artificial and managed creation of "belief-stuff". Such a metaphysical substance could read-ily replace Eddington's "pointer-readings" and "world-stuff"[1] as constructs of experience in a "virtual world". We have therefore, with massively in-creased suggestive power in our global Entertainment State, the dread pos-sibilities of completely engineered belief systems, growing "realities" as eas-ily as ideological Soya crops.[2] This fulfils Fort's view of the science of As-tronomy in particular as "a phantom-film distended with myth-stuff". Such "quasi-reality" as Fort described it, equates with Mann's "not quite sub-stance," and Newton's alchemical substance (the mother of all partial-sub-

• •

stances),[3] very well indeed.

Another significant writer of the epoch of Kafka, Fort and Mann was Al-fred North Whitehead[4]. He too, as distinct from that great practical bench-experimenter Rutherford (who called metaphysics "so much hot air", and relativity a "work of art"), saw science as being equally insubstantial, and he occasionally reflects Charles Fort's much-abused syntax:

> We have only got to look in the sky, towards Percy Lowell's moving point, and we shall see a new planet.[5] Certainly we shall not. All that any person has seen is a few faint dots on photographic plates, involving the interven-tion of photography, excellent telescopes, elaborate apparatus, long expo-sures and favourable nights. The new explanation is now involved in the speculative extension of a welter of physical laws, concerning telescopes, light, and photography, laws which merely claim to register observed facts. It is involved in the speculative application of such laws to particular cir-cumstances within the observatories for which circumstances these laws are not concurrently verified. The result of this maze of speculative exten-sions is to connect the deviations of Uranus and Neptune with the dots on the photographic plate. This narrative, framed according to the strictest requirements of the Positivist theory, is a travesty.[6]

Marketing Belief

Thus for Whitehead, as for Fort, "reality" consists of nothing more than layer upon layer of well-managed ideological *guano*: the difference between elements of these historical deposits is the difference between a small-scale "fantasy", and some projection of a much larger one, the endless war between the two being a war to secure the high frontier of an equally illusory "cer-tainty". Whitehead continues:

> The speculative extensions of laws, baseless on the Positivist theory, are the obvious issue of speculative metaphysical trust in the material permanencies, such as telescopes, observatories, mountains, planets, which are behaving towards each other according to the necessities of the Universe, including theories of their own natures. The point is, that speculative extension be-yond direct observation spells some trust in metaphysics, however vaguely the metaphysical notions may be entertained in explicit thought… meta-physical understanding guides imagination and justifies purpose. This urge towards explanatory description provides the interplay between science and metaphysics. The doctrines of metaphysics are modified, so as to be capa-ble of providing the explanation, and the explanations of science are framed in the terms of the popular metaphysics lingering in the imaginations of these scientists.

This is Sonnabend's voice: he too is full of the conflicts of a similar com-bative tension, and though at most times he can still laugh at both himself and science both, at other times he is very angry. Perhaps the best minds are born between two cultures, and the tension of such is certainly in Sonnabend: the quick tendency to laughter, the many changing masks, the almost-apologies, and the equally rapid change to nervous fear and dislike, that very state of *fin de siécle* historical consciousness which Huizinga pointed out so well in *The Waning of the Middle Ages*. When Sonnabend points out the constant putting forward by science of some great structured mundanity as a veritable cathedral of "truth" and "reality", it is as if he were referring to some monstrous medieval structure of consciousness, some anachronistic architecture of the mind, whose brief historical time has come:

> ... the pathos of the dull and uninspired, but courageous persistence of the scientific: everything seemingly found out is doomed to be subverted — by more powerful microscopes and telescopes; by more refined, precise, searching means and methods — the new pronouncements irrepressibly bobbing up; their reception always as Truth at last; always the illusion of the final.[7]

Writing in 1948, F. J. Hargreaves, President of the British Astronomical Association,[8] sees the future of astronomy extending infinitely in terms of bigger and better optical telescopes. He comments on the completion of the 200-inch reflector at Mount Palomar:

> Every time a great advance in telescopic power has been made, problems have been solved and unexpected discoveries have been made. Every time, also, these discoveries have presented further problems which have had to wait for their solution until a larger telescope could be made. We may expect that before many years have elapsed astronomers will be calling for a telescope of 300 inches aperture to supply the answers to questions raised by the observations made with the 200-inch. Such an increase in size would no doubt present many difficult problems, but so did Galileo's first telescope, Sir William Herschel's four-foot reflector, Lord Rosse's six-foot, the sixty-inch, the Victoria seventy-two-inch and the 100-inch.

Stan Augarten, in *Bit By Bit*[9] quotes the text of a speech given at the Napier Tercentenary in 1914, by John Fletcher Moulton, a Cambridge mathematician who visited the great Babbage a few years before his death. His insight into the tunnel vision of science combines Fort, Kafka, Mann and science in one:

> In the first room I saw the parts of the original Calculating Machine, which had been shown in an incomplete state many years before and had even been put to some use. I asked him about its present form. "I have not finished it because in working at it I came upon the idea of my Analytical Engine, which would do all that it was capable of doing and much more. Indeed the idea was so much simpler that it would have taken more work to complete the calculating machine than to design and construct the other in its entirety, so I turned my attention to the Analytical Machine." After a few

minutes talk we went into the next workroom where he showed and explained to me the working of the elements of the Analytic Machine. I asked if I could see it. "I have never completed it," he said, 'because I hit upon the idea of doing the same thing by a different and far more effective method, and this rendered it useless to proceed on the old lines.' Then we went into the third room. There lay scattered bits of mechanism but I saw no trace of any working machine. Very cautiously I approached the subject, and received the dreaded answer, "It is not constructed yet, but I am working at it, and will take less time to construct it altogether than it than it would have taken to complete the Analytical Machine from the stage in which I left it." I took leave of the old man with a heavy heart.

Thus perhaps it is not only Walter Mitty who provides part of the great moral comedy of two centuries, but also scientific geniuses such as Babbage.[10] As Fort points out, there is a searing tragic pathos about such very great men, who, trusting the "disciplines" given to them by their proud parent cultures, push their discursive tools to the limit of their focusing grain. They try to stabilise their gears and wheels, their pulses and fields, within what is still essentially a Cartesian framework,[11] somewhat dated, to say the least, since Descartes died in 1650. But the world will just not sit still long enough to be nicely photographed as a finished product in central focus, the one place where the co-ordinates are almost completely linear. If Charles Fort teaches us anything, it is that characters and actions, times and places, knowledge, facts, and belief systems are always slightly blurred at the non-linear edge before, like Babbage's last machine, they run themselves into chaos and infinity. The Fortean point is that without both Mitty and Babbage imagining beyond themselves, any system would lock and be quite incapable of change, in the sense that any tall building has to have a certain amount of elasticity or it will shatter.

Marketing
Belief

Fort's main complaint is that most scientific investigations commence with the assumption that the world is some corpse on a slab ready to be dissected. But given the mass of external evidence he gathered it is more likely that "reality," like the "average" person, is something not only widely oscillating about some theoretical central axis, but rather is fluid, alive in every sense, and like the dreams of Babbage, Mitty and Sonnabend again, forever incomplete.

the

new script

In the earliest years of our century, questioning writers and experimental artists in general were being pushed into a cultural *cul de sac*. It was André Breton, the author of the Surrealist Manifesto, who coined the phrase *avant-garde*, meaning those who experimented with strange new ideas. Such were in savage opposition to the prevailing intellectual and artistic tradition which in the 1900s, by and large, as in our own time, had looked at the new society, picked up its skirts, and had run for its life. In Breton's famous manifesto, war was declared on scientifically-organised mass mechanistic conformity, and subsequent developments much nearer our own time resulted in what we now term the literature of the outsider, a term almost tailor-made for Charles Fort.

But it is doubtful if Breton's call to arms was heard by him. The bustling New York of the 1900s was hardly a place for artistic or philosophical matters. It was being almost entirely rebuilt, and scores of thousands of homeless immigrants from all over Europe were arriving every month. Fort had probably never heard of the word "surrealism", but nevertheless he belonged to this movement in the sense that when he looked at anything at all, he did not see what he should properly have seen. Such dangerous and subversive people frequently live unhappy lives, but without them, mankind would not have gone beyond the single-celled stage of the amoeba.

The idea of an *avant-garde* was a concept which Tennyson, or even Yeats, would hardly have understood, and which today we may have equal difficulty in understanding since in our own time, most fiction writers in particular — as questioning figures — have fallen to being stylish entertainers rather than seeing their talent as a weapon in a war to the death against the prevailing culture, even less seeing such as a dedicated search for truth. But the first fifty years of this century were very different days for the innovative writer. There being no vast film industry, or media base to give them good jobs and sustenance, some of those who could be described as *avant-garde*, such as Ezra Pound, went mad, some retreated into pure aesthetics, some became wanderers and eternal exiles, such as Ernest Hemingway and D. H. Lawrence, and some took to mystical religion, such as Eliot. Later, others became the first of that great trail of floor-dwelling, sock-borrowing dropouts, from Henry Miller to Jack Kerouac.

As Eliot's *The Wasteland* tells us, after 1900 the writer was no longer an accepted and integrated part of the broad pattern of social, moral and political development as for instance George Eliot, Hardy, Melville or Whitman had been. The new culture that was transforming society utterly was science and its associated technology and industry, and of all human activities, science did least brook resistance. But by the time a copy of the newly published *Wild Talents* was laid by the bedside of the dying Charles Fort on May 3, 1932, both literature and the imagination may have been on the ropes, but at least they now had no less than four complete textbooks of cultural guerrilla warfare, and probably the best of such since Rabelais.

But despite Sonnabend's good humour, the fun is often that of a hardened con facing up to his sentence. The expression is tough, male, yet nimble, and superbly contemptuous of the patrolling guards. Often the impression is that Fort himself must have laid his head down for many early twentieth-century nights like some long-term fortress prisoner, feeling the walls for the most minute gaps in what he saw as the prison system of the scientific view. That may sound mournful compared with the totally misleading impression some commentators have given of Fort as a benign, liberal, hippie saint-cum-guru, for beneath the tolerant and humorous exterior there is seething all the resentment and political savagery of his age. Within Sonnabend there is detectable certainly the carefully-controlled and very deep violence of the bomber and the assassin, but rather like Alan Turing (whose deep frustrations came from an entirely different direction), Sonnabend's anger expressed itself in the driven intellectual savagery of the code-cracker and chess-player. Fort himself had perhaps the greatest hacker mentality of our century; his entire life was dedicated to entering the mainframe system of reference and utterly destroying it by introducing anomalistic viruses. He depicts Sonnabend as being very definitely the spy under cover, and like most writers of spy stories, Fort himself had neither a happy youth nor a happy adult life. Though he does not state it explicitly, in *The Book of the Damned*, which was composed during the mechanised slaughter on the Western Front, it is as if he is speaking through Sonnabend to accuse science of creating the whole damned twentieth-century mess. Both author and character know that they can do hardly anything about it, and at times both appear to be like the birdman of Alcatraz, giving their home-bred anomalies wings like the passing souls of the dead. Sonnabend talks of exclusionism, which includes of course his own separateness and alienation:

The
New Script

There have been lights like luminous surfs beating upon the coasts of this earth's atmosphere, and lights like vast reflections from distant fires; steady pencils of light and pulsating clouds and quick flashes and seeming objects with definite outlines, all in one poverty of nomenclature, science called "auroral." Nobody knows what an aurora is. It does not matter. An unknown light in the sky is said to be auroral. This is standardisation, and the essence of this standardisation is Exclusionism.[1]

There is also the phenomenon of inclusionism, which is just as perverse. Sonnabend quotes a correspondent to the *Scientific American* saying that he saw a silky substance falling from the sky at time when there was a distinct aurora borealis, and he attributes this substance to the aurora. Quoting from the Greenwich astronomer E. W. Maunder's recollections in *Observatory*, Fort discovers another of his "damned" animals which, in similar fashion, almost became equally "auroral" but not quite:

... Maunder was at the Royal Observatory Greenwich, Nov. 17, at night. There was an aurora, without features of special interest. In the midst of the aurora, a great circular disk of greenish light appeared and moved slowly across the sky. The thing had passed above the moon, and was, by other observers, described as "cigar-shaped", "like a torpedo", "a spindle", "a shuttle". Had the incident occurred a third of a century later, beyond doubt, everyone would have selected the same simile — it would have been "just like a Zeppelin". The duration was about two minutes. Colour said to have been the same as that of the auroral glow in the north. Nevertheless, Maunder says that this thing had no relation to auroral phenomena. "It appeared to be a definite body." Motion too fast for a cloud, but "nothing could be more unlike the rush of a meteor".[2]

This is typical of human beings, technology, and experience: scratch the surface of any twentieth-century product, and there will be revealed more mysteries than one would ever believe. As a newspaperman, Fort was skilled at teasing out not so much finite skulduggery, as an implicit self-censoring system within all human beings, products, and ideas. We know from our own time that when an event becomes truly fantastic and dramatic (such as the claims in our own time of alien abductions, the alleged finding of crashed UFOs and the apocryphal films of the dissection of dead aliens), and when the consequence of acceptance of it as such would easily upset the world paradigm, the event is quickly reprocessed: not rejected so much as made *mundane*. This is a word whose original meaning was to make "void of spirit", to make a thing belong to this world and presumably no other, thus giving the game away entirely. Whilst to a certain extent Fort accepts the mundane if only for certain kinds of psychological defence, it is an automatic equating of the mundane with truth that he rejects, if only because to make a thing mundane is to make it void of all spirit.

From this, we conclude that basic Fortean Law is that All Things are Equally Fantastic. Thus any piece of so-called "reality" when examined breaks up into folklore, this folklore being within as well as without both the observer and observed. But Fort would also have agreed with Borges in saying that "reality longs to yield", for like Borges, he also wrote a bible in which the imagination is seen as a kind of combative resistance which ensures that no slice of experience ever settles down into a perfect steady-state condition, no matter how hard such "planet Venus" or what Fort called "fishmonger" conclusions are pressed. Within the terms of this law, any encounter with anomaly shows "reality" on the move and the "concrete" to be forever liquid, updated rather like history as seen by Orwell's Winston Smith or perhaps Captain Mantell,[3] seeing something which they should not have seen. A person from a stone-age culture would smile at the unprecedented intellectual problems such reported experiences give us. He would merely accept that such manifestations are taboo.

There are now on record many thousands of such well-substantiated anomalous incidents on land, sea, and air, recorded in the post-war world alone. They question the very categories we think in, and confound the basic paradigms of discursive intelligence. They also excite our imagination and offer a constant revivification of the very idea of what we mean by the word *fiction*. Fort, like Hamlet, is at his best when he takes a word such as this, and drags it from the prison-house of its fallen definitions, where it has been reduced to concepts of passive entertainment.

The New Script

Therefore in the Fortean world model, fact and fiction feed off one another symbiotically. At this, our stone age person would nod a head, and perhaps do a dance celebrating this making of imagination active again, where it is rampant, dangerous — possibly putting lights in the eyes of fighter-pilots, and baffling doctors and surgeons when a part-brain functions as a full brain, or when our "fictions" take a walk outside ourselves.

We deny fictions in action, yes, but at the same time, we lift very slowly what Dylan Thomas called the "fabulous curtain" and see the first beams of new script, better described as a new and very strange view of both mind and world. The lifting has to be slow, it has to be carefully done, because there are new worlds without limit beyond the new world that we see immediately just behind the curtain of perception. George Eliot's Dorothea draws back from her tumultuous experience in the Rome gallery, lest she should "hear every squirrel's heart-beat". Lift the curtain too quickly and we might be blinded, we might not cope; we have seen what happens to primitive cultures when our own lights shine in their eyes.

If Fort did anything at all, he culled material sufficient to rejuvenate totally the concept of "mystery." Throughout the nineteenth-century, this word had gradually fallen from being associated with all kinds of religious and spiritual truths to describing the unravelling of detective tales, the solving of elaborate mechanical puzzles, and in the hands of the great Holmes of Baker Street, finally it came to mean something which, no matter how complicated, could be "solved" properly, therefore *explained* and put into a closed system of reference, rather like a newly-conquered country. This was the classical nineteenth-century deterministic position, and Charles Fort was to challenge this view, almost exactly at the same time as Einstein and others were doing likewise in particle physics. But whilst the theory of relativity relates largely to the microcosmic world, in that we still use Newton's laws to build bridges over rivers, Fort's view relates to the macrocosmic, in that he found endless anomalistic contradictions not in the abstractions of electricity and magnetism, time and space, but in everyday experience. Fort's celebrated "mysteries" emerge not from the inaccessible interiors of the atomic nucleus, the remoteness of interstellar space or abstruse mathematics which few understand, but from the full light of noon on a thronged high street, from crowded rooms, from reports of ship's captains, baffled farmers, puzzled housewives and scared families. He shows policemen and citizens often reduced to baffled and rather frightened silence, theologians offering instant interpretations and scientists offering often celebrated cranked-up explanations, these being great creaking intellectual contraptions, frequently far more fantastic than the things they would have explained: "the methods of science in maintaining its system are as outrageous as the attempts of the damned to break in."[4] Some of this atmosphere, given the history of the development of the UFO phenomenon, is more than familiar to us,[5] and gives Charles Fort's work a present-day relevance.

Fort, conceiving of "materialistic science" as a "jealous god", knew from the start that the kind of opposition he would encounter would reach a religious level of fanatical opposition.

By his idea of "quasi-existence", Fort means that our mental projections have a kind of working life, and these systems of loosely connected desires begin to have a destiny of their own, even when thinkers are deceiving themselves, or even when they are practising what appears to be outright fraud. Though such an idea has innumerable historical ancestors, revitalising it as he did very early on in the twentieth-century, Fort refashioned this idea using empirical methods, and cut away all the troublesome and largely antiquated apparatus of traditional occultism associated with it. In doing this, Fort updated fairyland; he dragged it from the darkening twilight shades of a fustian world of late nineteenth-century romanticism into the full light of systems analysis: the deviant event, whatever form it takes, is the built-in system destabiliser, the "noise in the system", be it the UFO or the "more than chance" element in laboratory-controlled ESP guessing games. In this sense the deviant event, so roundly condemned by mainstream science, becomes profoundly more political than any party policy or election manifesto.

In modernising occultism he cleared it of much decadent and over-elaborate ritualism, and replaced these traditional forms by a theory of creation, growth and flow of information and counter-information. The dynamics of this flow sculpt those part-forms which give science so much trouble as it tries to categorise and define: as Fort points out, scientific psychology being such, without a category, these refugee events cannot exist.

A Fortean "existence" is of course a very special dimension. We do not need knowledge of spells or incantations to know that when we imagine, we create a form of life. Such a minimal shape and form might be called a Fortean Animal. Such partial creations[6] are weak, primal forms; often a few paltry coincidences, or a short run of linked experiential coding serves to constitute the vaporous substance of such Fortean animals as the airships seen over America in 1896, or the falls of any and every kind of material from the sky. Events as well as objects may be called such animals.

This seeing of imagination as a third state of matter, between the concrete and the abstract, makes the imagination a kind of "third grid" between the anode and cathode of symbol and realisation,[7] and it is an intermediate form of existence which the ancient world and the Renaissance understood, but it is a state of matter and energy lost to us, largely. We pay lip service to its expression in Shakespeare, but the intermediate area between the concrete and the abstract is not regarded as operational in twentieth-century culture.[8] This is our loss, because such a view allows a malleability of matter and spirit, extending identity and personality into material and quasi-material realms, allotting many more degrees of freedom to both personality and intellect than "finite" politics or sociology (and particularly "factual" science) will allow. It is to be hoped that love can reach folk as well as do the death-dealing fires.

The
New Script

the

absent brain

A Fortean investigation has a unique character. It does not use the conventional mythology of the great evidence games that are now poured willy-nilly into every single campus mainframe on the planet. As a procedure, the first Fortean thing to do is think of something big, conventional, and of everyday substance. That is, something that does not have much need of an advertising campaign to construct and hard sell its illusion of objective solidity, permanence and "factual" truth. By *size* in the Fortean sense is meant something universally recognised as "real", unquestionable, such as the thought-equivalent to common icons of stability like the Statue of Liberty, or the Houses of Parliament.

Let us pick *brain*.

The brain has, like the black hole, and the older wave/particle controversy, become one of the most heavily sold public relations packages of our modern age. The labels of the jars on the shelves of the cultural supermarket tell us that this pulsating mass of bioelectric jelly contains all *mind* and is therefore the supreme control, which calculates, warns, judges, and is responsible for the Parthenon, Bart Simpson and *Hamlet*.

Or is it?

One of the few things certain about the brain is that all analogies for its purpose and function fail to describe adequately its anomalistic structure. Official science, modest and respectable as its essentially seventeenth-century roots, has always advertised the brain as an admirable and superbly efficient control mechanism that watches over and manages all aspects of the body's functions like a good and faithful nanny. Such implicit cultural persuasion is not uncommon in scientific propaganda, from worthy TV documentaries to a fire-breathing Richard Dawkins public lecture. It is a politically useful vision of the town clerk's myth of the "accountancy driven" universe, where all the windows of creative possibilities have simple closed-loop arithmetical boundaries. This is the grocery store vision of the brain as a worthy hard-working unit, ever ready to serve, and alert to a customer's every requirement. It is a Victorian hangover, this constant invitation by science to admire the wonders of creation such as the brain. It smacks of the last days of imperial and industrial hope, the time when great engines, mighty ships, and sparking locomotives promised complete fulfilment of nature's grand design. Such were the days when the great mathematician C. G. J. Jacobi (1804–1805) could say that his work was the result of "brain-splitting thinking" which was "hard work that has often endangered my health". Darwin was careful to talk of the results of his "unbounded patience", and Faraday was equally careful to qualify his ideas as being the result of "industry".

Neither Jacobi nor Faraday has anything to say of those inspirations that come from doing absolutely no work at all.[1] In this sense, both men fall into that Fortean category of people who know that they have extraordinary abilities, but who half-consciously invent a plausible world-cover as causation in order that the world might not ask too many questions about ideas of non-conservation of inspirations.

In this sense, "fact," as a most subtle mythological contrivance, can be made to perform a most useful social-psychological role as good cover-planning to prevent being burnt at the nearest convenient cultural stake. But certainly no nineteenth-century scientist ever conceived of fact and fiction being in symbiosis in any sense; to them, the imagination played not a functional, creative role, but was a positive hindrance; it was what T. H. Huxley (in a pre-Freudian age) called a "garment of make-believe", and the world was only truly revealed once this garment had been "stripped off" by "pious hands". This edifying view, when eventually fully developed, allied itself completely with that humourless, puritanical, fantasy-stripping dialectic called social-scientific communism, in which mind was seen as quite separate from nature. Lenin wrote, "... the sole property of matter — with the recognition of which materialism is vitally connected — is the property of being objective reality, of existing outside our cognition."[2] But what eventually emerges from these glowing, confident views and predictions is a corpse or a cripple — which is what usually emerges after any politically correct interrogation, of which the countless social-scientific mass graves of the twentieth-century bear witness.

Once the large-scale icon is selected, the second Fortean thing to do is deconstruct it: that is, to search for the hairline cracks in its advertising surface. Here is some such cultural "advertising" about the brain, picked at random from the books of various epochs. The brain is, as one Victorian encyclopaedia put it, "that blessed organ whose activity makes Man superior to all the rest of the animal kingdom." An early twentieth-century reference book describes the brain as "that Renaissance glory" and even as late as the 1930s a popular children's book of "science facts" describes the brain as that "Jewel of the Enlightenment", which is "God's gift to Man".

The trouble is that this "gift" appears to be a movable feast. An article by Bob Rickard, *Medical Curiosities*, [3] gives examples of brains pierced by falls on iron railings, brains shot through by a javelin, a crossbow bolt, a knife blade, a spear, and even the point of an umbrella. Accidents involving powered nail guns are frequent. In 1979, despite having his brain shot through with a nail from a powered gun, seventeen-year-old carpenter Kenneth Blount from Baton Rouge recovered completely. In 1982, injured by a similar missile, Burger King waitress Linda Archipolo of Massapequa, New York, made a partial recovery, against what neuro-surgeon Robert Degler said were "staggering odds", and was progressing rapidly at the time of the report.

Rickard gives two examples of where, despite extensive tissue damage, full cognitive functions were preserved. Despite having his brain pierced through with a 40lb seven-foot steel crowbar, which penetrated right through the mid-brain just above the brain stem, John Thomson, of Boston, made a good recovery, although experiencing some paralysis and some difficulty in talking. The example of what happened to carpenter Michael Melnick of Reseda, California in 1981 is even more illustrative of how resilient the brain is. He fell ten feet through the floor of a house under construction in Malibu, to find a six-inch length of a five-eighths inch thick rough-surfaced steel rod protruding from between his eyes. The rod had penetrated his head through the base of his neck, its other end being fixed into the concrete floor. As Melnick, presumably not in much pain, lay there "trying to figure it out", lifeguards from nearby Zuma beach sawed through the fixed end of the rod. At Westlake Community Hospital, neuro surgeon Paul Ironside said that he

The Absent Brain

> ... removed the iron from inside Melnick's skull, rebuilt his shattered nose and repaired tear ducts, nerves, muscles, and what tissue damage he could. Doctors, certain there would be permanent if not fatal damage, were baffled to find this was not the case.

After some seven months, although he suffered from nightmares, insomnia, a fear of falling, and some unstated "physical complications", Melnick made a reasonably full recovery. Rickard's conclusion is interesting:

> The question raised is just how much of our brain matter is essential to normal functioning at any time? Part of the answer may be the discovery of the ability to relocate specific brain functions in other parts of the brain, but whether this means that the available matter is shared out in a new proportion, or that there are unused or 'spare' areas of matter which could be cultivated in the event of accident to other parts is not yet fully understood.

Pacho Penaloza of La Paz, Bolivia, blasted off a quarter of his brain and a third of his skull when mishandling a pistol in 1984. He was in a coma for three

• •

months, his right side was expected to be permanently paralysed, and he was also expected to be deprived of speech. A new skull cover was reconstructed by Minnesota plastic surgeons Joseph Skow and Frank Pilney, using a section of bone taken from a rib and another part of Pacho's skull, and a scalp flap stitched into place. Apart from a clenched fist and a limp, Pacho made a complete recovery.[4]

The type of packing to replace the lost tissue is not mentioned in Pacho's case, but it is to be hoped that he fares better than did forty-five-year-old Pauline Nuttall, who had a benign tumour removed from her brain in the London National Hospital for Neurology in 1983. The brain survived that operation, but it didn't survive after the hollow cavity in her skull was filled with an unspecified "brain tissue". Pauline developed symptoms associated with Creutzfeld-Jacob's disease (the human equivalent of the 'mad cow' disease BSE), and died in May 1991. Professor Leo Duchen said there had been faults with the "sterilisation process". Dr Faustroll, author of a 1991 article on this incident, adds:

> Does this mean that sterilised brain tissue from (presumably recently deceased) people or foetuses (for all we know, perhaps even from animals) is being used to fill the heads of the living? Isn't this a brain transplant of sorts? Could sterilisation have dealt effectively with Creutzfeld-Jacob's disease even if it could be detected in 1983? The AIDS risk, the debate on foetus experimentation, and our interest in the anxieties dramatised in dozens of transplant horror films make these questions far from idle.[5]

Brains might not survive Creutzfeld-Jacob's disease, but they managed to survive pre-frontal lobotomies carried out in the 1950s by the notorious American psychiatrist Walter Freeman, who despite protests from the medical establishment, performed lobotomies by himself, although unqualified as a surgeon:

> He would perform them in his office, pushing a modified ice-pick through the corner of an eye socket and twisting it around inside the brain. The procedure was so gruesome that even a hardened surgeon fainted at the sight.[6]

Freeman himself said of his work: "lobotomised patients make rather good citizens."

Though deprived of these late examples, Fort wrote a tragedy of applied social-scientific "intellect" to be placed alongside Solzhenitsyn's *Gulag Archipelago*. In Fort's four books we see an equally breathtaking expanse of Western intellectual time as in Solzhenitsyn's work. Though this cultural time certainly moves more slowly than specific political or social time, it is as fashionable in its way as a twenty-hour change in the cleavage of a movie star, and Charles Fort's books show most of the "facts" we are given to be just about as meaningful. If Marx described the appalling "condition of the working class", Fort describes the equally appalling condition of the scientific intelligentsia. He first revealed a "science" which was to grow into that flourishing denial industry of our own time, of which the brain, partial, absent, or otherwise, was to become just one of the victims. The article in *X Factor* continues:

> Gradually, though, lobotomy fell out of fashion. Therapists began to believe that it was the shock to the brain rather than the removal of tissue that was producing the calming effect. Lobotomy was replaced by electro-convulsive "therapy" (ECT). Then, a new range of tranquillisers, including Valium, were found to have a similar effect to lobotomy. But this was not before tens of thousands of people around the world had effectively been turned into zombies.[7]

The maintenance of what we term "reality" in which a "proper" brain is commonly supposed to exist, requires all the technical energies of that continuous process image industry which allowed Freeman to operate in the first place. The projections which make up for the solidity of such a thing as a brain or indeed such a practice as Freeman's must be maintained by a flicker schedule of metaphors within an efficient denial industry whose main work is propagandistic persuasion. In the first years of the twenty-first-century, science, like the Church and courts of old, is revealing itself as essentially a massive public-relations exercise in which anything, such as the Auschwitz-like experiments of Freeman (and many more of associated colleagues, past and present),[8] is justified.

The Absent Brain

Science is looking a little lonely without its fallen partner, communism. Without its supporting "social" dialectic, it now spends inordinate energy merely managing itself, fencing off anomalies, giving increasingly nervous reassurances in the face of practices just as evil as that of Freeman. It has to face also the countless other disasters[9] wrought by socially applied scientific ideas and advice, many of which interface defence and intelligence interests. A system of denials has to be maintained also, as essential to scientific progress as breathing, and quite subordinate to any supposed role of "objective" research. At the same time, science has the burden of all the difficulties involved in having to hold its options open. In his own time, Sonnabend himself chortles with glee when he comes across a classic from well-respected Richard Proctor,[10] which is as good an intellectual almost-pregnancy as can be found, certainly as good as any phantom limb from the pages of Sheldrake.[11] Proctor, when referring to carbonaceous matter found in meteorites, said that such material was present in "very minute quantities", which is almost as good an as almost-abduction, and certainly as interesting as an almost-brain.

It was this kind of attempted vanishing (or psychological management) of anomalies which led Fort to conclude that any Newtonian matter-conservation laws are far less important than socio-cultural tricks of exclusion and inclusion. He concluded that such event shaping as the determined preservation of a right and proper brain in the skull (or indeed in Sheldrake's terms, a right and proper limb), is much more effective a force than gravity or momentum in deciding whether a thing is "real" or not, or indeed whether a particular event has "happened" or not, as in the controversy of cold fusion. As Fort points out, whether it has "happened" or is "real" or not, depends much on the relations between sets of complex taboos, sanctions, and those meta-physical elements of which mechanical forces are but the masks.

Sonnabend's Fortean eye winks: brains have two lobes, and occupy almost the entire volume of the skull; alien beings come from outer space, and that is therefore the only region from which their signals will be heard. Any pre-sumed "alien" signal therefore would be nicely tailored to respond to par-ticular equipment limitations, suit specific research requirements, fit set tech-nical parameters, and come in recognisable and nicely discreet quantities from some expected direction.

These examples all go to show that science is above all, the art of the cool. Time and again in Fort's work there is the feeling that the octave of technical allowances is governed by hot and cool principles of a techno-set, rather than fact versus fiction, which are becoming green-screen divisions of conscious-ness in an Internet age.

Like most bright folk who belong to an ordering elite, scientists like things (especially complicated things like people, brains, and alien signals) to stand still and be counted. If there is movement, they will slow it down, if there is complexity, they will simplify. If there is both complexity and movement to the point of incomprehensibility, they will, despite themselves, jury-rig a more sta-ble model, like the two-lobe brain, which will fit nicely the newly developing "cool" prestige tools of their particular era. Despite being an improvised and temporary thing, *this* model will filter down the media scales, and be land-scaped into the culture: it will be paraphrased, mimicked, and its advertise-ments (for fundamentally an advertisement is what the "brain" is), will be sold off as diagrams for elementary school textbooks. The night-side of nature is a thing not calculated to appeal to the writers of school text-books, nor the essentially well-behaved men and women in well-paid jobs in massive corpo-rate structures and institutions, who equally well do not like the night-side of town. Some of the more enlightened scientists part-recognise the part-brain, but they still struggle against their paymaster's corporate paradigm that a brain must be physically complete for full and proper functioning.

Whether that is true or not can be decided from considering a celebrated example from 150 years ago:

Phineas P. Gage, who at 25, was a railway foreman, somewhere in the USA. On 13th September, while placing a charge in a hole, a premature explosion drove the tamping-iron through his skull. The 13lb one-and-three-quarter-inch wide 3-foot 7-inch long rod entered point-first and passed completely through. He lost parts of his skull and some brain matter, but a few hours later was still rational enough to ask after his work. For several days he discharged bone and brain bits through his mouth, then passed into delirium and lost vision in one eye. Gage recovered rapidly, and even tried for his old job. His employers rejected him not because he wasn't fit, but because 'the most efficient and capable foreman' had changed into a truculent, brutish, untrustworthy simpleton. His friends said he was "no longer Gage".[12]

Thus despite massive brain damage, lost faculties return frequently, even when many or most parts of the brain do not regenerate. In the *Presence of the Past*, Sheldrake quotes E. R. John,[13] who says that in general, after traumatic head injury:

> Memory and skills return at a rapid rate during the first six months, with recovery sustained at a lower rate for up to twenty-four months. Defects in sensory, motor, and cognitive functions caused by brain injury due to penetrating wounds are characterised by an enormous resiliency of function in the great majority of cases, ultimately leading to little or no detectable defect.

The Absent Brain

Thus the hard-wired model, with specific physical areas of the brain allotted to specific activities, has to be rejected,[14] just as were the hierarchical computers of the 1950s. The emotional-locatable area idea is a perfect example of a theory that is in the twilight zone of cultural obsolescence. In a post-industrial age, where physical "location" and hard products are secondary to virtual organisation, scientists want a digital brain, and electronic-digital at that. Most researchers in artificial intelligence (AI) don't see the brain as biological-chemical, never mind metaphorical-analogous. The messy wetness of the brain's biosoup is out this season, victim of Tom Wolfe's principle of radical chic applied to science. Interest sectors, all metaphorical in themselves, of course fight like dogs to get into the mainframe of cultural realisation. To get into this primetime slot of active, physically manipulative full consciousness, Sonnabend pictures troublesome metaphors themselves having to go through a kind of Sweeney Todd barber's shop run by scientists. Though the hairstyle is pure sepia, the scene is quite suitable for our own Entertainment State:

> There was an investigation of phenomena in Assam. It was scientific, in the sense that the tonsorial may be the scientific. Dr Oldham enormously reduced a catastrophe to manageable dimensions. He lathered it with the soap of his explanations, and shaved it clean of all unconventional details. This treatment of "Next!" to catastrophes is as satisfactorily beautifying, to neat, little minds, as are some of the marcel waves that astronomers have ironed into tousled circumstances.[15]

Knowing perhaps a little more about what constitutes *information* since the time of poor Gage's accident, we might ask how such an example squares with the much-vaunted "computational" theory of mind, which according to Steven Pinker in the hubristically titled *How The Mind Works*:[16]

> ... solved millennia-old problems in philosophy, kicked off the computer-revolution, posed the significant question of neuroscience, and provided psychology with a magnificently fruitful research agenda.

Science appears to be the one field of cultural endeavour where such self-praise is allowed and encouraged. But in the face of the above quotation, we might well ask ourselves whether such a fruitful agenda has yet "solved" the problem of the total and coherent reorganisation of Gage's personality, its unpleasantness apart. Are such identity kits preformed? What centre recognises, re-dramatises, and generates the new integrated world-script when the need arises? Surely it would have been easier merely to replicate the older (pleasant) identity rather than go through the labour of creating an entirely new one, with the possibility of encountering a whole host of quite new computational problems. Paradoxically, in this damaged state, the brain, it appears, finds an inordinate amount of processing gigabytes which presumably were not available to poor uneducated workman Gage (bless him) during his life. Despite great loss of tissue, the brain obtained (or a great wonder, quickly manufactured), a profligate computing power sufficient to restructure totally a completely different identity, install its complete functioning, and maintain a consistent role and development. If it can borrow such organising power for the retrofit, why does the brain struggle with the rather simpler problem of 35.798×76.573 in the first instance? That is surely a small problem for any "computational model". Moreover, if the circuits are *down*, where does the computational power come from to organise the retrofit at all, no matter how faulty?

Each level, no matter how spectacular in itself, seems out of touch with all others. The remodelling consults neither the outer world nor the inner character as regards any particular preference, rather like Dr Frankenstein sticking any old face on his monster. After damage, the new personality can improve as well as degenerate, *X Factor* 43 reports. In one instance we have the case of a young boy, James, whose learning difficulties were cured when an entire hemisphere of his brain was removed. Thus mass appears to have no absolute connection to quality.

Another example of this independence is the change in character of Australian aborigine Reuben Poonkalya, whose head was pierced through from left to right with a hunting knife. His character was changed from being that of a "foul-mouthed, violent drunk" into that of one of Dr Walter Freeman's "good citizens" after the knife was removed by surgeons.[17] Similar severe head wounds however, can leave a person almost entirely unaffected, as was Alison Kennedy, after a knife was plunged right into the back of her head by a madman on a train.[18]

But surely the most searing example of brain damage is that suffered by

Kelvin Page in 1991 when working in a steel factory in Kent. A steel rod, heated to 700° centigrade, shot off its cooling bed and pierced his skull. Though his frontal lobes suffered serious damage, he survived; he did, however, experience serious personality changes.[19] The nice Fortean point is this: the psychologists might be pleased at the connection between frontal lobe damage and personality changes, thus avoiding completely the question of why, in view of the temperature, poor Kelvin's entire brain was not fried instantly in the first place. This is a perfect example of the Fortean principle of the lesser (manageable) *wonder*, being preferred to the higher (incomprehensible) *wonder*.

Looking at the brain even in its "normal" state, its "computational" management system is even more anarcho-schizophrenic. Yes, the management of heartbeat, circulation, and the organisation of the senses demand enormous computational power, yet little of this strength can be reallocated when the senses convulse with fear sufficient to cause a heart attack and death. In the "strong computational" model, surely such a state has the priority to borrow some RAM, close unnecessary windows, and pump calming signals to wherever they are needed. But that does not happen, except on rare occasions. More often than not (say, during examinations), the brain freezes up when it is most needed, indicating that we are not dealing with anything like a model, say of a rationalised economy with linked computable resources. If the brain is a computational device, then it is a very old-fashioned one; it appears to behave in an analogue manner rather than digital, with no guarantee that the matching analogues will find one another. The whole point of computerisation of any kind is the rationalised sharing of available resources, with the aim of quickly integrating available assets into some common purpose.

The Absent Brain

Three-year-old Hannah Thomson of Portsmouth, Hampshire is a living example of how the brain ignores, or does not recognise such logical paths, hence illustrating the "weak computational" model. Hannah had to have all her teeth removed in May 1996, because she could feel no pain at all. She had bitten her thumb to the bone, gnawed off the ends of her fingers, damaged her arm, and also bitten her tongue in half.[20] In this case, scientists reached immediately for the hackneyed phrase "genetic disorder" (failing of course to define exactly what that means), and left alone the far more disturbing idea that the "computational" elements had failed in their computations. Though the discovery of the structure of DNA is one of the great discoveries of our century, neither Crick and Watson had much to say about why the double-helix goes out of alignment on many occasions, producing inefficiencies such bad eyesight or diabetes with as much aplomb as it produces great strength, beauty or mathematical ability. Scientist have only just begun to have a look at failure in systems, wrong answers, and malfunctions, instead of merely dismissing such things as the result of "random noise". Taking a hint from Charles Fort, we suspect that the next thing to go overboard will be the "random mutations" of Darwin's great theory.

If in any way brain processes *are* computational, either weak or strong, then surely the whole point of such is flexibility — yet the brain cannot easily switch calculating energies and procedures to other domains, even in a life-threatening emergency. Whether weak or strong, the brain as computer appears to have great difficulty in negotiating with gross physical elements. One would assume that if body and brain were linked in quite a rational manner, the brain of Professor Hawking for example would be more than capable of allotting some of its intensely computational energies to calmly work out what has very obviously gone wrong in the management of his body, and proceed to carry out full repairs, rather in the manner of the maintenance of a space station. But his brain appears quite oblivious to the needs of its user. It does not even appear to recognise that if Hawking's body were repaired, then his brain might well work more efficiently than it does already. Thus his clever brain does not recognise that which would certainly be to its advantage.

Again, why does the brain struggle with 35.798x76.573, when other, far more complex "computational" problems have been solved within the body itself? The bio-electric computer that makes sense of light falling upon the eyes, for example, would not even blink the tiniest fraction of a nanosecond at 35.798x76.573, yet it remains aloof, unaware of the needs of a host body. It remains such even when that body, given even a momentary extra computing power, could avoid death, and thus we presume, the extinction of every physical centre within which all computational operations are surely based, or are they?

According to Rupert Sheldrake, even when bits of the maintained body are cut away, it appears that the "shapes" of such are still being run through the main program, even to the extent of *feeling* being registered, though created by no physical nerves. Ronald Melzack, a leading American neurologist,[21] comments: "It is evident that our experience of the body can occur without the body at all. We don't need a body to feel a body."

Thus we might conclude that the "computational model" of the brain is about as useful as the Victorian "careful housewife" model of "Dame Nature". In "her" kitchen, there are certain mismanaged scarcities and such superfluities as would bring shame to her homely managerial cheeks.

This writer has never ever had a TV set, and has seen a grand total of three films in his entire life. But nevertheless he is aware that in a cultural fluid, there is no "off" switch, and he once woke in the small hours with a complete TV series in his head. Beyond the sequence I could remember best, were innumerable rows of other episodes of this same series, stacked in the memory like shuffled cards, each sequence undergoing several different rates of memory decay. The sequence I recalled on waking was ready for showing: it had been cut, edited, was complete with commercial breaks and was entitled "Cyril Leicester's Burger Bar". The dream-story was pitched stylistically between *Roseanne* and *Frasier*, and showed a large young family who were being forced into vegetarianism by their father. Members of the family stole out at different times of day to eat at the local McDonald's. The husband and wife went there separately, heavily disguised, and in the episode best remembered, they tried to pick one another up whilst eating huge steaks at the same diner.

Let us just think of the superfluous computational power here. The whole creation was perfect: the realisation was that of a top professional writer in this class. Something also knew of the complete array of modern TV studio techniques, management and technology. "I" had not only cast the series well, "I" had created the actors, storylines and developments, not to mention shots, costumes, sets and editing. "I" knew also of the market requirements, and had command of all the subtlety of commercial styling: not too heavy, not too light, no long words, simple soap-opera thoughts, and a polished commercial level was achieved and maintained. Certainly no turkey within its own terms, the whole thing was of pleasant, light, comic subtlety, out for prizes and awards. Beautifully accurate, but if I tried consciously to do this kind of thing (as many do, and fail), I would probably fail, too. I would find out very quickly that lightweight popular TV writing is as difficult as any other kind of writing. Without any experience, my jokes would not be balanced; I would go under or over the top, and the whole thing would be an amateur mess, if only because I know that my personality and any talent I might possess are not suitable for this kind of thing at all.

The speed alone with which the whole multi-dimensional completeness was assembled was nothing short of miraculous, beyond all practical outer-world realisation. Within an hour, say two hours out of eight hours' sleep, the whole thing had been started and finished. A TV professional friend of this writer was asked how long, say, ten episodes of such a thing would take to create from scratch to broadcast. The reply was at least a year. Pencil and paper will verify that my dream of say, two hours, was in 0.045 percent of that time! I have also the idea that the achievement in the dream was just a party trick. I recall momentary scraps of many other things present: fragments of my almost-forgotten deepest past, and fragments of the almost-known present, and on the most distant horizon, scraps of scenes from a wonderfully spectacular opera, sung in Italian, by a cast of well-scrubbed pigs!

The Absent Brain

Unfortunately for my bank balance, such skills as seen in the dream are unavailable to me. Here is mystery piled on mystery: though I have had four books published, I have never ever had the desire to create such a series as described; I am not interested in the form, and the few hours of TV I have seen in my life have been accumulated from passing from shop windows, or seeing programmes in the houses of friends.

What have such dream creations got to do with "fact" or input/output? Yes, the psychologists might be right, some sublimated ego desires might be there, but a modern age asks a different and much more interesting question: where does the computational power come from? I know that on other nights, I may glimpse myself as a general, an astronaut, or some bozo swigging beer in a doorway. The creation of the characters is not so important as the question of where does the accurate and up-to-date knowledge of these very different worlds come from? Good guesses won't do. Good guesses could not have created my dream series, the texture was too fine. Good guesses would have conceptually bitmapped the whole creation of my dream programme called "Cyril Leicester's Burger Bar".

But the mystery compounds itself again: there was built into the whole thing two deliberate mistakes. Though the series was one hundred percent American, the commercial break showed an Egyptian pyramid made of hamburgers, with a sales commentary created by a man with the unmistakably British name of "George Dong of Batsford". Now there's a nice one from Dreamland! A nice primetime turkey of a title, that, perhaps a deliberate mistake, an automatically generated error signal, a wrong strand in the architecture of the entire structure, if only perhaps to stop its endless fractal-like expansion becoming a kind of blooming pond-algae in the brain.

Television soaps of course are the ultimate in modern non-significance; they belong to categories far beyond those of "real", "unreal" or "meaningful". In the face of burgeoning insignificance, the generating algorithm blew itself up, which does not sound promising for the Theory of Everything. George Dong of Batsford was a piece of "noise" which created yet another mystery within the "computational model". We are faced with the idea that provided with enough of Turing's "rough paper", the unconscious, like a Turing machine, would write soap operas to infinity until the algorithm self-destructs in the face of its own burgeoning chaos.

As a final party trick, I remember a few drifting fragments which showed that the process had the cheek to award itself some marks. It had generated a paste-up of newspaper reviews of the series, all of which contained raving praise! If infinity has a face and feel to it, I was convinced that this was it. Perhaps, thought I, the same process could sketch out the complete private lives of the performers and their relatives, and like a fractal, open all and any possible histories from any direction, point of view, or set of possibilities.

These image-creations within each and every one of us are far more meaningful than sterile concepts of atoms, neurons, or quarks. Such a dense structure of organised imagery as this writer experienced by accident relates in no way to linearities of industrialised time and space, or the input/output universe of finite economics, or those liberal-democratic nightmares called facts. The energy flow in these vast dream-constructs did not obey any kind of conservation law. In no way did the process rationally relate itself to any spectrum of my personality or social needs. And the process hinted of party tricks on the very limits of human perception. Both Borges and Proust tell of characters that momentarily become surrounded by the creations of their own imaginations.

I guess that most readers of this book will know what is going to happen next. At a train-station, in a restaurant, in a crowded bar, I will hear a busker give out a few bars of the introductory theme of "George Dong of Batsford", or I will see the face of one of the actresses across a busy road from which she will vanish quick as the busker, both like two frightened pike into reeds. I will not bother indulging in the paper chase of verifications. I will accept that a possible universe has formed, only to burst like a bubble. I will let such incidents bury themselves in the infinities[22] of the day, knowing that when we imagine, we create a form of life. The existence of a face, or a few bars from my dream soap-opera will mean that a process of recognition has been enacted before going on to its own illimitable purpose.

The whole point of what both the biologist Kammerer[23] and Carl Jung called acausal events, is the delight and wonder they arouse: through them, a human being is once more attached to a rich *mysterium* of nostalgia and inspiration, an area of growth and meaning beyond all fact, and perhaps before birth and beyond death. They construct an existential freedom worked by analogy and metaphor rather than by materialist and mechanical systems, and they represent a politics of the imagination beyond fixed categories of left or right.

Shakespeare would wonder why we have problems with this kind of thing: why we need it, yet are conditioned to mistrust it. But Shakespeare lived in the last age when there was a unity between mind and nature. Throughout his work, the coincidences, the conspiracies, simulacra in events and relationships, the foci and balance of human and material significance, all flow in and out of that vastly expanded being which Shakespeare saw as both state and cosmos combined. Cursed as we are with the utter vacancy of the random, the factual, and the objective, we are convinced that we are alone, surrounded by enemies and low on ammunition.

The Absent Brain

Such dreams show a typical Fortean comedy of striking wrong notes in organisational perfection. Signals indicated that the process I glimpsed in my dream had gone on long enough; it had reached exhaustion, it had run through all the fertile possibilities (as soap operas do, very quickly), and "I" had decided on a new series of games. It is pleasing to know that sometimes that process which puts an end to its own self-started, accelerating natural selection has sometimes a broad Fortean smile on its face.

My television drama comes from deep subjectivities that I would not like destroyed. I have that Fortean "damned" thing called an intuition, which says that should such a fascinating and delightful game fold its tents within me, I would be in deep trouble. The intellectually terrifying thing about this secret life, glimpsed by accident, is that it is not offensive or threatening, pathological, or destructive, but neither is it particularly profound. These are clues as to why AI is in so much trouble. The images of the described dream are amusing, but they come from a high organisation dedicated to a seemingly absurd purpose; they are therefore within an area where not a single biologist, philosopher, psychologist or mathematician has yet dared to tread. The very idea of something that is superficial, lightweight, non-intellectual, something that is such an impractical waste of time as I witnessed in my dream, is the very reversal of all the elements in Western input-output cultural expectations. Where the AI approach is wrong is not so much for the very deep mathematical reasons given by

Roger Penrose, Robert Wilensky and Joseph Wiezenbaum, but that no algorithm can generate superficiality, whimsicality or such active deception as a
cover for possibly much else. Even the very best modern thinkers, from Jung
to Sheldrake,[24] make the mistake in thinking that "intelligence" is a worthy,
"hard-working" and practical entity, dedicated to historically "forward" expectations which are worthy of the best kind of social-democratic heroes
(who are of course, themselves). That what we call "reality" has the infernal
cheek to misbehave itself as a function of the brain's very lotus-eating
superfluities, that it is indeed so deeply subversive as to include a waste of
time, and vastly extended jokes in its makeup, makes Fort a most valuable
philosopher. The best thing that can be said about this situation is that some
bright folk are beginning to be just a little suspicious. Thus Professor Robert
Wilensky, one of the leading lights of artificial intelligence research at Berkeley,
watches the old George Burns and Gracie Allen Show "partly from an AI
point of view".[25] Wilenski said that he didn't understand how people who
didn't study AI could understand Burns and Allen, because so many of the
things that Gracie got wrong were pronominal[26] references.

If my dream is any indication, Wilenski, in his attempt to crack humour for
AI purposes, has a long way to go. Such intense tribal dreaming makes modern
mysticism and intense subjectivity a very cool affair, devoid of apparatus and
tools, drugs, prayers, and extreme mental and physical states. For the first time
I recognised my community in the very deepest sense, though it was a community I didn't think I belonged to.

That both the forces of destiny and the surreal pathways to authentic discovery involve such complex and paradoxical recognition[27] seems to support Arthur Koestler's opinion that, with regard to the brain, "evolution has
wildly overshot the mark".[28] The brain is said to have 10^{10} cells in the cerebral cortex alone. Knowing what Shakespeare did with some possible connections of just twenty-six letters of the alphabet (even shredded of all
redundancies, such as "udfpb"), the number 10^{10} contains possibilities beyond all conception. When we know that the brain of the sperm whale is far
bigger than that of humans, then no one will fancy the chances of future
Ahabs if the whales ever get such things into action.

Yet despite all this potential:

> For all our expertise in unravelling the genetic code and the miracles of nerve
> conduction, muscle movement and blood clotting, we still understand noth-
> ing about pain, sleep, growth and healing. We are ignorant about nearly
> every aspect of consciousness, and even find it hard to diagnose death. The
> truth is that we know life only by its symptoms.[29]

Thinking is perhaps the result of the brain trying to comprehend itself.
But in this process, we have anything but a programmatic utilitarian democracy involved. Why, instead of such wondrous play as we have seen, does
not such a computer direct its computational power to, say, improving my

short sight, or curing an illness? But a greater mystery is that I was not supposed to see the dream I described in the first place. In general, people only encounter dreams by accident. The body turns many times in sleep; if for whatever reason the body experiences discomfort (such as pain, thirst, or wanting to urinate), the brain switches on, and some fragments of the vast hidden dramas of our secret lives are glimpsed. The optic nerve is hardly involved, yet the whole drama is visually available internally.

A good question, therefore, is who or what is watching it?

George Dong of Batsford?

According to traditional scientific thinking, specific areas of the brain are responsible for certain kinds of function. But there is a condition called hydrocephalus that frequently contradicts this view. This affliction means that the brain volume of the new-born child is filled with cerebrospinal fluid, which can be drained off by modern surgical techniques, but which frequently leaves sufferers with sometimes only five per cent of the normal amount of brain tissue. According to a recent article in *X Factor* 43, Professor John Lorber of the University of Sheffield discovered that there is appears to be no relation between the *volume* of brain tissue and IQ:

> Of the 253 subjects in the study, nine were found to have approximately only five per cent of the normal amount of brain tissue. Despite this, four of the nine had IQs of above 100, the national average, and the other two had IQs above 126. One subject, a twenty-six-year-old man, proved himself to be every bit as intellectually adept as the researchers investigating him — he attended Sheffield University and graduated with a first-class degree in mathematics.

The
Absent
Brain

Typically, the mind-body anomalies here are ignored by a cultural rather than strictly a scientific process, well described by Richard Mattuck's ideas about absent particles:

> A reasonable starting point for a discussion of the many-body problem might be the question of how many bodies are required before we have a problem. In eighteenth-century Newtonian mechanics, the three-body problem was insoluble. With the birth of general relativity around 1910, and quantum electrodynamics around 1930, the two- and one-body problems became insoluble. And within modern quantum field theory, the problem of zero bodies (vacuum) is insoluble. So if we are out after exact solutions, no bodies at all is already too many.[30]

The assumption here of course is that God's gift called the brain properly arrives to play all these games in the first place. Most human beings have at least some parts of a physical brain, even if those parts are damaged. But all these questions pall when we consider *no brain at all* to calculate anything. It would be nice to know what the comments of Jacobin, Faraday, or Huxley, or

Marx and Darwin (Newton excepted — the Great Alchemist would probably have been up to it), would have been in the face of the "fact" that some humans are born *without any physical brains at all*. Surely we say, such unfortunates are deprived of all metaphor: they have no engine-room, no fount of all philosophy, no multi-track control panel or railway signal box or any kind of bioelectric or circuit analogy to register the suffering or hypocrisy, not even the truths and the lies. Surely a person who has no physical brain has nothing even to generate vengeance, summon up evil, nothing to make a curse, nothing to erect the stage-fronts of hatred, love, forgiveness, and knowledge, never mind *manage* the body's complex systems? Perhaps we always feared that the universe was more anarchic than ever we thought, but no brain *at all*? Most people are agreed that there is a lump of grey matter within the human skull which functions as a kind of control box without which it would be quite impossible for a human to be "alive" in any proper sense, never mind think, decide, or act as an integrated personality.

In *Medical Curiosities*, Bob Rickard quotes from a TV programme[31] in which this was shown:

> Sharon — during a routine check on a brain fluid valve, a huge cavity where brain tissue should have been was discovered. Professor Lorber said her brain had disappeared or become paper-thin in the frontal cortex region. She otherwise functioned normally.

> Roger — who had only five percent of his brain left, but who still got a first-class degree in maths. The whole area where speech and feelings are usually located were missing.

> Stephen — his absence of brain was demonstrated by holding a light behind his head, [which lit up] like a dull pink goldfish bowl. He nevertheless obtained five O-Levels.

Charles Fort would probably have said that unfortunately for the admirable struggle for perfect accuracy within reference books, encyclopaedias, and even operating theatres, there were also other disturbing rumours:

> ... there's the fellow who wrote a will the night before he died in a New York hospital whose body — allegedly, though I don't have any references — on autopsy showed only half a cupful of dirty grey water in his skull.[32]

Within the Fortean scale, such an apocryphal rumour shades into the much more "solid" experience of Homeland, the German brain specialist, who performed an autopsy on the body of a paralysed man who had been in full possession of his faculties to the last, but instead of brains the man had only eleven ounces of water in his skull.[33] But at least there was *something* in this head, as distinct from the quite empty head of a baby that was born at

St Vincent's hospital in New York in 1935. This baby had no brain whatever yet lived for twenty-seven days and appeared to be quite normal until it died suddenly, the autopsy revealing that its skull was quite empty of brain tissue.[34] To bring us almost up to date, *The Sun* reported eight years ago that Andrew Vandal, of Wallingford, Connecticut, had lived for five years without a brain, and was about to start nursery school:

> Andrew was born with his skull filled with fluid. A cyst had formed at the stem of the brain, and stopped the rest of it from forming. The stem contains the nerves that control breathing and circulation. But the parts which allow humans to think and co-ordinate are missing.[35]

Andrew, born on July 12, 1984, suffered from a condition known as atelencephalic aprosencephaly. This is the most extreme form of hydroencephaly, resulting in a cranium filled with nothing but fluid. In some cases, no brain tissue at all is detectable. Dr Robert Leshner, professor of paediatric neurology at the Medical College of Virginia, in an interview in *X Factor* 43,[36] said of this condition: "In those circumstances, cognitive awareness is physiologically impossible."

In the same article, when asked about the influence of his research on hydrocephalus, Professor Lorber said that it had "suffered a fate like that of much of the literature of phenomenological science: it was ignored".

The Absent Brain

A modern Fortean might say that since *The Sun* picture shows Andrew laughing his head off, though *sans* brain, he still co-ordinates. Here we have one of those beautiful and edifying mysteries that make Forteans rejoice. What, we might ask, in this case, happened to the twin-lobe control box which was God's gift, and the cause of the Enlightenment? What happened to the "areas" of the brain allotted to specific emotions? As Leonard Stringfield learned[37] when trying to locate crashed and captured UFOs, rather than the simple idea of "facts," there is encountered a grey-scale of half-being and semi-substance, starting with rumour, looping through the intermediate tones of early and late journalism, and concerning the brain, what better to continue such a progress than that high-quality consumer convenience, the designer reassurance of the academic fact, given by biologist Professor Steven Rose:

> The concentration of neurons in ganglia is perhaps the first step towards building a brain, but even the appearance of a large head ganglion does not ensure that the brains that humans and other mammals possess are the only design solution that can result... even without their head ganglia, insects can show some behaviour which could be called learning. In the 1960s, Gerald Kerkut, in Southampton, described a series of experiments in which he suspended a headless cockroach above a bath containing a salt solution. Kerkut arranged it such that whenever the leg touched the liquid an electrical circuit was completed and the cockroach was shocked; when it withdrew its leg from the liquid the circuit was broken and the shock ceased.

. . . .

> The residual cockroach, even without its head, eventually ceased putting
> its leg into the liquid — it had "learned" how to avoid being shocked.[38]

But do we need more evidence of intelligence functioning without a brain? What does "more evidence" mean? Do we need evidence of three-quarter brains, or of full human functioning on a *single* lobe? There are reports on the Web of a five-lobed brain; at the time of writing, there is a rumour from France of three lobes; who can say that there will be no examples of fourth or fifth lobes, but again, how much evidence do we need? A seventh lobe, perhaps? How high shall be built the house of cards? The latest report from Reuters is of a boy born in Chaoyang city in the north-eastern Liaoning province of China whose brain scan revealed that he had *two* complete brains.[39] According to the Xinhua news agency, this healthy child did not need surgery, and hardly sleeps even for one hour a night. This is because his brains, apparently, work in rotation!

This "gift" from God now appears to be something of a disappearing Pandora's box, or should we say a Trojan horse with we know not what inside? As an example of how we humans think about anomalies, a letter[40] to the *Fortean Times* in response to news about this two-brained child is illustrative:

> The Chinese baby "with two brains" is almost certainly one born with the
> two cerebral hemispheres lacking their main connecting channel, the *cor-
> pus callosum*, resulting in a "split-brain". Presumably the report lost some-
> thing in translation from the Cantonese!

Split-brain. Lack of connecting channel. Perfect explanation, and complete with the correct Latin term, indicating insider knowledge, and with a nice touch of vaguely facetious undergraduate "cool" humour at the end. We all walk away satisfied and not a little impressed, if only because every single human being indulges in this kind of cultural advertising to advertise other things. That these two brains (miraculously) work without their "connecting channel" is side-tracked, like Kelvin Page's 700° centigrade insertion; it becomes secondary to the *style* of the general expression.

Another example of a preference for the lesser wonder rather than the greater is to be found in a recent article in *X Factor*, entitled *The Hounds from Hell*.[41] In talking of mysterious appearances of black dogs, the unnamed writer says that there are some theories connecting these sightings with UFO activities, adding that other researchers see such things as the modern forms of old gods. The writer then goes on quickly to add that Graham McEwan, in *Mystery Animals of Britain and Ireland*, has a "more earthbound" explanation that such black dogs are "thought-forms". That the writer sees "thought-forms" as being more "earthbound" than "old gods" is a perfect example of the Fortean idea that explanations are often equally as fantastic as the things they would seek to explain. Again we come up against the Fortean idea of time itself existing in terms of updated changes in presentation of information rather than any forward moving rationalist "progress".

What, a true Fortean might ask, in the middle of all this folklore in crea-tion, is a "fact"? Do we need yet more evidence of brains functioning, though crushed to pulp,[42] brains working though pierced through by iron railings and shot through with steel bolts,[43] and brains which are little more than complete cancerous growths,[44] before we realise that the physical size, mass, and indeed condition of the brain need not necessarily relate to the com-monly accepted functions of either cognition, control or even common sense? Given this "evidence", whatever became of the almost phrenological idea of the "emotions" in one lobe, and the "rational faculty" in the other? In Fortean terms, that ark of the human scientific covenant, the much-propagandised quest to know, is accompanied and counterbalanced by what appears to be a very human need not-to-know. The divine comedy of this is that one has a funny Fortean feeling that the amount of evidence is as unimportant as the amount of grey matter within the skull. Thus as far as the brain is concerned, we trust the school book diagram just as we trust the pointer-readings on the impressive-looking electroencephalograph and lie detector. We care not to know that apart from the addition of a few buffer amplifiers and better displays, these instruments are no more than tarted-up versions of the high-impedance voltmeters of round about 1890.

In Fortean terms, the no-brain situation is "damned" and for the same reasons as is the Loch Ness Monster and the UFO. Fort teaches us that it is not a question of truth versus falsehood, but what kind of level of universal mess we are prepared to accept. To accept that "reasoning" can take place within animal death, and without any grey matter at all, would ruin our science, con-taminate ideas of human destiny, and make nonsense of our dearest religious thoughts and philosophies. The very absurd and often grotesque playfulness of many incidents Fort describes is insulting to all our ideas of the universe being a serious design with proper purpose. Thus we make the extraordinary event mentally off limits. It is the other side of town. That is the basic Fortean position. Thus we do not consider "factual objectivity", so much as what is *allowed*. In the library of every school in the world, there will be found no doubt beautifully coloured illustrations of the human brain. *This* brain will no doubt be whole, have only two lobes, and will be described in a knowledgeable and well-written text as being the generating centre of that celebrated twenty-first-century institution called the Official Reality.

The
Absent
Brain

The anomaly is difficult to live with; we fence it off like encroaching chaos, and we cross our fingers. There are many mansions. We cannot live in them all. But then it is equally difficult to live with the excruciatingly mundane nature of many "fair and democratic" evidence games that lead to nowhere. The "evi-dence" which is "damned" in the Fortean sense and not incorporated in the general system of reference, is that evidence which goes on saying that we cannot learn without a "proper" brain and that children cannot bend metal at a distance. Is Professor Hasted of Imperial College therefore mad?[45] Is he an impostor? Was he confused, were his metal-bending experiments not set up properly, was he completely tricked by the hundreds of children tested in his laboratory in Imperial College?

At the time of writing there are a growing number of highly respected writers from very different countries who have gone on public record stating that they have been shown evidence by official government organisations of the retrieval of crashed UFOs, the recovery of alien corpses, and even co-operation with live aliens. Are *these* people mad? Are they all liars, impostors, laughable eccentrics and complete idiots? If they are the victims of jokes and deceptions, then this is a damned expensive and most perverse way to raise a laugh by authority, never known historically either for its charity or its sense of fun. It would be more expensive and even more peculiar to arrange the thousands of cattle mutilations that accompany many UFO sightings,[46] and also the increasing number of claimed abductions by aliens. If we consider that the countless recollections of such under hypnosis are also rigged in a similar manner, then we are again getting near to that Fortean threshold where the explanations are more fantastic than the phenomenon itself.

But do we need more evidence, when there is almost *too much* evidence already to indicate that something most peculiar is (perhaps always) going on? The matchbox in the kitchen may be in front of the eyes when searched for, but if we are not thinking about it, it will be invisible. The conclusion is always the same. The evidence may be there, but it is ruled out of court: banned, exiled, imprisoned, damned, not so much by some corporate Big Brother, but by a completely automatic self-censoring system implicit in a set cultural frame-work. As always, such a framework consists of warring domains of interest, is tribal in its intellectual organisation, and quite demonic in its role as persona to preserve its own interest sectors and identity.

A few pages on from the picture of the brain, we can only surmise what a school textbook will contain alongside the right and proper and respectable pictures of other important things. Pain as a warning alarm perhaps (when it continues long after we have got the message, or when it can do more damage in itself than the very thing it is "warning" about), or that a liberal-democratic arts culture is a civilising and humane influence, when at least five of the major fiction writers of the twentieth-century were outright fascists and racists. Per-haps the relevant passages[47] in the works of Céline, D. H. Lawrence, T. S. Eliot and Ezra Pound, and many others, become Fortean anomalies them-selves in that they are "not seen". This is pointed out here not in way of moral comment, so much as a reminder, in the spirit of Charles Fort, of the difference between the world as it is and the world as we would like it to be. Perhaps similar textbooks will also *not* tell the children about Isaac Newton, the epitome of Enlightenment and Reason, spending much of his life involved with metaphysics, occultism, mystical theology, and having possibly the very last fully equipped alchemical laboratory and furnace in Europe.[48] We can only assume that the existence of this laboratory was kept a secret from Voltaire, who visited Newton frequently during Newton's last years. If Voltaire had inadvertently opened the wrong door, it could have changed history, just as history might have been changed if it had become generally known that British schoolchildren from 1945 onwards were given 11-plus intelligence tests based on the influence of allegedly fraudulent statistics compiled by a celebrated psychologist, whose work in every other respect was never anything less than quite brilliant.[49]

The same schoolchildren will also not be told about the implicit political sympathies of the great physicists Otto Hahn and Werner Heisenberg. These two Nobel Prize winners (who, like Neils Bohr, had genius second only to Einstein), stayed on as heads of the Max Planck Institute in Berlin during WWII, supposedly, according to popular report, to "hinder" Nazi nuclear research. Undoubtedly, these men were the twin fathers of the embryo Nazi nuclear bomb,[50] and their reputations are fine examples of edited history, as are Newton's alchemical preoccupations. Also concealed by default, will be the intense metaphysical involvements of Clerk Maxwell, the Pythagorean mysticism of Benjamin Franklin, and the spiritualism of J. J. Thomson and Oliver Lodge. Faraday's involvements with a bizarre fundamentalist sect probably caused his lapse (between 1841 and 1845) into complete madness, from which he fortunately recovered, will also be left out.

The world as conspiring advertising structure (which Fort believed it was) has therefore made sure that the glittering names of Hahn and Heisenberg have long ago obliterated the names of the Norwegian Resistance workers and the thirty-four British commandos from 1st Airborne Division who tried unsuccessfully to sabotage the heavy water manufacturing facility at the Norsk Hydro plant in 1943. Many of these unbelievably brave heroes were shot whilst prisoners, some died in concentration camps, and three badly wounded British commandos were killed by poison injections administered by German doctors.[51] In the world of Orwellian-Fortean "edits", we are asked to assume therefore, that if Hahn and Heisenburg had got their Krupp-manufactured[52] equipment in time, and had also obtained their heavy water (fortunately successfully sabotaged in a later attempt in 1944), they might have "hindered" the Nazis even more. Perhaps, waiting in the historical wings, is a claim that ex-Nazi Werner Von Braun, the founder father of the American space programme, "hindered" the work at Peenemunde. He hindered this work by showering the South of England with V1 and V2 rockets, and he hindered it yet again by energetically supervising the design of a long-range winged V-weapon with an eye to it coming straight down between Broadway and Fifth Avenue.

No wonder Von Braun and the rest of the imported Nazis were kept well down-range in Houston.

The Absent Brain

knife-edge
systems

Using this powerful technique of making the discursive method take a good look at *itself*, Fort shows how our reactions to anomalies shed light on how we think and organise our concepts. In this sense, he demonstrates contradictions in thought as well as matter. He works the "strangeness" he uncovers into a unique essay in the psychology of perception, at times using the discursive technique almost against its very self. In that though, Fort's frequently tongue-in-cheek Sonnabend is always careful to give dates, times and places, together with statements of authority and technical assessments of experts, he is still wary of even his own formulations. There is often some confusion, even amongst very knowledgeable Forteans, about Fort's "theories" of such things. Whilst it is true that he puts forward many theories to "account" for the things he records (such as telekinesis, teleportation, space-visitors, other worlds drifting near Earth in the past), he mocks his own theory formation just as he mocks its equivalent in scientists. At the very end of *New Lands,* he comments:

> We assemble the data. Unhappily, we shall be unable to resist the temptation to reason and theorise. May Super-embryology have mercy upon our own syllogisms. We consider that we are entitled to at least thirteen pages of gross and stupid errors. After that we shall have to explain.[1]

There is great ironic strength here: he views brain as being far more subtle an entity than a something which merely contains codes which, when solved, are simply added to an existing store of other codes which have been previously "solved." From the Fortean point of view, this reduces nature to a passive game of finite clue hunting, the clues being added to that kind of continuously expanding store, which the books of the nineteenth-century frequently call a "treasure house" of knowledge. Fort rejects such a supine culture; he cannot accept the passivity of the idea of a continuously updated system of "improvement" made by joining fixed and predictable states of reference together to form a "universal" system whose growth supposes a closer and closer approximation to some final truth. Such a system is in no manner capable of leading to an understanding of those countless thousands of fractures in the scheme of things which Fort points out to us. As far as he is concerned, science, far from opening out "wonders" to us, often closes them. Using the idea of "the system" again (how strange that word in that context must have sounded in those days), he indicates some ominous changes since 1860:

> We take most of our data from lists compiled long ago. Only the safe and unpainful have been published in recent years. The restraining hand of the "System" as we call it is tight upon the sciences of today... the protecting hand strangles; the parental stifles; love is inseparable from phenomena of hate. Nature, at least in its correspondent's columns, still evades this protective strangulation, and the *Monthly Weather Review* is still a rich field of unfaithful observation: but, in looking over the long-established periodicals, I have noticed their glimmers of quasi-individuality fade gradually, after about 1860, and the surrender of their attempted identities to a higher attempted organisation. Some of them held out as far as 1880; traces findable up to 1890 — and then surrendered, submitted. After the death of Richard Proctor,[2] all succeeding volumes of *Knowledge* have yielded scarcely an unconventionality. Note that the great number of times that the *American Journal of Science* and the *Report of the British Association* are quoted: note that after 1885, they're scarcely mentioned in these inspired but illicit pages — as by hypnosis or inertia, we keep on saying.
> About 1880.
> Throttle and disregard.[3]

Knife-Edge Systems

Just two of the threatening things about anomalies are their frequency and size. Fort's terrifyingly large-scale examples have appeared on a world-stage; he jokes about the difficult task of finding any "mystery" which is shy, furtive, or obscure, and he takes great care to make weird incidents and experiences verifiable by good report, often joking that therefore they are "normal", as against the "mundane", which Forts says is quite rare in his experience, sometimes being almost an impossibility in itself! In this, he shows quite clearly that psychologically we do have a problem with the sheer macrocosmic size of some anomalies, and their often outrageously dramatic entrance into the china-shop of Official Reality. This unique institution is always managed by authority, to which science, for material and financial reasons alone, must always belong. The idea of an *avant-garde* science is so absurd it might even belong to a Fortean category in itself, and therefore it might *just* be possible. In this sense, Fort is more liberal than science, since science has yet to pay his discoveries the same compliment.

Like the examples of non-existent brain, 500 tons of material, though reported by *Chemical News*[4] as falling specifically within a rectangle some fifty miles by ten miles, didn't even get recognised as a common anything by the so-called experts. In this respect, Fort presents a wholly novel theory of fiction as related to the psychology of experience as related to *fact*.

Five-hundred tons of stinking substance apart, when the anomaly appears in test tubes or in particle-accelerators, the scientists have no problem. As long as countless billions of intelligent creatures that look like a million different nightmares exist quite unseen snug in every newly laundered bedsheet, and deep in the cleanest living room carpet, everything is under control. Some of these creatures need no oxygen, no light, and some again have no detectable brain. Yet they are intelligent enough to procreate, recognise danger, form social groups, and some also have the power to inflict damage on human beings. Such things well illustrate a rationalist crisis of focus: as long as these creatures remain in the carpet that is alright, but when a larger version appears cruising alongside Concorde, and performs intelligent manoeuvres, there are no terms of reference, no controls, and the receptor processing of almost the entire culture has a problem. The difference between Fort and the scientists thus concerns the information levels and dialectical focusing of the macrocosmic frame, rather than the microcosmic; in the latter, the scientist is more than ready to accept all kinds of quark-like degrees of strangeness within atomic structure.

Quite at the other end of the scale, the scientist is also prepared to accept black hole-like strangeness at a terrifying distance away from the Earth, that is the super-macrocosmos. But should we see in this some reconciliation with Fortean views, it is, as Fort pointed out, the scientist's much more localised *kitchen* as it were, which gives him the most problems. If, against all sane and proper assumptions, a brain is absent, or a spoon waltzes up towards the ceiling, the event simply *cannot* have happened. That, in 1995, some four million Americans disappeared without trace, together with another two million world-wide,[5] is similarly a non-event, as is the admittedly "unaccountable" loss of $18 billion recently announced by the US Defense Department. In addition to this, *The New York Times* reported that the New Reconnaissance Office (a department of the CIA) had lost $2 billion "between the cracks."[6]

The human psychological management framework hardly makes place for such things along the scale of what Fort's Sonnabend would call "allowances". Such vast things are therefore subject to an almost automatic shrinking (if not a complete vanishing), which is implicit in the way we all process our perceptions. As a Fortean model of elementary consciousness, "degrees" of truth are subject to "normality" contrast-control.

Although for the most part Sonnabend does indeed report the unbelievable event, and the utterly fantastic occurrence, it is therefore most important to realise that he makes most of his discoveries within the terms of the "normal" scale of this working "kitchen" world, that is in ships, cars, aircraft, rooms, streets, fields, police courts and even cupboards. It is this part of the scale of experience in which scientific denials most cluster, denials which Sonnabend frequently reveals as being often wondrous anomalies in themselves in that there are constant strangely quantum-like contradictions amongst the physicists, as if they themselves are living metaphors of their theory. Here is Leon Rosenfeld writing in the early 1960s:

> ... as Pauli was quick to remark, Heisenberg had overlooked situations in which trajectories did fall within the range of observation; after all, we do observe the orbit of the moon, although there is no reason not to apply the same rules of quantisation as those of the electrons around the nucleus of an atom.[7]

This is in direct contradiction to Paul Davies, writing at almost exactly the same time, in his introduction to Heisenberg's *Physics and Philosophy*:

> ... quantum effects are generally only important in the atomic domain. We do not notice them in daily life.

Knife-Edge Systems

As well as such a blushing and weak qualification as "generally", these contradictions and denials show that in science, as in everyday life, there is the drama of a constant struggle for a stable language of description. Language is power, and without a successful *naming* of things, there can be no "existence" in any accepted sense of cognitive recognition. Modern anthropology and the studies of language structures show the naming of things as being very important. The way we think, allocate identities, distribute techno-tribal power architectures, and above all the way we name things means admission into the spectrum of sanctions, as Sonnabend says, "Or oneness of allness: scientific works and social registers: a Goldstein who can't get in as a Goldstein, gets in as a Jackson."[8] Or, when the quantum world, with no apologies for political incorrectness, is taken from its precious little academic nest and made to perform on Broadway:

> I predict that next Wednesday, a large Chinaman, in evening clothes, will cross Broadway, at 42nd Street, at 9pm. He doesn't, but a tubercular Jap in a sailor's uniform does cross Broadway, 35th Street, Friday, at noon. Well, a Jap is a perturbed Chinaman, and clothes are clothes.[9]

It is typical of Charles Fort that at almost exactly the same time as Heisenberg and Planck were concerned with applying "degrees" of truth to the extreme limits of the human spectrum of consciousness, he was demonstrating *degrees* of "strangeness" within the perfectly "ordinary" level of experience.

He uses these degrees to describe the structure of what might be called knife-edge systems. These are systems which, like the almost-brain again, *almost* work, indeed which *do* work on occasion, but which nevertheless do not work every time on demand, or when activated. Though chaos theory and fuzzy logic have just begun to take a look at such systems,[10] in general, traditional mainstream science still rules them out completely; experiments must work on every occasion, they must be repeatable when carried out by different people, and complete stability within the bounds of reasonable possibility, *must* be secured for the word "scientific" to be used at all.

This idea of something being "almost real" (collectively strong imaginative forces) as against something that is hardly real (collectively weak imaginative forces) holds the key to one of Fort's main ideas: *that there are no completely false systems,* just as there are no completely "real" ones. There are embryo states, which are possibilities, not falsehoods; there are partial truths that are only half-lies and so on. This fundamental Fortean axiom allows for fuelless engines, the almost-brain and a host of other "damned" things, to at least enter the spectrum of possibilities at the low-energy end of the scale of imaginative realisations. This is quite the opposite view of established science, which even today is still locked in absolute yes/no, real/false paradigms.

Fort thus created a much-needed general theory of the anomalous event which is largely devoid of the antiquated and largely degenerate apparatus of goat's feet, rituals, and spells, although in speaking of such things, we must not commit the Fortean sin of exclusionism, and create our own system of "damned" or excluded things. In Fortean terms, "not working" means, as we have seen in the case of the fuelless machines, and the absent brain again, not working *very often*, or even not working *very well*. Typical of such "damned" and "rejected" systems are the ouija board or astrology; these might be called knife-edge systems in that parts *might* work in part, as almost-discarded paradigms. Like batteries, such things may still have a little cultural life-sap in them.

Thus Sonnabend sees scientific truths not as necessarily true or false, but as faltering things in a withering context of dying cultural approximations. It goes almost without saying that a lot of people would not want a fuelless engine, just as they would not want a partial brain. But the fact that they patently do not enables Sonnabend to see poltergeists for example, ghost rappings, appearances, as *system-strains* rather the "normal" versus the "paranormal," and the forces which determine what thing is more or less "real" than anything else are forces in a kind of war within the collective imagination. Hence Sonnabend has got rid of the absolutely wretched idea of the "paranormal" versus the "normal". For him, the Amazing Randi would have just as much difficulty in showing that what he did was *not* "paranormal" as Geller would have in showing that what he did *was* "paranormal". The onus of proof is therefore equal for either party, for in a Fortean world model, everything is a question of intermediate degree:

> Some trees have buds that are not permitted to develop. These are known
> as dormants, and are held in reserve, against the possibility of a destruc-

tion of the tree's developed leaves. In one way or the other, there are reservations in every organism. We think of inter-mundane isolations that have been maintained, as once the Americas were kept separate from Europe, not by vast and untraversable distances, but by belief in vast and untraversable distances. I have no sense of loneliness in thinking that the inorganic sciences that are, by inertia, holding out for the isolation of this earth, have lost much power over minds. There are dissatisfactions and contempts everywhere.[11]

Thus the interesting consideration from his point of view is not whether a thing will work or not, *but by how much.* In this sense, he is a most non-Aristotelian philosopher, and this kind of thinking is very near to what today we call fuzzy thinking in computer programming. In these Fortean terms, whether something works, or is "real" (to any degree), or is true, or false (to any degree), depends on what might be called the state of the institutionalised forces within fields of belief, governed by the state of the prevailing resources of the imagination. Therefore Fort replaces what we usually experience as "real" by allowance schedules consisting of fields of belief sanctions that are anything but uniform and static. He sees the imagination as an almost-live animal grazing on such fields. Such a belief-animal chews the cud of the entire complex of social, psychological, and intellectual formulation, and is a creature

Knife-Edge Systems

> ... that is working out its development in terms of planets and acids and bugs, rivers, and labour unions and cyclones, politicians and islands and astronomers. Perhaps we conceive of an underlying nexus in which all things, in our existence, are different manifestations — torn by its hurricanes and quaked by the struggles of Labour against Capital — and then for the sake of balance, requiring relaxations. It has its tougher hoaxes, and some of the apes and some of the priests, and philosophers and wart hogs are nothing short of horse play; but the astronomers are the ironies of its less peasant-like moments — or the deliciousness of pretending to know whether a far-away star is approaching or receding. This is cosmic playfulness; such pleasantries enable Existence to bear its catastrophes. Shattered comets and sickened nations and the hydrogenic anguishes of the sun — and there must be astronomers for the sake of relaxations.[12]

Under a Fortean microscope there appears to be not a single scrap of the world which could be called mundane; because when we look at it closely, what we would like to call the *ordinary* or the *conventional* splits, cracks, falls apart as great gaps in knowledge, received experience, and factual perception, are revealed by Fort's relentless Sonnabend. Both the explanation and the mundane, in his terms, emerge as pure *control*. As such, both are pieces of cultural camouflage, and to see anything purely in terms of them is rather like seeing British life and culture solely in terms of the changing of the guard at Buckingham Palace.

cosmology

as

consumerism

James Ussher (1581–1656), Archbishop of Armagh, Primate of All Ireland, and Vice-Chancellor of Trinity College, Dublin, claimed in his book *The Annals of the World*, that Man was created by the Trinity on Sunday October 23, 4004 BC. Sir John Lightfoot (1602–1675), Vice Chancellor of Cambridge University, claimed even greater accuracy: "heaven and earth, centre and circumference, were created all together, in the same instant, and clouds full of water... this work took place and man was created by the Trinity on October 23, 4004 BC at nine o'clock in the morning."[1]

Lancelot Hogben comments on Ussher's astonishing claim for both physical and metaphysical accuracy:

> The limits of land and water were settled on that date by divine decree. The marine fossils, inconveniently, collected at greater distance from the coast, were either deposited by Noah's flood, inserted, where found, to test the faith of believers, or left there by itinerant merchants and armies with a partiality for fish diet.[2]

Good Fortean examples of modern science piling similar obscurity upon obscurity can still be found in abundance. The toothpaste smiles of the New Cosmology grinned at us in a recent article in *The Sunday Telegraph*. The mathematical physicist Paul Dirac (1902–1984), the writer tells us, came across a "curious cosmic coincidence":

> In 1937 [Dirac] pointed out that the characteristic strength of gravity in our universe is roughly equal to the result of dividing the time needed for a ray of

light to cross a sub-atomic particle by the age of the universe.[3]

But if we smile at all, should we smile at Ussher, Lightfoot *and* Dirac? These pieces of pure intellectual consumerism, though vastly apart in time, are as good as anything found today in Hawking or Gell-Mann. In his description of Dirac's almost mediaeval theology, after inadvertently forgetting to give us the age of the universe, and also failing to tell us which particular "sub-atomic particle" he is referring to, the *Sunday Telegraph* writer also forgets that no "sub-atomic particle" has a simple Euclidean circular "diameter" in the sense of $c \div \pi$; they have quantum orbits, which are, supposedly, very different things altogether. But later, the same article contains almost an apology for the profusion of such spectacular omissions, and the writer, become suddenly a Fortean, appears to smell a rat within the whole house of cultural cards:

> Many physicists will give the idea of oscillating gravity a very wide berth — because it will offend their sense of aesthetics. Altering the strength of gravity to fit observations smacks of medieval attempts to patch up the Earth-centred model of the solar system by adding more gear-wheels.

This example is given to show the Fortean view of the follies of so-called "scientific statements" which suffer a meltdown in the face of a decision complex of compromises, allowances, and sanction-rituals whose labyrinthine obscurities are as false as any system of social manners, that is things to say, and not to say, things to wear and not to wear. As Robert Matthews finally has the courage to point out, Dirac's statement is shot through with such tangible monastic decay as to rival many similar such suspicious "profundities" handed out by the copywriters of our own New Cosmology. A modern Sonnabend would have much fun with this kind of thing, easily culled from contemporary scientific journals; it makes the Inquisitorial lists of the names of the thousands of devils "cast out" from tortured unfortunates look almost like a relatively sane option, by comparison.

Cosmology as Consumerism

Given such verifiable incidents from respectable sources, Sonnabend sees humanity in general, and scientists in particular, as deep-sea fish trying to account for the fall of wreckage from a huge ship that has exploded. The fish have no concept for a five-year diary, a wooden leg, an umbrella, or a split steel door of a cargo hold, never mind the myriad of other unidentified objects descending into their particular bandwidth of perception. Yet, as Sonnabend would say, if fish think at all, just like the astronomers, they will systemise, they will interpret; they will produce accuracies and certainties beyond the sun and moon based upon scraps of inconceivable cosmic wreckage, some electrical bits of which might even respond with a last bleep or two, producing endless fishy scrolls of prophecy and revelation concerning aquatic destiny. What the reactions of a fragment of live coral, or a passing eel would be to such a voice from on high is anybody's Fortean guess:

> I'm in the state of mind of a savage who might find upon a shore, buoyant
> parts of a piano and a paddle that was carved by cruder hands than his
> own: something light and summery from India, and a fur overcoat from
> Russia… the higher idealist is the super-dogmatist of a local savage who
> can hold out, without a flurry of a doubt, that a piano washed up on a beach
> is the trunk of a palm that a shark has bitten, leaving its teeth in it.[4]

Just one of the reasons why Fort became a popular author some fifty years
after his death, is that his basic picture of mind appeals to moderns: he sees
mind as a media-filled entity. This is the equivalent to the above fish seeing
veritable blizzards of dumped Pig'n'Chicken Party-Boxes, crashed 1.4 Mb
floppies and stolen mobile phones, instead of the occasional flint-lock pistol,
horse-collar, bronze sword, or leather-bound set of Trollope. In this, he does
not see the wholes, unities or harmonies of his time; he sees a kind of transforming fragmentation which is anarchic, yet moral in its comedy, and inform-
ing in its implicit suggestions of endless new possibilities and structures of
alternative modes of consciousness achieved by seeing the structure of mind
in a highly original way. In a Fortean world, when we make an almost-decision
(what decisions are otherwise?) acting on part-information (what information is
otherwise?), bits of our semi-decisions *almost* arrive on the main sensory stage.
These fragmentary new arrivals are his original view of coincidences, and as
such, they mirror the hazy nature of our part-decisions, shaped by the pushes
and pulls of quarter-beliefs, almost no-beliefs, and three-quarter almost-be-
liefs. Coincidences (which Einstein called "intersections of world-lines"), are
only pieces at first, approximations, half-tries, failures, almost-successes, the
thin body of a wish; in Fort's terms, they are even what might be called rehearsals of possible beliefs, like Goethe's "shadows of history" which come before
the events themselves.

The anomaly as a Fortean animal, therefore, whether it be the Surrey Puma,
or the extra-terrestrial, is a "fuzzy" media creation, a partial shell full of coincidences, mixed with those mistakes, wastes of time, comic episodes and even
self-deceptions inherent to brain which researchers in artificial intelligence
have so much difficulty with. The entropy of this mass of "noise" changes as
the realisation-body begins to be more fully-formed, that is if it ever gets to
that stage at all, and does not vanish like the unstable part-ghost it always
tends to be, like the force which drives the perpetual motion machines described in *Wild Talents.* In a Fortean domain therefore, it is not so much that the
machines patently do not work, or the mystery aeroplanes are not up above,
but that they are not *allowed* to work, that is fully work, or indeed be fully up
above; they are indeed half- and quarter-forms, subtle forms of energy suspended between symbol and realisation. Such things are almost like traders
from the wrong side of town. As part-born embryos, Sonnabend suggests that
the time has not arrived for their seemingly absurd principles to appear as

anything but nonsensical:

> ... there never has been an art, science, religion, invention that was not first out of accord with established environment, visionary, preposterous in the light of other standards, useless in its incipiency, and resisted by established forces so that, seemingly animating it and protectively underlying it, there may have been something that in spite of its unfitness made it survive for future usefulness. Also there are data for the acceptance that all things, in wider being, are held back as well as protected and prepared for, and not permitted to develop before comes scheduled time.[5]

There follows the outline of a daring idea which suggests replacing finite economics and concrete social and political "causation" with a kind of acausal machinery:

> Langley's flying machine makes me think of something of the kind — that this machine was premature; that it appeared a little before the era of aviation upon this earth, and that therefore Langley could not fly. But this machine was capable of flying, because some years later, Curtiss did fly in it. Then one thinks that the Wright Brothers were successful, because they did synchronise with a scheduled time.[6]

Cosmology as Consumerism

This is the theory of both fact and product as information-animals that are a function of time itself as well as human energies and ideas. They are creations that are not "objective" in that they suffer birth, life and death just as does a human foetus:

> Cells of an embryo build falsely and futilely, in the sense that what they construct will be only temporary and will be out of adjustment later. All are responses, or correlates, to a succession of commandments, as it were, of dominant, directing, supervising spirits of different eras: that they take on appearances that are concordant with the general gastrula[7] era, changing when comes the stimulus to agree with the reptilian era, and again responding harmoniously when comes the time of the mammalian era.[8]

This sheds light upon the frequently shattered lives of those folk who create fuelless motors and perpetual motion machines. Let no-one think that such Fortean half-formed creations do not bite. A good modern example of such a Fortean animal "living" as pure information-plasma is provided by the saga of the AIDS industry. It is perfectly possible to see this as a modern virtual reality construct, a bubble-product, built of pure media, manufactured information, the "product" of an out-of-control good cause machine, using all the empathic pressure points of glamour, forced high-powered sentiment, the intrigues of deviant sexuality, and white-coat scientific credibility. If we speak therefore of AIDS being "manufactured", it is "manufactured" through the kind of Fortean forces described, and not primarily through some madman in some secret genetics laboratory, although such a person may have been the ultimate focus of these forces. Shakespeare always points out the difference between the idea and the finite instrument, as such.

That both time, idea, and instrumented endeavour are subject to often tempestuous collective mental seasons is an idea that both the ancient world and the Renaissance fully understood. Against the two-way traffic of mind and nature described by Sophocles and Shakespeare, our own witless and simple-minded objectivity is not an advance, but a fall. Objectivity not only prevents us understanding the UFO for example, but also prevents us from hearing the screams of countless laboratory animals, sounds that may well be the Furies announcing our downfall. Any good theatre manager is a Fortean: he knows that mass formulaic mechanisation creates a desert: the best possible cast, script, resources and advertising will not guarantee the required number of bottoms on seats. Down the road, a single unpaid performer will pack them in. That this can happen shows something indefinable about atmosphere and nuance. The anomaly allows us to enter the mysteries of form and expression, the enigma of created character. Networks of singular and unique events (whether those events be a rain of frogs, a president asking for forgiveness for not knowing what constitutes a sexual act, or the not-so-funny death of a British princess which warrants no British investigation) are our own present day *Inferno*.

This could be called the modern Fortean view. This sees any social or technological realisation as a part-creation of implicit allowance schedules or belief quotas. These in turn concord or conflict with human ambition and endeavour, national politics and moral panics[9] which govern the part-realisations of almost-possibilities, and interface them with taboo sanctions. But fear of things happening too quickly stirs up a complex of deep-rooted fear and expectations within the national group:

> Shores of North America — nowadays, with less hero-worship than formerly, historians tell us that, to English and French fishermen, the coast of Newfoundland was well-known, long before the year 1492; nevertheless, to the world in general, it was not, or according to our acceptances, could not be, known. About the year 1500, a Portuguese fleet was driven by storms to the coast of Brazil, and returned to Europe. Then one thinks that likely enough, before the year 1492, other vessels had been so swept to the coasts of the western hemisphere, and had returned — but that data of western lands could not emerge from the suppressions of that era — but that the data did survive, or were preserved for future usefulness — that there are 'Thou shalt nots' engraved upon something underlying all things, and then effacing, when phases pass away.[10]

This is an original approach to many familiar stories, from Charles Babbage's ignored 1842 digital computer, to the national mysteries connected to the cancellation of the British TSR2 aircraft in 1965.[11] Acceptance of it means that the processes of historical causation are anything but rational. The fundamental Fortean question is, "What shall we allow ourselves to experience?" Any decision is taken not on "facts", or empirical or pragmatic examination of "evidence":

> There is no intelligence except era-intelligence. Suppose the geo-system be a super-embryonic thing. Then, by the law of the embryo, its parts cannot organise until comes the scheduled time. So there are local congeries of development of a chick in an egg, but these local centres cannot more than faintly sketch out relations with one other until comes the time when they may definitely integrate. Suppose that far back in the nineteenth-century there were attempts to communicate from the moon; but suppose they were premature: then we suppose the fate of the protoplasmic threads that feel out too soon from one part of an egg to another.[12]

Even taking a charitable view, it is difficult to think that of something more nonsensical than such signals as Fort describes here. The attempt to "communicate from the moon" described by Fort above, may appear to be quite ludicrous, unless one sees it, like our absent brain, as an almost-real Fortean event, not so far removed from the navigational anomalies experienced by such well-known and respected figures as Alan Cobham, Admiral Byrd and Lindburgh, as described by Fort in *Lo!* Yet another famous flyer of the inter-war years, Captain Eddie Rickenbacker, also saw an unknown luminous object near the sun, as did indeed the great astronomer Asaph Hall, but such things are not uncommon in history. Fort gives dozens of observations of objects seen near the sun or crossing its disk. De Rostan in Basle, France, and also Croste in Sole observed a "vast, spindle-shaped body, about three of the sun's digits in breadth and nine in length" on August 9, 1762, in Switzerland.

Cosmology as Consumerism

After giving thousands of examples of such things throughout his four books, Fort concludes that the subtle relationship between mind and nature is such that these things are "embryo" echoes of those many half-thoughts that are always occurring within direct experience itself. From Galileo onwards, the new optical technology turned the thoughts of man to space. Much vital expectancy was therefore focused out in space, and a typical Fortean joke dialogue started. These runs of diluted desire pulses will run out very quickly, just as do the runs of the sighting of strange animals, the almost-impossible aeroplanes, or, in our own time, those social workers with no credentials who try to collect children from baffled families, but who are never caught. Yes, the pulses are "real" enough, but there is never enough will-energy to make the desire complete. But was it such a low-powered echo of fairly high-powered desires that caused the astronomers Francis Bailey, the Rev T. Rankin, Professor Chevalier, Lockyer, Secci, Dr Galle, Dr Sage and others too numerous to mention, to observe moving lights on both the moon and Mars at different times throughout the nineteenth-century?

Perhaps it was. The Fortean domain is a kind of information field structured not by simple causal foundations, but consisting of half-tries, almost-theres, rehearsals, trials, jokes and mimicking fragmentary dialogues. His *deus ex machina* is hence a frightening clown; there are mistakes, blind alleys, pieces of majestic brilliance, a hole-in one, a miss by a mile; here is a nice design, or, in the case of the human evacuation system, not a particularly good design at all. Within both mind and nature there is every shade of stupidity and brilliance that imitates the infinite varieties of plumage, wing-hue, size and shape in the animal kingdom. His theory is all-inclusive; if we choose, there is even the almost-complete fantasy of an almost-complete objectivity.

The Big Brothers in a Fortean universe are live domains of interest which thread through that very stuff we call group or individual "personality", whether we know it or not, still less whether we prefer it or not. The Fortean domain is a kind of story-dimension in which coincidences, and anomalies are *dialogues*, and they appear to be networked by simulacra. In the Fortean "space" of this dialogue-dimension, there are no such things as *complete* falsehoods.

The dread term "virtual reality" wants to intrude here, and indeed the Fortean animal, that anomalistic half-form, is almost certainly built of somewhat adulterated information. It moves therefore in a "space" which is a conceptual region parallel to our modern ideas of Internet "cyberspace". The question might be asked who, or what, are such Fortean dialogues between? Immediately an individual or a group has even only a partially unified idea, the thinnest shell of this begins to form, just like an embryo; a word Sonnabend uses many times. In his most succinct passages it is as if we almost see matter in creation as function of ideologies. This Fortean thought is well described by Werner K. Heisenberg: "What we observe is not nature herself, but nature exposed to our method of questioning."

The dimension of the Fortean body is stretched across, and supported by those almost-bullseyes called coincidences, to become a kind of gigantic pulsating brain, rather like the Internet, the same metaphors moving through major sectors of human activity and expression:

> I will engage to write the formula of any novel in psychochemic terms, or draw its graph in psycho-mechanic terms: or write, in romantic terms, the circumstances and sequences of any chemic or magnetic reaction: or express any historic event in algebraic terms — or see Boole and Jevons for economic situations expressed algebraically.[13]

In all the above reflections, those philosophical jokers, the prime mover, first cause, or fact, are activated by something like that capacity of an ordinary human being for terrible violence, that is by the anomalies, which though rejected, wait for the day when there is no possible alternative but to let loose the dogs of intellectual war. That time arises when the prevailing game has exhausted all its possibilities. The great game of cathedrals, steam trains, stone circles and pyramids, lies limp and drained, devoid of the possibilities of metaphor:

> Our data are glimpses of an epoch that is approaching with far-away explosions. It is vibrating on its edges with the tread of distant space armies. Already it has pictured in the sky visions that signify new excitements, even now lapping over into the affairs of a self-disgusted, played-out hermitage.[14]

This is an outline of the Fortean model of consciousness: an ever-evolving body of multi-faceted abstractions which invade and possess mass mentality through life or death of metaphor, acting rather like a fifth column hidden in all the modes of seeing and mental formulation. Causation or indeed non-causation is the "Old Dominant and its jealousy, and its suppression of all things and thoughts that endangered its supremacy". As distinct from Kuhn's paradigms, (which are largely of intellectual construction), Fort's "Old Dominant" is a live animal, ready to get up to all kinds of tricks, rather like a joke character whose name does not appear in the cast-list. By comparison, Kuhn's paradigms are chess-moves rather than "virtual" dialogues between semi-substantial intermediate states. Some of the confusions in scientific definitions, and indeed some of the very strange accusations of fraud and misrepresentation, seem very much to have acted on people who have been "led astray — as if purposefully — as if by something directive, hovering over them. Just so, in any embryo, cells that would tend to vary from the appearances of their era are compelled to correlate."

Cosmology as Consumerism

This Fortean view makes both the mind and experience much more interesting structures than yes/no and true/false structures, or Hawking's "consciousness is recategorisations all the way down", Dawkins' "extended phenotypes", Edelman's "neuronal Darwinism", or Penrose's "quantum coherence within microtubules". As with strange deaths and fires Fort examines, the "confession" of factuality may be there, but there is still something very odd about the scene; the framework of details around the circumstances show the events are *as if imagined*. The "confession" serves only to conceal some "wild talent" which the victim half-knows that they themselves possess, but which they can hardly control, and wish, for many obvious purposes, to conceal.

In Fortean terms, the false "solidity" such structures may create is replaced by overlapping and fragmented *imaginations*. These are approximations, partial events, semi-accurate guesses, half-realisations, some things that almost come off, but others that miss out by a mile. One man says fairies do not exist; he reads in a newspaper the next day that another man has sworn an affidavit that he saw one in Central Park, six inches high, complete with silver wings and green hose. In Fortean terms, the subtractive tension between the absolute denial and the absolute affirmation creates a half-form, a statistical wave along the scale of a kind of octave of appearances. Others have seen similar things;

not quite as clear and solid, not quite as perfect, say, as this man's fairy, or another man's ghost. Fort sees the "strange" as always having this major characteristic of being constructed of active, projected imaginative elements which are just as "detectable" as viruses, molecules, electrons, atoms or protein-strings, bearing in mind that these things lack all "absolute" definitions in themselves, and are little more than *imaginative* conventions that have secured, through advertising and public relations, more secure positions in consciousness.

With these Fortean animals, there are always some essential parts left out of their "reality picture", just as with UFO sightings, and as with poltergeist effects and spontaneous combustion. There may be spoor marks, but there is certainly no food-swathe left by such large beasts, and the small animals presumably killed by these strange creatures look as though they were toyed with, rather than killed for food. There are no droppings, just as there are no vapour trails or soundbarrier booms with UFOs. The effect is rather like that of a bulldozer travelling through a house and leaving only a "proper" (or "expected") hole in an internal bathroom wall, the rest of the wall being (and this is a very important point) *almost* intact, as if the very matter of the wall tried to conceal such a laxity of stiffness, but didn't quite have the energy to make the proper appearances. Sonnabend, in a good mood (he is not always in a good mood), quotes Einstein in support of such an idea of macrocosmic quantum action:

> The only reason why the exponents of ultra-modern mechanics are taken more seriously than I am is that the reader does not have to pretend that he knows what I am writing about. There are alarmed scientists, who try to confine their ideas of magic to the actions of electronic particles, or waves. But in *The Physical Review*, April, 1931, were published letters from Prof. Einstein, Prof. Tolman, and Dr Boris Podolsky that indicate that this refinement cannot be maintained. Prof. Einstein applies the Principle of Uncertainty not only to atomic affairs, but to such occurrences as the opening and shutting of a shutter on a camera.[15]

In a Fortean world then, on occasion, matter itself may not make its proper onstage cues. Very different writers have formed the same conclusion. On occasion, physical fragmentation comes in far more frightening forms than UFOs, crushed or even absent brains, or walls trying to avoid the stern gaze of some kind of paranoid drill sergeant. Jules Eisenbud, the American psychiatrist who wrote *The World of Ted Serios*,[16] and an extremely sober man, talks of "hair-curling reports" of nineteenth-century psychic researchers, Geley, Richet, and he of the daunting name Schrenck-Notzing:

> ... numerous varieties of partial and incomplete embryonic forms were reported (and sometimes photographed) by observers of alleged materialisations produced by certain types of mediums in trance. These forms

too are described as often never progressing beyond their initial in-between stages before they recede and disappear, and forms closely resembling well-known embryological monsters, with fragments of skin, bits of hair, glandular tissue, all jumbled together.

In Fortean terms, such terrifying visions are a fragmented waste, rather than any profundity; this comes near to modern terms in that they appear to be dumped information fields gradually decaying, like the contents of the wastebin of a hard disc. The idea of the mind needing such vast rubbish dumps and such wastes of time in order to do anything at all is another Fortean reflection that is only just entering AI discussions about brain function. But understandably, as human beings, when we research anything, we expect to find that high seriousness which is a compliment to ourselves and a reward for the expenditure of our energies. But frequently with the strange, what is most psychologically disturbing is the effect of savage primal play, as in the previous illustration. Like the many things discovered by Fort, and like images described by Eisenbud, we get the impression of a fairy tale gone mad, of a riotous anarchic nonsense, perfectly representative of the imagination of a growing child, with its cartoon horrors, its surrealistic thrills and spills, its shadowy corners, stairs which lead nowhere, its cupboards to be avoided, and its mysterious houses and magic gardens. Fort's point is that we far underestimate the imagination; that even the most infantile whimsies such as these have transforming power.

Cosmology
as
Consumerism

The philosopher H. H. Price[17] describes such a possible Fortean animal:

A hallucinatory entity, the celebrated pink rat, for instance, is composed of sense data or appearances just as a "real" object is. What is wrong with it, what inclines us to call it "unreal" is the fact that there is not enough of them. For instance, the hallucinatory rat can be seen from the front, but not from the back; it is visible but not tangible; it can be perceived by one percipient but not by more; and it endures only for a minute or so. But some hallucinations do better than this. Apparitions, for example, are sometimes public to several percipients, can be seen from several different points of view, and endure for considerable periods of time — though not as long as they would if they were "real" human beings. Now suppose there was an apparition which was public to an indefinite number of points of view and an indefinite number of observers: suppose there are tangible as well as visible particulars among the appearances which are its constituents; suppose it endures for half an hour and then disappears. We should not know whether to call it an unusually prolonged and complex hallucination, or a very queer "real object". In point of fact, it would be something between the two, but not quite complex enough to count as a complete material object. Now imagine this process pushed to the limit. We might expect that occasionally a complete material object or a complete physical event would be produced by purely mental causes.[18]

This pink rat of Price is a typical Fortean half-form. It is an example of almost-creation that abolishes the category of "unreal", and exists in the intermediate Fortean domain. J. P. Chaplin in his book *Rumor, Fear, and the Madness of Crowds*, tells of a similar situation in which fearful things came almost fully formed from that very domain in America. As the result of Orson Welles' broadcast play of H. G. Wells' story:

> There were some in New York who "saw" or "heard" the battle of the Martians and Earthmen that was being waged in the neighbouring state. A man equipped with binoculars could "see" the flames of the holocaust from his vantage point on top of a tall office building. One "heard" the bombs from aircraft fall on New Jersey, and was convinced they were heading for Times Square. Another "heard" the swish of the Martian machines as they plummeted through the atmosphere to earth. In Brooklyn, a man called the police demanding that he be issued a gas mask; he had "heard" the distant sounds of the battle going on over in Jersey and believed a gas attack imminent. When informed it was a play, he shouted "We can hear the firing all the way here, and I want a gas mask. I'm a taxpayer.[19]

Lest this be confused with the psychosocial view, it must be pointed out that most psychologists and sociologists (and sceptics in particular) miss the point here: systems such as witchcraft and indeed great world religions on occasion, are rejected and persecuted not because they are theologically incorrect, scientifically invalid, or considered evil, or immoral, but because, like fuelless motors, or no-brain brains, *they might just work*. They might just do this in the sense that a row of rusted and empty US Army jam tins, or B-29 bombers found by natives on remote Pacific islands, may function as perfectly valid objects of worship, *and might achieve the same manifestations as more obvious and "legitimate" foundations of belief*. In the face of this, science advertising itself as an objective, demythologising Mr Clean is a marvellously comic distortion, and often just about as profound and valuable as a smile from a commercial break. In Fortean terms, as long as scientists have to use language, they are telling stories. Kathleen Raine, in her book[20] *The Inner Journey of the Poet*, says of the French phenomenologist and scientific historian Gaston Bachelard:[21]

> ... he set out to purge the language of science from all such animistic implications as gender, or of such phrases as acids 'attacking' bases, and the like. But in doing so, he perceived, as in a flash of revelation, that the very terms he was seeking to eliminate from pure scientific discourse constituted no mere residue of inaccuracy, but a whole poetic vocabulary expressing our living *experience* of nature. He later wrote his famous books on the poetics of the four elements — of Shelley's use of the element of air; of the sombre stagnant water-imagery in which Edgar Allan Poe discov-

ered the objective correlative of his dark vision; of Blake's mythological characters seeking to break out of the constrictions of a world of "rocks and solids".

In other words, the "Martians" of Orson Welles were *almost* created.

In this respect, in our new millennium, we may have to redefine fundamentally what we mean by *life*. We may have to accept the somewhat Fortean view that the corporation and the laboratory are forms of life, as are the media complex, the military-industrial spectrum, and also that rapidly evolving systems-animal we call the World Wide Web. If we recognise that life may not be confined to the molecular, and that both information and ideas have lives of their own, we may then begin to understand the UFO and all its ancillary manifestations as an intermediate state between strong fictions (almost matter) and weak fictions (almost idea). Fort's thinking is not so simple as being merely a plea to replace one theory with another, so much as a general plea to try and see both mind and world in all their wondrous and very often subversive and paradoxical complexity, rather than seeing the cosmos as essentially mundane, conformist, objective, uninhabited and void of all spirit.

In that entertainment state which has become the Western world, "concrete" political resistance in the old-fashioned sense to a sterile official reality has almost vanished. It has been replaced by something uniquely suitable to an Internet age: a structure of implicit denials on principle alone. These range from the extremely disturbing hot denial of the Holocaust, to cooler denials of the original moon landing, and even cooler claims for the "face on Mars". We have thus an imagination war: a series of massed guerrilla attacks on the high frontier of fact, which has become an intellectual Hadrian's Wall. This battle takes place not on the streets, but in cyberspace, and though some assaults are almost suicidal, we can be sure that at least some of the granite face of dominating "factual" oppression will be chipped away.

Cosmology as Consumerism

In the new twenty-first-century, where no doubt good and monstrous things both lie in wait for human kind, Charles Fort is one of the few useful guides. Many of his thoughts warn against official explanations. They were formed whilst the great "explanations" about the casualty lists of the Somme, Verdun, Ypres and Passchendaele battles were pouring from the British, French and American press alike. In a Fortean world, the only thing explanations do is make you go away. Belief in explanations sucks in willing candidates, and whilst they can be seen home from the belief wars without physical wounds, in believing, they have joined what James Joyce called The Dead. What the Sirens were to Odysseus, *beliefs* are to Charles Fort. "I have freed myself of belief." He does not trust belief (not even his own tendency to theorise and make up ideas such as "teleportation"), if only because human beings have a tragic tendency to institutionalise such things. Once constellated as a system, belief becomes a tyrant, killing everything that does not fit in, and frequently dining off countless millions of human beings before the generating algorithm self-destructs, either in dreams, Auschwitz, Verdun, or on the blasted heath of *King*

Lear, revealing that truth is scandalous beyond all possible conception, and that in the so-called "information society", the last thing which will be available is information.

Fort's great anarchic sin is that he shows the vulnerabilities of our beloved leaders in that they do not hesitate to fall into such brawls as would not disgrace greasy spoons, alley joints, dunkin' diners, or even the Boar's Head Tavern in Eastcheap as midnight strikes. In this sense Fort's comedy of intellect is as moral as any comedy of Shakespeare. If he teaches us anything at all, it is to laugh at science, the "greatest human adventure"; of course we are not supposed to laugh at great truths revealed from above, but inevitably we do, though in secret colleges, and long past the hour of any clock.

THE QUEST FOR OSWALD

Sometimes I am a collector of data, and only a collector, and am likely to be gross and miserly, piling up notes, pleased with merely numerically adding to my stores. Other times I have joys, when unexpectedly coming upon an outrageous story that may not be altogether a lie, or upon a macabre little thing that may make some reviewer of my more or less good works mad. But always there is present a feeling of unexplained relations of events that I note, and it is this far-away, haunting, or often taunting, awareness, or suspicion, that keeps me piling on.

Wild Talents

accuracy

as

myth

Charles Fort's method of analysis may be usefully applied not only to the sightings of sea monsters and UFOs, but also to the major mysteries of our own time. *Assassinations*, published in 1976,[1] is a book he would have loved. It shows many awesome brains spinning webs of purely "factual" investigation, and, like Babbage's machine, these writers almost disappearing into a theoretical infinity of their own making. This book contains over thirty fascinating articles about the major American assassinations, many by brilliantly astute minds drawn from a wide range of professional disciplines. As these superb analysts (all American) feel along the fault lines of their vanguard nation, the impression is of a beautifully constructed masterpiece by absolutely superb technicians of a first-class intelligentsia, but who are in the grip of a paranoid training which has stripped them completely of any wider perspective. It is an amazing process to watch. They are desperate for a single elegant solution which will sum the non-summing parts. And there must be no jokers in the pack. Without the Fortean joker therefore, these writers must cite nothing but facts; they must contribute nothing but objective evidence; unsupported opinion, speculation, intuition, rumours and even good guesses, these are all are quite taboo. And of course, metaphor, that most troublesome subversive joker of all, is banned, or at least his presence is denied, or minimised, since in Western legal and scientific terms, metaphor has almost no meaning at all as far as analysis "proper" is concerned. To any such investigators, the idea of a mechanics of metaphor-as-causation as suggested by Fort, would be looked upon as a gross intellectual indecency, going right against their hard-won and bought-and-paid-for education, to be cast to the darkness beyond that circle of campfire light called the discursive intellect. None seem aware that the idea of "fact" (as compared to the idea of metaphor) is a fairly recent appearance on the historical stage. Become in our own time more *managers*, rather than investigators, scientists would like to see the evidence games given the accuracy of machine tooling. The world could then be processed and controlled, designed, modulated, programmed and re-programmed.

But coincidence troubles them deeply. They simply have not been trained to ask the kind of question posed by the old tracking language of synchronicities, for example. The best of them suspect that there is a transcendental leakage of information somewhere, a movement of people and materials and a release of energy that does not add up in any sense of pure factual information, but the set paradigms being such, they are *verboten* to even hint of such things. Anyone who has ever worked for a large corporation such as the BBC will know the atmosphere. The writers of *Assassinations* are corporate minds, scuttling about the corridors, shoring up and patching and repairing the great armour-plated leviathan called Acceptance. But as in any soap opera, the bandwidth has been set long before the script is even conceived: their education has been expensive, their reputations dearly bought, and their responsibilities deeply impressed upon them. They must not let what Fort called "the system" down.

One could expect such super-technicians as Sylvia Meagher,[2] Peter Dale Scott,[3] and Paul Hoch[4] to enter Hamlet's Elsinore or King Lear's castle, and ask the characters in these plays to reach rationalised agreements, demythologise themselves, their class, identity, power structure, relationships, take the democratic view, and hence clear up situations which have become quite unnecessarily too complicated, wholly politically incorrect, and certainly destructive of time, energy and lives. Perhaps they would ask the characters to look at the "facts" of the situation, and hence try to form a single solution that will combine and resolve all the conflicting elements. Perhaps they would recommend stress counselling for both Lear and his daughters.

But a proper solution has been in existence for a long time. The Greeks called it tragedy, but today the concept has degenerated to being knocked down by a supermarket trolley full of multi-coloured facts. The idea of tragedy is avoided because it contains metaphysical assumptions. If he does anything, Fort points us back to these things as trackers. The researchers have lost the ability to let the track talk to them. As always, intellectuals (and if a scientist is not an intellectual he is nothing) are usually far too well protected.

As essays in late twentieth-century avoidance, the articles in *Assassinations* are gems of Fortean perfection. Most are works of art in themselves as concerns how to engineer a way around a complex of experience and avoid all metaphysical questions and implications. For that is what these essays are really about — getting round mysteries, rather than solving them. The "facts" are processed, put into a structure, taken apart again, new facts added, then structured, reassembled, looked at from another point of view, some errant facts "corrected," new interpretations added, this structure joined to others; there is then a refocusing, new interpretations again added, perhaps more mistakes are found, and the whole progress is updated in the light of new information. It is all glossy intellectual product management to perfection, guaranteed to substantiate and confirm all those impressive bourgeois affectations of hard work, concentration and commitment to finding the "factual" truth. The book is a monument to the world of the working skills of the genuinely gifted intelligentsia, who are, rather like their equally oppressed industrial equivalent, equally forbidden to look up resentfully from their benches full of structured specialisations.

However, unbeknownst to them, what they *have* constructed is a fascinating new genre. *Assassinations* reads rather like a long novel by Borges, or perhaps a novel by Charles Fort, if his life had taken quite another turn. Here are some of the finest brains of the mightiest nation, rationalists all to their fingertips, implicitly subverting themselves and their approach by the wonders they are producing. A literary museum could be constructed to hold these essays. Shimmering planes of facts twist and turn, flutter and dance before being swallowed up by ever-widening penumbras of uncertainty. Such beautifully ironic works could well be a wholly new area of speculative fiction, since each good writer has a strongly developed style, and is also a master of the subject matter. More powerful and up-to-date compared with equivalent pure "literary" efforts, *Assassinations* is an unconsciously self-mocking masterpiece, a delight to read in that these superb rationalists have constructed a story in which there does not appear to be a single rational hour of any single rational day in which Oswald (and many other assassins mentioned)[5] do not push the patterns of their fractured lives through the walls of all rational causation.

Accuracy as Myth

lee harvey oswald
as
fortean man

According to *Assassinations,* there was so much packed into a typical Oswald week, an innocent observing alien could be excused for thinking that any one week was the first week of all creation. Oswald proceeds, with his cartoon mind, rather like Leopold Bloom, through the separate "night towns" of Russia, the Marines, the Mafia, the CIA, the FBI, the Cuban sector, corporate conspiracies and a *very* strange marriage. He has an equally strange rifle with badly behaved rounds, and a death weirder than all those things put together. To assume that any single entity could so time and integrate these somewhat complicated schemes of matter, movement, and motivation, down to a two-shot six-second bolt-action manual/lay framework, is the height of rationalist optimism. The distance between some well-understood (and for once quite rational) overlap between the Cuban émigrés, the Mafia, the CIA and the strange dynamics of whatever bullet(s) struck President Kennedy, is simply far too great to be tactically managed. Similarly the dimensions of some simple external mechanical plot could hardly extend to complete control of the high degrees of strangeness involved in angles, times and movements. That this same degree of strangeness accompanies many other major assassinations as concerns rounds, times, and movements makes the Fortean point — that *every* particle of the social embryo is a smoking gun. The strange patterns of the last phone calls of Jack Ruby before being arrested, and also the last phone calls of Marilyn Monroe, present much the same problem, and in the second case, bring in a whole creaking stage apparatus of Bobby Kennedy's hired helicopter, U-turning ambulances, hospitals which have no records, and the whole seen by other, quite independent observers from other covert networks, shows that the rational view is like the short-run formula for primes:

some strands of it work, they indeed continue working, until, like Fred Hoyle's view of the downfall of Stonehenge as a wound-down clock, they become increasingly inaccurate. Their ticking begins to falter where the rational elements that make up personality meet the interests of the general ideological field and its own separate domains, interests, and developments. Historically, figures that command much attention often die strange deaths. They are close to the much-troubled area where rational elements interface with systems mythology. Shakespeare had no problem at all with this idea: for him, the "system" is always a *dramatis persona* whose name is not on the list of players, yet who is tangibly present in every single scene that is played.

Yet, spurning tragedy, the writers in *Assassinations*, like the pre-Copernican astronomers, still stick further epicycles onto previous epicycles in order to discover a single, general objective systems solution. In *The CIA and the Man Who Was Not Oswald*[1] a double-Oswald, of all things, is brought in to correct the orbit-wobbles, as if one Oswald was not quite enough for one lifetime. Here, the assumptions about the timing are quite something; knowing how many mistakes can be made in tying a shoelace, we may permit ourselves a Fortean smile when we know that throughout his life, this Marine, this politically confused (and increasingly schizoid)[2] drifter, had defied any and every attempt to organise himself and his life. In this, he quite defeated the attempts of an American mother, the United States Marine Corps and even the entire might of Soviet Russia to organise his day, not a bad achievement in one short lifetime, especially for a person who after he left the Marines voluntarily, could hardly be relied upon to pull on a second sock after he had pulled on a first.

This Mitty-like inability to pull on two socks one after another was, as it were, Oswald's Fortean "wild talent". The world of course, is always looking for two-socked folk, those wearing one sock not usually regarded as being of great account. Walls, borders, laws, are therefore transparent, irrelevant, or inoperative to those who do not obey the rules precisely because they do not see any rules. The grain of the seeing of the many and varied cultural filters, no matter how fine, remains coarse for the one-sockers; they enter the target system like minnows through a net, and one thing is certain: the killers of the two Kennedies, Martin Luther King, and John Lennon, and the man who tried to kill President Reagan, were all dedicated one-sockers. That is, they were back-bedroom heroes who sprang out from their cartoon frame and, trailing wires and smoke, they pressed the tinsel triggers of almost cut-out guns.

Trying to fit Oswald into a "real-time" frame is impossible. From a Fortean point of view he is a wall-eyed tapestry figure; a living Escher drawing of a human being, we cannot square him off because a dimension is missing; like Walter Mitty, he lives in perspectives that we have long discarded. A true anomaly is a one-sock event.

Oswald is thus a Fortean figure. He illustrates how useful is the Fortean method of analysis. Many of the essays in *Assassinations* try to reconstruct the basic common sense "real time" sequence of his simple physical progress

(marginal note) Lee Harvey Oswald as Fortean Man

from one week to another; they fail completely. As an ex-marine radar operator (and dishonourably discharged from the Marine reserve), he practically walked into Russia, married a Russian girl, and calmly walked out with her back to America, even managing to avoid being debriefed when he returned. During this utterly fantastic progress (which very few twentieth-century characters ever came near to matching), and which must have made him more obvious than any screaming siren, not a single sector of the American intelligence community admits to having targeted him as a possible threat to anything at all. Here is Anthony Summers giving us some idea of the difficulties of trying to discover some kind of integrated mundane baseline for the Oswald dimension:

> Oswald's progress is marked by visits to the employment office, the cashing of unemployment cheques, and the withdrawal of library books. Even these are not necessarily valid for charting Oswald's movements; the FBI was able to authenticate Oswald's signature on hardly any of the unemployment documents. Of the seventeen firms where Oswald said he had applied for work, thirteen denied it, and four did not even exist.[3]

Then there are the fake addresses of fake branches of extreme sections of the political spectrum; a series of fake change-of-address cards filed to various mail offices, but the most disturbing of all are the Oswald sightings made *before* the actual assassination took place. On September 25, 1963, an "Oswald" walked into the Austin (capital city of Texas) offices of the Selective Service System (the American military draft organisation), and asked if he could have his dishonourable discharge revoked on account of his two years' good conduct. The assistant could not help because the name Harvey Oswald was not on her records.[4] Two weeks before the assassination, another "Harvey Oswald" visited a supermarket at Irving, Texas, and tried to cash a cheque in the name of "Harvey Oswald". Twenty-four hours before the assassination, the FBI received a report that a "Lee Oswald" had behaved strangely (making anti-government remarks) in a Dallas car showroom. Of course these three reports are only of interest because they do not line up with the verifiable movements of the so-called "real" Oswald at the times concerned. These examples are drawn from Summers' book, and he goes on to give many more examples of strange Oswald appearances at shooting ranges, gun shops, and even the good old YMCA had a visit. But the mighty Oswald defeated even this mundane organisation; neither his telegrams nor his money orders could be traced, though witnesses swore that Oswald identified himself by his now famous "library card", this wretched slip of paper being just about the only constant "fact" he ever had anything to do with.

Like Fort's examples of Princess Cariboo and Cagliostro, Oswald seems to have put anything and everything he ever had contact with under a kind of enchantment: the space-time around the incident of the shooting of patrolman Tippit[5] only some few hours after the assassination seems hardly to be consistent. The round(s) that killed Tippit is as controversial as the round(s) that killed President Kennedy,[6] though it was of course fired from an entirely different weapon. It seems that when Oswald pulled a trigger (as when he undoubtedly took a previous pot-shot at General Walker[7] some time before the events in Dallas), only one thing seemed rationally certain: that is that the whole event would certainly dissolve into a kind of infinity of tragic burlesque.

There are times when Summers, a sober rationalist to the core, appears to be quite overwhelmed by the bizarre nature of the quest for Oswald. As his investigation proceeds, he confesses he just cannot account for the high strangeness he experiences at every turn. Deeper into the system, and yet deeper again, he understands less and less about how it works. Refusing to accept anything but fact for his guide, in Fortean terms, this superb investigator will understand less and less again.

Assassinations represents a crisis within the great Information Society, a society in which, paradoxically, there is surprisingly very little information available. Given the present situation concerning UFOs alone, nothing less than the validity of the entire rationalist complex is at stake, and rationalism will no doubt shame itself to death, booted off the cultural scene to universal laughter, a fate it has wished upon its flat-earth opponents many a time. In *Assassinations*, as each and every Oswald hour splinters, lesser investigators than Summers have no problem in introducing yet more clockwork. One article[8] even speculates that there may have been no fewer than *three* assassins acting in concert. Here, to resolve our cosmological inconsistencies, we might suppose then, that the possible Oswald "double" acted with the three supposed assassins, at which the entire situation becomes like Fort's example of the millions of periwinkles scattered all over Worcester in one night by many hundreds of charitable fishmongers. There comes a point when it might as well have been ten further assassins, five more doubles, or some equally fantastic delta-mouth of possibilities involving all the ghosts of every Western consumer's Christmas past: Marilyn Monroe, Jayne Mansfield, or Elvis Presley.

As women and cars, nations and performers, products and events, are all multiple mirrors we might well think upon a somewhat Fortean story by Borges, *Theme of the Traitor and the Hero*. This story is related by Ryan, the great-grandson of the assassinated Fergus Kilpatrick, described as "a secret and glorious captain of conspirators," and whose name "illustrated the verses of Browning and Hugo," was killed "on the very eve of the victorious revolt which he premeditated and dreamt of." As the first centenary of Kilpatrick's death draws near, Ryan, writing a biography of the hero, discovers that "the enigma exceeds the confines of a simple police investigation." Other "facets of the enigma" disturb Ryan:

> ... they are of a cyclic nature: they seem to repeat or combine events of remote regions, of remote ages. Caesar's wife, Calpurnia saw in a dream the

Lee Harvey Oswald as Fortean Man

destruction of a tower decreed to him by the Senate; false and anonymous rumours on the eve of Kilpatrick's death publicized throughout the country that the circular tower of Kilgarven had burned, which could be taken as a presage, for he had been born in Kilgarven. These parallelisms (and others) between the story of an Irish conspirator lead Ryan to suppose the existence of a secret form of time, a pattern of repeated lines. He thinks of the transmigration of souls, a doctrine that lends horror to Celtic literature and that Caesar himself attributed to the British druids; he thinks that, before having been Fergus Kilpatrick, Fergus Kilpatrick was Julius Caesar. He is rescued from these circular labyrinths by a curious finding, a finding which then sinks him into more inextricable and heterogeneous labyrinths: certain words uttered by a beggar who spoke with Fergus Kilpatrick on the day of his death were prefigured by Shakespeare in the tragedy *Macbeth*. That history should have copied history was astonishing; that history should copy literature was inconceivable...

It this sounds familiar, it is certainly like similar books written in the past thirty years on the UFO phenomenon, particularly those concerning the "Magic 12" documents.[9] As yet, for none of these areas is there is the beginning of an explanation. The rationalist fury is appreciated. Neither the Oswald system, the UFO system, nor the Fergus Kilpatrick system can be entered.

If a system cannot be entered, then we must consider that the entire and fundamental relationship we have with such a system has broken down. We have been asking the wrong questions. It will get worse until the elegant Fortean solution will have to be faced: that what we term "reality" within a transient complex of knife-edge events is a movable feast.

Concerning the death of Diana, Princess of Wales, as every Fortean knows, the first anomalies and contradictions, the first wave of unanswered questions and unaccountable coincidences, were not long in arriving. Connoisseurs of explanations looked askance at the police claim for the 122mph of her car, equivalent not so much to being driven, as to being fired from a cannon point-blank at a wall. The fast autopsies, the even faster reopening of the tunnel, whose exhaust fumes would very rapidly destroy all forensic evidence, have also been noted, along with the first claims of doubles seen, official denials, and typical chain of associated deaths. These are the tones of the only really authentic twentieth-century sonata-form: the figures acting suspiciously nearby, the figures seen along the tunnel walkway, the time and speed contradictions, the bending of all levels of perception in the strong Camelot image field. And perhaps we may have the bonus of even a "real" UFO over the Tuilleries, reported by few, denied by many, wanted by all, expected by some, and part-recorded by radar. Tonal variations will be provided by amateur still photographs: some fogged by the local chemist, others lost in the post, and a few with photos of an old aunt who happened to be in Canada at the time the camera was pointed at the family dog.

It is such dream-like elements that defeat the absolutely superb analysts of

Assassinations. Whenever these fine new late Roman minds come across these modern mysteries, the real problem is that they cannot cope with the breaking of the heart of that near-religion called continuous product development of a completely stable reality. They must mass produce denial structures to defend the idea of clean-limbed and continuous intellectual progress. There is thus induced a crisis of belief and explanation within that ark of the consumer covenant, that Boolean colonisation of inputs and outputs, which is at the heart of those modern vanishing rituals called rational explanations. The pride of all these analysts is that as they have grown up, they have also fully woken up, and that the car they have just been sold that looks like a spaceship is not really a spaceship, and that a rationalist is not really another mythological performer, like everyone else.

Oswald, Fort and indeed Shakespeare's Hamlet, were great outsiders. Fort's idea of imagination as the supreme prime mover of all philosophy is well described by another of the same ilk, Luis Borges, who in rewriting the end of the story of that other great outsider, Walter Mitty, might well have been writing of our three characters:

> The greatest magician (Novalis has memorably written) would be the one who would cast over himself a spell so complete that he would take his own phantasmagorias as autonomous appearances. Would this not be our case?" I conjecture that this is so. We (the undivided divinity operating within us) have dreamt the world. We have dreamt it as firm, mysterious, visible, ubiquitous in space and durable in time; but in its architecture we have allowed tenuous and eternal crevices of unreason which tell us it is false.[10]

Lee Harvey Oswald as Fortean Man

scepticism

as

mystique

Talk given
by Colin
Bennett at
the Fortean
Unconvention
on April 6,
2002, at the
Common-
wealth
Institute,
London.

There are two kinds of scepticism: local and cultural. Local scepticism is wholly healthy. Charles Fort was a sound believer in this. It shields us from the state-ments of politicians as it protects us from the claims of the second-hand car salesmen and the bovine simplicities of the *News At Ten*, or whenever. Chronic cultural scepticism on the other hand is a dangerous intellectual allergy, and it is this kind of scepticism that we meet in the claims that UFO sightings are psychosocial fantasies, and that all experience of the paranormal or the anoma-lous is an illusion. On this level, sceptics question our mystical and religious beliefs, our intuitions, our dreams and our visions. They question every single human insight that is not founded on those historically arriviste impostors called facts, and would like to leave alternative cultures with outright denial as their own only political weapon. But these facts are things that are rather new and callow arrivals on the historical scene, and are cultural screens that suc-cour little more than the gross deterministic materialism of cellular corporat-ism, resulting in death by a million car parks.

Despite its protests to the contrary, scepticism usually allies itself with established Authority, and as a tradition, it has a long history. In the nineteenth-century, there arose fear in the upper strata of British society that the clever but dirty folk of industry and technology somehow disturbed the *status quo*, if not in a communist sense, then certainly in a social democratic sense. Nearly two hundred years later this cultural fear is still very much with us, and it is the emotional force behind traditional British scepticism. Britain has traditionally always had an uncertain and rather schizoid relationship with its very own individual creation, the Industrial Revolution, a revolution that changed the world utterly. Even in modern times, British culture still takes good care that its beloved liberal arts are well preserved from such an influence.

This native scepticism is often used as an implicit political tool in the broadest sense. In its most potent form, it can cause doubt and uncertainty and therefore can destroy inspiration and enterprise, not to say original genius.

Many British men and women of undoubted genius have been unfortunate in being born in a country where brains and innovation (particularly technological innovation) are regarded traditionally with an almost religious fear. Even in the times of greatest peril, when the British nation was within days of being destroyed, sceptical fear nearly lost us the tank, radar, and the Spitfire, never mind the entire British Army stranded on the beaches of Dunkirk.

Of the many folk who were ritually crucified in the name of scepticism, the name Alan Turing stands out. Turing, whose first code-cracking digital computer was absolutely vital to victory in the Second World War, was given aversion therapy in 1947 because he was a homosexual. Instead of a knighthood, a blank cheque, and the resources of a great university, he was drugged and tortured to death by electric shocks when shown pictures of male genitalia. The result was that one of our greatest scientific geniuses killed himself by biting into an apple laced with cyanide. Turing was given this concentration camp treatment not by Nazis, but by the British Medical Establishment supported by certain departments of His Majesty's Government.

D. H. Lawrence, perhaps our greatest novelist, was crucified in a similar way because he was, on the contrary, heterosexual. Even those geniuses with sexuality between Lawrence and Turing didn't get away. Our greatest soldier-intellectual, Lawrence of Arabia, had great difficulty after WWI in getting into the Royal Air Force as a mere recruit. The hackneyed phrase "no sex please, we're British" seems to fit this situation.

From the Fortean point of view, there is something most odd about the very nature of the high level of sceptical fear aroused by such people. The fear aroused can result in a kind of sceptical panic. Even though the very life of the nation is in danger, it appears that these people must be put down, nevertheless. General Hobart, the genius who formed the British pre-war tank force, was, on the eve of WWII dismissed as commander of 7th Armoured Division in Egypt for his outrageous technological enthusiasms. Back home he joined up as a corporal in the Home Guard. The horse-mounted British generals of the First World War certainly fought the tank pioneers with almost as much mistaken energy as they fought the German armed forces. Such characters and such innovations appear to excite some hidden switch in nature; individuals don't act against them so much as a Thou Shalt Not command deep within nature and human forces both. Thus though indeed the people I have mentioned do use facts, they do things with facts that apparently should not be done. It is this, and not their mere use of facts alone that appears to organise forces against them. Charles Fort called such powers *era forces*. These era forces are destructive, negative sceptical emanations that can destroy lives, discoveries, and reputations and all creative visions and inspirations. Sceptical forces can destroy intellectual life, restrict

Scepticism
as Mystique

knowledge, and cause national decline. In that they restrict imagination, sceptical forces can cause that economic and political inertia called decadence. Scepticism is therefore essentially the mystique of reaction: it produces nothing but hesitancy and timidity in the broad fields of manufacturing, technology and national enterprise. It fills us with fear about our own capabilities, it destroys our faith that we can change ourselves and the condition of our lives. We can only change if our imagination is in a healthy state ready to take the enormous risks that national and individual progress demand. With scepticism triumphant, we squat on the ground as existential prisoners, blindfolded, tied and shivering with mental fear.

ii

The life of the aerodynamicist Leonard Cramp is illustrative of this very Fortean idea of scepticism on the attack. Like the makers of perpetual motion machines and fuelless motors, Cramp produced fairy things — half-forms almost from another world — that hopped, skipped, jumped, and sometimes even flew, often in apparent defiance of the laws of Faraday and Newton. Sceptical prophets of mechanical certainty, who happened to be standing near, were frequently astonished when some impossible thing swooped and manoeuvred.

But any hero who makes claims for "paranormally related aerospace technological developments" and writes four books about a kind of technological mysticism is bound to run into Anglo-Saxon trouble very quickly. Cramp, like Barnes Wallace the designer of the bouncing bomb, suffered vicious put-downs from far lesser men. Both Cramp and Wallis were ignored whilst the modern equivalents to Leonardo's futuristic drawings poured from their head. The engineer Eric Laithwaite and Professor Hastead, both of Imperial College, and also the cold fusion physicists experienced a similar opposition by sceptics certainly equivalent to a medieval witch-hunt.

Like the cold fusion devices, some of Cramp's "damned" devices were what might be termed knife-edge systems. This means that some worked, some did not, and some worked only partially, earning a visit from our old Fortean friend, the partial explanation. Others, like John Worrell Keely's machines, earned no explanation at all. To add to his problems Cramp, like George Adamski before him, had a mind that ignored small-time distinctions between small-time facts and equally small-time fictions. Like Uri Geller and indeed like Lee Harvey Oswald, Cramp's wild talents enabled him to walk through twentieth-century walls on occasion with no problems at all. It goes almost without saying that Cramp, like Adamski, was a UFO contactee.

Such destructive cultural scepticism as almost destroyed both Leonard Cramp and Barnes Wallace smacks strongly almost of national self-hatred. People like Cramp and Wallace could have taken us into space ahead of the Americans without the help of scores of evil Nazi SS scientists, but they were ignored almost completely, as were the brilliant designers of the revolutionary TSR2 fighter of the 1960s. This was an aircraft that nearly half a century later could still be in squadron service and still be ahead of anything in the skies.

iii

Of late, organised scepticism has been evident in books, magazines and articles that have launched a co-ordinated attack on all aspects of New Age thinking. In particular, the icons of ufology have one by one been consistently ridiculed in magazines and books to the extent that one is justified in using the word conspiracy. The Betty and Barney Hill abduction, Travis Walton's experience, the Roswell affair, the incident in Britain's Rendlesham Forest, all these have all been the targets of attempts by sceptics to try and show such incredible events to be the results of self-deception, hallucination, and disinformation, often coupled with outright fraud and hoaxing. There has even been an attempt, organised and published by people who should perhaps have known better, to trash the original Kenneth Arnold sighting. This particular author, in the *Fortean Times*, attempted to transform the crescent-shaped discs Arnold saw in 1947 into supersonic high-flying pelicans. One author has attempted to reduce the Roswell event to crashed box-kites, and another has attributed the Rendlesham Forest incident to mistaken observation of a local lighthouse. Whilst these things might indeed be good one-frame jokes and cartoons for the prep-school common room, the mental level they represent as plausible analysis is appalling. Such silly claims remind us of the days of the "swamp-gas" UFOs. If sceptics think they earn credibility by perpetrating such nonsense, they are wrong.

Scepticism as Mystique

Thus the debate between believer and sceptic is no longer a friendly liberal free-for-all. A violent and sometimes vicious struggle is now taking place. Often those who say they represent so-called "objective factual truth" have been guilty of the most extraordinary underhand chicanery in order to try and destroy reputations. For example, there have been many attempts to destroy the reputation of those leading American academics such as John Mack and David Jacobs who have examined abduction claims and found them to be quite genuine experiences. Even the *Harry Potter* and *Lord of the Rings* movies and the *Mothman* film have been criticised for turning young folk to occultism, fantastic mythology, and pagan beliefs.

From this desperate rejection of all wonder and magic on any and every level, we conclude that sceptics, like the communists and English Puritans before them, can be defined as people who have a terrible psychological problem with wonder. They hate things that don't fit, but unfortunately for them, as Charles Fort reminds us, there are *always* bits that don't fit in life, experience, and the external world.

Anything extraordinary, or even curious, anything transcendental, odd, or anomalous, all these things tend to irritate sceptics to death. It is as if some deep alarms are set off within them when confronted with the extraordinary. An automatic call goes out along the tribal lines of rationalism to level off all that could be labelled as fantastic, radically different, creative, or new. Sceptics appear to react to new ideas as the early twentieth-century reacted to sur-realistic painting. Indeed many sceptics look upon the UFO experience as a First World War cavalry general looked with horror upon the first tanks.

Thus we have a battle not between easily separable old industrial fact and fiction, but a battle between different kinds of socially transforming mys-tique. Often the debate reaches such a level of demoniac intensity that we have the impression not of a search for some mythical "truth", but of a war between various levels of counter-ritualisation. This is a war indeed at times that quite transcends anything in *Harry Potter* or *Lord of the Rings*.

Effectively, we have in ufology versus scepticism, not the old industrial real versus the unreal, or fact versus fiction, but a war between belief-sys-tems. Horse-mad generals in clean smart clean uniforms and shiny boots who refused to climb into the driver's seats of greasy tanks were completely symbolic of opposition to new paradigms. Their cultural fear that their entire social group was doomed is the same fear that is aroused by a claim of having met a man from the planet Venus. Such claims trigger very deep alarms in certain parts of a common culture. Often, mundane violence and ordinary criminality can be quickly rationalised, but the man from Venus claim arouses anger, fear and ridicule out of all proportion to its physical threat, or even its physical substance.

Most sceptics want to stay in their first simple world as First World War generals wanted to stay with their horses and their idea of old-fashioned roman-tic military chivalry in the face of gas and machine guns. Perhaps sceptics even believe that what we see is what we get. Perhaps they believe what the generals of Wind in the Willows England believed: that governments govern, policemen pro-tect, doctors cure, and that we are all the finite sum of our finite parts.

Sceptics are fond of talking all too easily about what they term reality, which is certainly their favourite word. According to sceptics, this reality is as easy to find as a packet of sweets hidden behind a cushion at a children's party. As mechanicals, their technique has not advanced much beyond good old Sherlock Holmes: follow the clues, go to the Public Records Office, and discover the "real" information. The idea of the real is, as I have said, relatively modern. Charles Fort certainly showed that the real is a piece of clapboard philosophi-cal fakery used to construct those metaphysical harpies called "accuracy", "objectivity" and "precision". By means of such concepts we are supposed to measure the infinities of being human.

Such factual innocence is highly dangerous. On the way to rational enlight-enment, sceptics and rationalists might just get rid of the nutcases and the bits that don't fit, throw them into trucks and sealed trains and pack them off to the outer regions of a conceptual inferno inhabited by people who say they have met men from Venus. Next, they might get rid of what they call lies and decep-tions, hoaxes and fantasies. Straightening out of the twists and turns of the human character, and there is the shining truth: a clean and pure thing as terrifying as monolithic Nazi architecture.

iv

The French writer Jean-Paul Sartre tells of how, as a young man before WWII, when after writing all night, he ventured out in the early morning to a nearby bistro for coffee. Some dozen men came into the café in an absolutely filthy state. They sat down and ordered breakfast. Sartre was told by the *patron* that these men were sewer cleaners and they always came in at exactly this time early in the morning after having finished a shift of work. Sartre asked the patron how he could possibly tolerate such filthy men in his café. The proprietor replied: "Ah, but you see monsieur, they are honest men..."

We imagine an astonished Sartre, in the middle of developing his ideas about existentialism, seeing the coffee and rolls put before him in a totally new light. Thus one of the greatest French philosophers of the twentieth-century was left with the somewhat pre-molecular thought of how a truly honest man was incapable of giving infection, though his hands were soiled with *merde.*

This edifying example of a direct connection between moral worth and what any sceptics would call external reality is a surprisingly late remnant of what was once a magical connection between cause and effect. It demonstrates perfectly how even in the middle of the so-called "scientific" twentieth-century, the stage constructs of fact and reality can easily collapse. When they do so, they reveal far older systems of knowledge and experience that are still very much in dynamic action in this case, based on the principle that there is no necessary connection at all between dirt and possible infection.

Scepticism as Mystique

The idea of the real must have come central to Sartre's mind as he gazed at his early breakfast. He would have known of course that the idea of the real is a late and rather callow arrival on the European stage. Whilst eating his rolls with some hesitancy, Sartre might have had the thought that Shakespeare for example would have found the scientific idea of the "objective real" almost meaningless, and he didn't do too badly without it.

Shakespeare might well have asked: are we really the sum of our finite parts? Is what we see what we getting? The British writer Andrew Darlington, in his book *I Was Elvis Presley's Bastard Love-Child* gives a good example of a vital connection between belief, moral worth, and mystical inspiration:

> My biological father died on Sunday, November 28, 1993, after falling downstairs drunk and never regaining consciousness. My real father was discovered on the bathroom floor of Graceland, August 16, 1977, and was pronounced dead at 3:30pm having never regained consciousness.[1]

Rationally, the assumption that his father was Elvis Presley could be seen as ridiculous a claim as having met a man from Venus. Both such claims are valid examples of trying to construct a magical relationship with consciousness, experience, and external events in place of a merely mechanical connection. In Andrew Darlington's terms, what we call fantasies are not the pathological things of the sceptics. They are attempts to reconstruct older and more creative transcendent relationship between mind and nature. In this relationship, there is no necessary connection between dirt and disease, if only because the molecule and the cell, like the real indeed, have not yet arrived or shall we say, have not yet been created.

But of course, as rejected assumptions, both the stories of Sartre and Darlington represent somewhat unstable and unpredictable world models compared with the objective-mechanical. Of course it must be admitted that the objective-mechanical has won the historical round. For a short time in history, the objective mechanical experience has battled successfully to occupy the prime time advertisements within consciousness.

This victory, of course, is temporary. To maintain and secure the prime advertising time of full consciousness, an appropriately ritualised vocabulary must be safeguarded. Thus we have the voodoo-chant words such as "solid", "cold", and "realistic" which must be securely attached to the ideas of truth and reality. In the sceptical vocabulary, there are whole Christmas trees aglow with such metaphors as "waking up" from "dreamland", and "the thinker must come out of his fantasy". These trees must be trimmed and watered by a whole process of cultural intimidation. Clichéd phrases are repeated in the manner of a mystical ritual: "imagination" must give way to "fact", and "myth" must be separated from "lies". The "truth must be faced up to" as if the truth were some mortal enemy and not a companion, a light in a techno-scientific dark age that is destroying all sea, air, and land. That the scientific "truth" as "revealed" is also contaminating breast milk, affecting the male sperm count, and lowering the intelligence quotient of the soap-watching young is not mentioned. Help to destroy the world, humanity and all else, and you get the Nobel Prize. But say you met a man from Venus, or claim that Elvis Presley was your real father, and the whole world will try and make sure you are never seen or heard of again. Within these networks of "truth" and "reality" and "fact", no wonder we just can't wait for the benefits of human cloning, genetically treated food, and the results from the next super collider, or whatever cloned monster may next emerge from the scientific dark.

This "objectivising", or "clearing of fantasy and illusion" of the sceptics is the rationalist equivalent to ideas of psychoanalytic "deprogramming", and the old communist idea of brainwashing. For the sceptics, in these terms, the "truth" is almost nearly always "terrible"; it is also vicious, destructive, and cruel. Like the rationalist view of outer space, the truth is dark and empty. The "truth" within these systems of coercion is not seen as friend and guide; nor is it seen as a thing wonderful, lovely, or magical; rather is the truth conceived as a great mental prison-house from which there can be no escape.

In the time of Margaret Thatcher BSc, the only Prime Minister who has ever had any kind of knowledge of science or technology, the common phrase used to be "Thou Shalt Not Go On Strike". Now, in a much later development of our consumer society, it is "Thou Shalt Not See Intelligently Controlled Flying Discs in the Atmosphere of Mother Earth". It sounds familiar: such a systems-blindfold was not only applied to witches, it was applied with vastly more terrible effect in Mao's villages, and in the prisons and concentration camps of Stalin and Hitler.

In this sense, scepticism in its purest form is an intellectual allergy. It is a condition that reacts violently to anything that is in the least way out of the ordinary.

The sceptical condition enters perception as a virus that mounts a powerful attack on that infinite capacity for wonder that defines human beings. When the virus acts, the truth is seen not as a blessing, protector, and saviour, but as a tyrannical scourging after which we stand naked and ashamed, "stripped" of all our "illusions" that Elvis Presley was our true father or that we have met a man from Venus. Once so isolated, an individual is cut off from all sources of occult and spiritual inspiration. Therefore, scepticism is a power-ful attempt to achieve the very deepest political alienation without reference to wages, social class, or economics.

The one target of all cultural scepticism is the human imagination. As the military saying goes, once you have them by the balls, their hearts and minds will follow. This negative bias as regards all transcendent thought is pure root and branch communism, whose roots stretch way before Marx to Martin Luther. Such a highly organised attack on fantasy, dream, and imagination is an attack on the individual as a sacred institution. We need men and women from Venus, Christ walking the water, UFO contactees, and Elvis as a father as we need the rain forest and the great barn owl. Lacking such things, the brain, like the planet, will become a televised car park of infinite episodes. Sceptics simply do not understand the function of the claims of George Adamski, Sartre's filthy workmen, or Andrew Darlington's extra-curricular father within a healthy psy-chic ecology. The sceptical fear is not that "wishes" are untrue so much, but that such things as intense desires might leave something of themselves be-hind in their swift passage. If we replace old industrial true and false by a battle of cultural allowances, we have a classical Fortean world picture.

When a thread is put through the eye of all the "nasty little truths" of the sceptics, it would appear that a great "no" has been massively engineered through all the interstices of our mental reference systems. It has taken gen-erations to do this, and the conspiracy is implicit as well as explicit. The scep-tics are the mere semi-automated managers of a process generated by a deep control-system within both language and consciousness, and the culture of industrialisation and technology.

Therefore Coleridge's "shaping spirit" of imagination is still political dyna-mite. Sceptics, like communists and scientists, priests and psychoanalysts, hate the great human Imagination. It is messy, imprecise and fundamentally unstable, and its transcendental freedoms are politically dangerous. It is not that sceptics are right or wrong, so much as they are not going to allow certain claims to come about. "Objectivity" has performed its trick in screening out what can be described as the implicit conspiracy, as distinct from the explicit one. Therefore "facts" are not about honest demystification. They are part of

Scepticism as Mystique

the propaganda technique of that black art of the North European middle class called rationalism.

But Sceptical Rationalism is not about truth. At its best, it is a defence against what prowls beyond the outer rim of the cave-mouth fire. This is the single idea that unites all the many themes that run through the books of Charles Fort. The quest is to try and rediscover the universe as a live animal. That this idea has been stolen, falsified, curtailed, and restricted is behind his implicit political anger. This is the force creating the raw emotional energy running about in a Fortean world model, which is a structure in which feelings can disembody themselves, affect whatever areas are convenient or accessible as symbolic foci of resentment:

> I feel the reliability of two scenes:
> In Hyde Park, London, an orator shouts: "What we want is no king and no law! How we'll get it will be, not with ballots, but with bullets!"
> Far away in Gloucestershire, a house that dates back to Elizabethan times bursts into flames.

V

The heart of rationalism as a philosophy is the idea of mechanical "progress". Yet there is something very odd about this clean-limbed "upwards" ascent from a pit of fools and madmen who were not "scientifically enlightened". In this sense, the one thing that betrays sceptics is the universally mundane nature of their "explanations". Whether sceptics replace UFOs with spots before eyes, supersonic pelicans, or marsh gas, they show that the one thing explanation does is make you go away. This process does not produce new knowledge; it is a means of inducing sleep, of diverting attention from the original target. Sceptics man this semi-automatic doubt-machine. They oil it and clean it, improve and develop it. They are slaves of this machine, and worshipping slaves at that. As such they are part of the machine itself of Doubt itself. It is this image-making power that is the target of all sceptics. Like those other control freaks, the priests, the sceptics know, if only unconsciously, that the making of images is the first alchemical stage of creation. They are not against "untruths" so much as "possibilities". Those oddballs, cranks and eccentrics who just happen to think that the truth is not only wonderful but thankfully scandalous beyond all belief, have on many occasions found themselves the very first to be put into sealed trains en route to places to face the "reality" of forced labour with the additionally "reality" of death as wages. Thus armed terrorists are often Public Enemy Number Two as compared to those who think of strange new possibilities.

How threadbare this view is when compared with renaissance thinking. Certainly Shakespeare had no concept of "objective fact". For him, mind and nature were a seamless robe. In this, he would have had no problems with UFOs, or such a concept as the "paranormal". He had a number of far classier options. He had the entire Bible plus his own fragmented national history. He had also the whole apparatus of Greek Tragedy, which included such ideas as the transmigration of souls, the musical harmony of the heavens, and all kinds of mystical ideas about destiny, and character, thought and action implied by Andrew Darlington's selection of a surrogate mythological father.

For many aboriginal natives and Carlos Castenada's "sorcerer" Don Juan, thinking never ceases to be a form of dreaming. The principle behind many Eastern philosophies is the idea that we are never fully "awake". Hamlet himself could be described by his attempts to try and wake more fully. For Shakespeare again, mind and nature are one entity. This is identical to that symbiotic process which Jung called "participation mystique" in which all matter becomes peopled again, and in becoming so matter can be regarded as a form of life, rather like the active imagination. In the Shakespearean machinery, the non-human world of pure idea and external matter are just as much dramatis personae as the characters themselves. In Shakespeare's sense, matter of all forms (and we can extend this to Hardy's Egdon Heath, Forster's Marabar caves, or Kafka's Prague) have their own weather, mood, their own eco systems, ambitions, and desires.

Shakespeare's idea of individual personality was that it was a system of ideas whose quasi-material structure interfaced with the animal, vegetable, and mineral elements of the "outer" cosmos. Therefore a human being had a super-body whose makeup was the more "airy" (or thinned out) elements of character. The great examples of this are *Hamlet* and *King Lear*. These plays show a dialogue between these inner and outer states. In the latter play, just prior to the storm scene, we have the "real" madness of Lear played against the "false" madness of Edgar, played against the "sanity" of Kent, all played against the inanities of the Fool. Similarly, Goneril and Regan become more animal than human because they invoke metaphors of animalism throughout their language and being. Thus there was traffic between non-human and human elements. This connection also included the non-animate world. Indeed our very own Mothman could have been from either *Macbeth* or *A Midsummer Night's Dream*.

Scepticism as Mystique

Try matching all this with the sceptic's impoverished theorising about "factual objectivity"! Our culture simplifies states of very complex affairs until we get the equations to work, and we call this simplification "reality". Science for example reduces a 52 bus full drunks, fighting skinheads and an ecstasy-head trying to leave by the luggage compartment to a mass moving down an inclined plane. It cannot describe the spew on the floor, the piss-sodden photo of a Tellytubby in *The Sun*, the hag trying to assault the driver, the smell of curry and chips, and the racist screams from Millwall supporters slashing the upstairs seats, all to the wail of pursuing sirens.

But all these images of our modern inferno are reduced by science to a point in space moving under the action of those historically arriviste harpies of mass, force, and acceleration. This vanishing of images and information by ignoring them to get a pet theory to work leads of course to one big scientific hoax after another. The joke is that the amount of information about the 52 bus event is decreased by science rather than increased.

If that isn't political, nothing is.

In the post-modern equations of Entertainment State the billiard-ball atoms of fact and fiction will become Personalities. Our coming Web world will be based on our re-invention of Plato's concept of the real as shadow play of matter and essence, ideology and quasi-material manifestations.

vi

The books of Charles Fort endorse these concepts. He shows that the sub-jective-objective stance gives us so many philosophic difficulties we have to hoax our way around the problems. But the hoax re-assures us. We know we are being tricked, if only by ourselves, but we need oversimplifications in order to get some sleep at night. George Adamski told some lies. Most reassuring. Interpret a man in terms of the lowest levels he falls to, and we can sleep tight. Accusing someone of being a fantasist is an old tribal way of vanishing or controlling fantasies themselves. This is fantasy-management more than truth versus falsehood. Perhaps we should ask the question of why we even bothered at all to accuse Adamski then, and why we still bother a half-century later. Yet early contactees such as Adamski, Howard Menger and Truman Bethurum still make sceptics angry. They still cause losses of temper, supercillious laughter, denials, and accusations of imposture. Adamski in particular is still seen as a ridiculous figure, a clown, someone to be de-spised, a permanent embarrassment, a person who showed just how silly and devious human beings can be.

Yet there is something very odd about our anger. Hurts of the deep past (infinitely more vast than those inflicted by the harmless Adamski) have gone with the world of Adamski. We no longer get angry about the Korean War or Pearl Harbor. Yet Adamski's wound does not heal. Something within us has been profoundly disturbed by his claims. They still frighten and amuse. He entered the unconscious and he went deep. He (amidst others) is a permanent reminder that the world is not a stable place. To go deeper than Pearl Harbour in American consciousness is quite an achievement. Even ten-year-olds relate to Adamski's pan-shaped flying saucers seen on the side of their cornflake packs. Certainly no other single joke remains from the 1950s. Quite an achieve-ment that. Far more clever men have achieved far less. His hoaxes (if indeed they were hoaxes) do not appear to be going stale, as distinct from the hoaxes of science, such as psychoanalysis, particle physics, health care, or environ-mental "improvement".

As we know, history picks the most unlikely heroes. There has to be a fulcrum for change and perhaps Adamski's mind was the focal point. Truman Bethurum was too simple-minded, and Howard Menger too limp. Only Adamski had the proper hunger, was in the right place at the right time. His mind was a kind of metaphor bomb, trying to reverse the automatic denial-bacillus of mental colonisation. In this sense his simple bourgeois worth in terms of "solid" achievement is irrelevant. Adamski was able to penetrate high-powered cultural levels (on many continents) with his new metaphors. There is now emerging the post-modern view that such interpenetrating metaphors are alien life forms in themselves in that they represent invading systems of new kinds of reference. Within the framework of such arguments, the old-fashioned "real" versus "false" arguments become somewhat irrelevant as compared to the idea of systems trying to out-advertise themselves. Most human problems are not actually "solved" so much as engineered around, re-programmed, or re-imaged. We need the aliens if only to provide the superb Anglo-Saxon comedy of a great number of Miss Marples on bicycles going around the country taking notes on searchlights and ball lightning.

vii

The going of the Fool from Western culture was a great loss. The function of Shakespeare's Fool as he sits at the feet of the mad Lear is to remind us that the world as Thought and Idea is never complete, and that the hoax as a system of deception is part of a very early psychology of a shamanistic technique of reaching and understanding the unconscious. The joke comes back to us as a reminder that the mind reasons by hoaxing itself. This is a healthy process. It enables us to handle danger, and is a vital element in the learning process, which is largely a process of self-deception. By convincing ourselves that we can master formidable problems, we eventually master them. Thus the "concrete" solution comes from an utter fantasy, as do most "solutions" in science and technology, these being the results more often than not of what Arthur Koestler calls, for instance, Kepler's "fantasy prone intellect". Koestler showed in *The Sleepwalkers* that so-called "falsehoods" are an essential part of any reasoning process. In great genius in particular, the degree of self-deception may be enormous. We live in a culture so commercially brutalised and with such a simple-minded media that such subtleties have been lost to us in any communal sense. Facts are the ultimate conspiracy. Look at a so-called "fact", and it will split into a thousand elements like the landscapes of Jonathan Downes or Doc Shiels. Those elements in turn will split again like a Fractal. In a trice, we are gazing into infinity and falling through space past shelves on which are stand jars of orange marmalade. The "isolated" fact is like the idea of the lone assassin. Few believe it, nobody likes it, and even fewer want it. The "facts" about a person tell us as much about that person as our mass moving down an inclined plane tells us about our 52 bus. Being part of a highly developed apparatus of mental control, they represent a deep negative politicisation of all thinking. Like the much-vaunted digital process, "facts" are not found in nature. They are manufactured screens, a fraudulent convenience to enable us to reason in yet more fraudulent terms, for this, according to Fort, is how the mind reasons:

Scepticism
as Mystique

> There is something of ultra-pathos — of cosmic sadness — in this universal search for a standard, and in belief that one has been revealed by either inspiration or analysis, then the dogged clinging to a poor sham of a thing long after its insufficiency has been shown.

The loss of the idea of the Fool has caused many people, sceptics amongst them, to have a very simple-minded idea of hoaxing and imposture. A hoax is an enactment of something; as such, it is not "false" but a kind of rehearsal. For a minute, a new "reality" (or rather part of a new world) comes about. True, this is a transient bubble-world, a kind of virtual construct, but nevertheless the hoax is powerful enough to change totally the entire complex of a deep-rooted group identity.

If "reality" is the favourite word of the sceptics, then the word "hoax" is certainly their second. A number of reasonably well-adjusted people, say, are in a room talking quite naturally in a relaxed atmosphere. One of the group leaves the room, only to rush back and announce that the entire building is on fire. Before it is quickly discovered that this person has a juvenile sense of humour, the group will momentarily have changed its fundamental identity. True, this new act will be only a very temporary one, but it will be sufficient to change social and personal masks forever. Within the new performance schedule, weak people will become strong, the strong weak. Leaders will emerge as well as equally unsuspected cowards. Though these new roles will appear not to last, memories of the changes will be permanent; the collapse of the strong will be remembered, as will the new-found confidence of the weak. The old positions then will have been undermined, and those leaders who try to regain their original position in the hierarchy will have lost face irrevocably.

For a moment a "fantasy" has had just as much effect as "actual" smoke and flames. True, perhaps it did not last very long, but that it lasted at all shows that here we are not dealing with iron-age "truth" versus "falsehood", but frequency and duration. In all likelihood, the more fantasy-prone members of the target-group will admit that they smelt smoke, and the even more fantasy-prone may well swear that they glimpsed a flame, if only a small one.

J. P. Chaplin, in his 1959 book, *Rumor, Fear and the Madness of Crowds*, comments on the notorious broadcast of Orson Welles:

> There were some in New York who "saw" or "heard" the battle of the Martians and Earthmen that was being waged in the neighbouring state. A man equipped with binoculars could "see" the flames of the holocaust from his vantage point on top of a tall office building. One "heard" the bombs from aircraft fall on New Jersey, and was convinced they were heading for Times Square. Another "heard" the swish of the Martian machines as they plummeted through the atmosphere to earth. In Brooklyn, a man called the police demanding that he be issued a gas mask; he had "heard" the distant sounds of the battle going on over in Jersey and believed a gas attack

imminent. When informed it was a play, he shouted, "We can hear the firing all the way here, and I want a gas mask. I'm a taxpayer."

It is difficult here to avoid the idea that both our hoaxed fire and the suggested Martian invasion were not "false" or "true" things at all, but things that were almost fully created in the Fortean sense. Science, with its absolute insistence of ON or OFF switches, its distinctions between real and false, yes and no, alive or dead, does not recognise as meaningful the idea of there being intermediate states between hard and soft separations.

This is part of the psychosocial equation sceptics never talk about. The appearance of small fires, say, along the line of the dreaming. Systems such as witchcraft and indeed great world religions on occasion, are rejected and persecuted not because they are theologically incorrect, scientifically invalid, or considered evil, or immoral, but like fuelless motors, they might just work for a time. Thus we have to consider the idea that the fire previously mentioned was almost created. An increase in the strength of the suggestion, and perhaps even small fires may well appear along with stigmata and "paranormal" effects in quite different contexts to imagined fires. Fort gives many examples of mysterious deaths where the scene is as if imagined. By this he means that if the socks are left perfect on a body that has been burnt by spontaneous combustion, this is because when we imagine killing a person by such a means, we harbour no resentment against their socks!

Scepticism
as Mystique

Thus we have to replace the working/not working paradigm with "not working very well" paradigm. In other words Darlington's umbilical to his Presley super-self is a noisy channel, as is the connection between dirt and infection as regards Sartre's sewer-workers.

Darlington's world is not an objective world. This means that it represents a system that can be entered. The only possible way we can learn something is to enter a system as ourselves. In Tennessee Williams' play *A Streetcar Named Desire,* Blanche Dubois is a ruined woman of transcendent beauty. Low-key, practical, mundane, simple-minded characters who are sceptical about anything and everything surround her. Stanley Kowalski (played by Marlon Brando in the film) sarcastically asks Blanche what is her use in the world: she cannot cook, sew, or do anything practical. Blanche replies that the only reason for her existence is to provide magic. She has done this almost as a vocation. Brando's face is a mask of astonishment: this cynical, sceptical, world-weary materialist mask of a face drops as if Blanche had hit him on the jaw.

Blanche's last piece of magic has worked.

Stanley Kowalski has learned something.

Perhaps Darlington's counterfeit father serves as our only true intimation of immortality, and perhaps the UFO contactees and visionaries are like Blanche Dubois, the broken poets of our time. Provision of magic is a holy thing, a sacred act, for without magic and poetry we all enter the great infernos of the utterly damned.

notes

FOREWORD

1 Charles Fort, *The Complete Books of Charles Fort*. Dover Books, NY, 1974, pp. 548–549
2 Fred Warshofsky is the author of ten books about science, medicine and technology, most recently publishing *The Patent Wars, The Chip Wars* and *The Control of Life*.

INTRODUCTION

1 Mayflower, 1971
2 University of Chicago Press, London, 1962
3 Richard Milton, *Forbidden Science*. 4th Estate, 1994
4 Murray Gell-Mann (1929–) is Professor of Theoretical Physics at the California Institute of Technology. He is responsible for what is termed the law of conservation of strangeness, and he predicted the existence of what he called the quark. This quark, as distinct from all other particles, has a fractional electric charge. Six quarks were predicted by Gell-Mann, and five have so far been indirectly detected. Readers of this book can decide for themselves whether Gell-Mann is a Fortean by considering the names he has given his supposed quarks. The names are up, down, strange, charm, bottom and top, and they have been ascribed properties of strangeness, charm, bottomness, and topness.
5 *Mr Coleridge* (essay in Hazlitt's *The Spirit of the Age*)
6 Article in *The Daily Telegraph Magazine*, June 11, 1994
7 Fort, however, was well aware of the latest ideas of his time (up to 1932) as regards electromagnetism and atomic physics, see *Wild Talents* p. 905. Also, in this same book there is a continuous satirising of Heisenberg's uncertainty principle.
8 *Prophet of the Unexplained*. Victor Gollancz Ltd., London, 1971
9 He wrote *Ages in Chaos* and *Earth in Upheaval*.
10 *The Velikovski Affair* (ed. Alfred de Grazia). See also Damon Knight's chapter on Velikovski in *Charles Fort, Prophet of the Unexplained*. Gollancz, London, 1971
11 Ibid. p. 133
12 See article *Wilhelm Reich, Guru of The Orgasm* by Neil Mortimer in

Fortean Times 107, February 1998.

13 Alex Constantine in his book *Virtual Government* (Feral House, 1997) reveals that Timothy Leary was a CIA double agent. Since he also accuses John Mack and Art Bell of being similar animals, his opinions, though eruditely expressed, are to be treated with great caution.

14 Now so discredited apparently, that his name no longer appears in the 1994 *Hutchinson Dictionary of Scientific Biography*, but then neither does the name of Thomas Kuhn!

15 S. G. Soal was, like Burt, a former President of the Society for Psychical Research. The statistical results of his card guessing experiments have given grounds for accusations of fraud. A. J. Carrington in *The Unexplained* (p. 1497) suggests, as did Charles Fort, that in the face of such disreputable action by such a highly-respected individual, an alternative to the simple idea of conscious fraud may have to be considered.

16 M. Gardiner, *Fads and Fallacies in the Name of Science*. Dover, NY, 1957

17 See *The Skeptic* magazine, Vol 5 No 2 and Vol 4 No 6. See also, Arthur Koestler's *The Case of the Midwife Toad*. The experience of the biologist Kammerer is interesting in respect of what happened here, and is mentioned by Fort.

18 Fort, *op. cit.*, p. 546

19 *A Fire on the Moon*. Weidenfeld and Nicholson, 1970, p. 251

20 John Hastead, *The Metal-Benders*. Routledge & Kegan Paul, 1981

21 Fort, *op. cit.*, p. 863

22 Ibid., p. 860

23 Ibid., p. 858

24 *The Presence of the Past* and *A New Science of Life*.

25 Professor of Theoretical Physics, Birkbeck College, London. He wrote *Wholeness and the Implicate Order* (1980).

26 Stephen William Hawking (1942–) is Lucasian Professor of Mathematics at Cambridge University. His *A Brief History of Time*, published in 1988, explained his ideas in visual terms and re-mained on the UK bestseller list for more than three years, longer than any other title. As a leading authority on quantum mechanics, he explained the action of black holes in terms of what he termed "virtual particles". Such particles are created fleetingly in empty space out of "nothing" and cannot be detected by a particle detector. Hawking, for obvious reasons, is almost entirely dependent on his metaphor-hungry editors and the frantic enthusiasms of graphic artists. This is probably the reason why his popular books are vastly inferior in quality as compared to those of his equally distinguished colleague, Roger Penrose, the author of *The Emperor's New Mind* and *Shadows of the Mind*.

27 *Wrinkles in Time*, p. 111

28 Fort's 1919 *Book of the Damned* was composed well before such prophetic films as King Vidor's *The Citadel*, the British early documentary *Coalface*, René Claire's 1931 comedy about robotic factory life, *A Nous la Liberté*, and books such as Upton Sinclair's *The Flivver King* and H. G. Wells' *Things to Come*. Like Fort, all such people gave warnings about increasing robotisation of human beings within the factory system that was to get its final expression in Nazism. In 1920, behaviourist studies in "time and motion" were already being carried by the British National Institute of Industrial Psychology. The Rowntree company was one of the first to attempt to assess worker intelligence without using language, using form-boards and pattern-fitting diagrams.

29 *The Secret Agent*, chapter 1

30 *Skeptic Magazine*

31 Brian Wynne, *Between Orthodoxy And Oblivion: The Normalisation of Deviance In Modern Science*. Keel University Sociological Review Monograph, No 27

32 Fort, *op. cit.*, p. 250

33 *The Sunday Telegraph*, November 4, 2001, p.9

34 Now, like any other evolving control system, science is preparing to

NOTES FOR
PAGES
15–25

change the goalposts. Roger Highfield in a recent article in *The Sunday Telegraph* (August 26, 2001, p. 29) talks about how science is getting to a stage where it may have to recognise that its "eternal laws of Nature" may change in themselves over time.

1900: STRANGE EVENTS IN THE BRONX

1 Fort, *op. cit.*, p.160.
2 Louis Pauwels and Jacques Bergier, *The Morning Of The Magicians*. Mayflower, 1971, p. 93 (first published by Anthony Gibbs and Phillips Ltd, 1963, as *The Dawn of Magic*)
3 Damon Knight, *Prophet of the Unexplained*. p. 203
4 Damon Knight, *op. cit.*, p. 168
5 Sussman also published Tiffany Thayer's first novel, *Thirteen Men*. Thayer (who introduced Fort's work to Sussman) was the founder of the Fortean Society. The first meeting of this Society was on February 26, 1931. According to Damon Knight, Fort was lured to this meeting by means of forged telegrams. He afterwards refused to join, saying that he would "rather join the Elks".
6 Knight, *op., cit.*, p. 179
7 Pliny (AD 23–79) was the Roman compiler of a "encyclopaedic rag-bag of popular science". Drabble, *The Oxford Companion to English Literature*, OUP, 1985 (fifth edition), p. 772
8 Marco Polo (1254–1324) wrote an account of his travels that caused much excitement in Europe as a description of worlds quite unknown at this time. His work is said to have inspired Columbus.
9 The English clergyman Edward Topsell (?–1638), wrote *The Booke of Foure-Footed Beasts* which appeared in 1607. This depicts many fantastic animals, including a dragon and many "serpents".
10 This is the Latinised name of Bishop Olaf Magnusson (1490–1557), Archishop of Uppsala. He was a Swedish historian and geographer, and drew the first comprehensive map of Scandinavia.

11 *The Seventeenth Century Background.* Peregrine, 1962
12 Basil Willey is here referring to Browne's *Certain Miscellany Tracts*, published posthumously.
13 Fort, *op., cit.*, p. 231–232
14 Damon Knight, *op. cit.*, p. 28–29
15 Quoted from Damon Knight, *op.cit.*, p. 168
16 Ibid.
17 Fort, *op. cit.*, p. 23
18 Louis Pauwels and Jacques Bergier, *op. cit.*, p. 90
19 He wrote *Ubu Roi*, perhaps the first "absurdist" play. The knockabout style of Fort's novel, *The Outcast Manufacturers*, is reminiscent of the style of Jarry, and also the work of other early French absurdists and surrealists such as Arteaud, Cocteau, and André Breton, the author of the original *Surrealist Manifesto*.
20 Introduction to *The Books of Charles Fort*.
21 Damon Knight, *op. cit.*, p 180
22 Founded in the US by one Jan Fort, otherwise Vanderfort, La Fort, or Van Fort, also known as Jan Libbertee, whose marriage in New Amsterdam was recorded in 1641. Damon Knight, *op. cit.*
23 See Damon Knight, *op. cit.*, p. 6. Knight gives a most affecting portrait of the early life of Charles Fort and his two brothers, Raymond and Clarence.
24 Fort, *op. cit.*, p.67–68
25 Roland Barthes, *Mythologies*. 1953
26 Fort, *op. cit.*, p. 753

THE YARNS OF DICKINS AND EUCLID

1 Fort *op. cit.*, p. 863
2 *The Fortean Times* has, over many years, shown that many of the things which Fort recorded are all very much still in evidence. See also Damon Knight, *op. cit.*, chapter 7.
3 Damon Knight has made a very useful and considerably detailed analysis of the frequencies of such phenomena and the cyclic connection. See *Charles Fort, Prophet of the Unexplained*.

NOTES FOR PAGES 30–43

4 Fort, *op. cit.*, p. 89: *The Monthly Weather Review*, for May, 1894.
5 Fort, *op. cit.*, p. 864
6 Ibid, p. 863

STORIES ABOUT STORIES

1 Fort, *op. cit.*, p. 30
2 Fort, *op. cit.*, p. 111

ENTER SONNABEND

1 Fort, *op. cit.*, p. 42
2 Frederick Karl & Leo Hamalian, Picador, 1973, p. 14
3 Damon Knight, *op. cit.*, p. 67
4 Damon Knight, *op. cit.*, p. 39
5 Damon Knight, *op. cit.*, p. 182
6 Weschler has been a staff writer for The New Yorker since the early 1980s. He is the author of the Passions and Wonders series.
7 This book was awarded the Pulitzer Prize for "General Non-fiction", and the National Book Critics Circle Award for "Non-fiction". Readers are advised that they may have to make up their own minds as to whether these two claims for reality are valid. To help in this, perhaps they should know a little more Sonnabend. According to Lawrence Weschler, " in 1936 the great mid-century American neuro-physiologist Geoffrey Sonnabend" was convalescing from a combined physical and nervous breakdown brought on in part, by the collapse of his earlier investigation into memory pathways in carp". *Mr Wilson's Cabinet of Wonders*. Vintage Books 1995, p. 5
8 Fort, *op. cit.*, p. 628
9 In his acknowledgements to this book, Leslie mentions (though somewhat briefly) his debt to Charles Fort.
10 See this author's own book, *Looking for Orthon*. Paraview Press, NY, 2001
11 By Kenn Thomas and David Hatcher Childress, Adventures Unlimited Press, 1999
12 By Jim Keith, Adventures Unlimited Press, 1997

RELIGIO AMERICANA: SYSTEMS ANALYSIS

1 The contactee Antonio Villas Boas claimed to have been seduced by a small white female humanoid with red hair who emerged from a landed alien ship. See Gordon Creighton's essay in Charles Bowen's *The Humanoids*. Neville Spearman, 1969
2 Fort, *op. cit.*, p. 617
3 C.P. Snow, *The Physicists*. Macmillan, London, 1982, p. 26. Snow is referring to the physicist Henry Mosely, who was killed in the trenches of the Great War.
4 Fort, *op. cit.*, pp. 258–259
5 Fort, *op. cit.*, pp. 30–31
6 On May 19th, 1919, Harry Hawker (CW 521) is reported to have picked up wireless messages "meaningless in the languages of this earth"; the *New York Tribune* of September 2, 1921, quotes (CW 526) J. C. H. Macbeth, London Manager of the Marconi Wireless Company, as saying that Signor Marconi had picked pulse-coded regular signals on 150,000 metres wavelength, which was far above any wavelength used on the earth at that time, that being on average 14,000 metres. See also CW 494, where "Night of Dec 7, 1900 — Tesla announced that he had received, upon his wireless apparatus, vibrations that he attributed to the Martians. They were a series of triplets".
7 Fort, *op. cit.*, p. 838
8 The discussions in Wells' short story *The Time Machine* (1894) of what were at that time the new ideas about non-Euclidean geometries, show Wells to be that rarity of rarities — the "literary" writer who is aware of mathematics, physics, and technology. Would that he were living at this hour.

THE DAMNED IMAGINATION

1 Fort, *op. cit.*, p. 3
2 Even in the last years of the Middle Ages, calling the king a fool was treasonable, as it might lead to the "imagination" of the king's death. See J.

NOTES FOR PAGES 43–65

NOTES FOR PAGES 66–78

G. Bellamy, *The Law of Treason in England in the Later Middle Ages*. Cambridge University Press, 1970, p. 121–2

3 Unsuccessful suicides have reported that in mid-air, whilst the emotions are frenzied, and the intellect paralysed, the imagination is still producing material hardly suitable to the occasion.

4 As any soldier who has been on night reconnaissance will bear out.

5 Louis Pauwels and Jacques Bergier, *op. cit.*, p. 92

6 *The Personality of Man*. Penguin, 1946, p. 41

7 *Varieties of Religious Experience*. Fontana, 1971 edition, p. 413

8 Science now appears to be changing its mind about cold fusion. Researchers at SRI California when passing a current between palladium electrodes through heavy water claimed to see more heat produced than could be explained. When examined by physicist Brian Clarke, the electrodes were found to contain 1015 atoms of tritium, a heavy radioactive isotope of hydrogen. In a wonderfully Fortean moment Clarke commented, "There's no question of the tritium being real." (*New Scientist*, September, 2001)

9 See Nigel Watson's excellent *The Scareship Mystery*, Domra Publications, 2000.

10 MacGibbon & Kee Ltd, 1957; Granada (Paladin) edition, 1970, p. 235

11 In our own society, perhaps the equivalent to this tribal transgression is not to have a television set, and hence at least minimise the consumption of trash images. But any would-be hero who thinks she or he is free, should bear in mind that it makes absolutely no difference whatsoever whether a TV set is present or not, since in a cultural fluid, there is no "off" switch. The physical witnessing of the broadcast of a group of characters is unnecessary, since one is made to live parts of their lives through many other means. Thus trying to avoid soap operas is quite impossible, just as in communist Russia it was impossible to avoid the local Commissar, or in Nazi Germany, your local friendly Party member. Thus a particular technology is only used to launch a particular self-sustaining "state of mind". After that, being subject to the particular technology itself in the gross sense becomes somewhat irrelevant.

12 Fort, *op. cit.*, p. 727

13 See *Eros and Civilisation* by Marcuse for example, Sphere, 1969

14 Fort, *op. cit.*, p. 572

WALTER MITTY STRIKES BACK

1 *The Love Song of J. Alfred Prufrock* (*Poetry*, 1915)

2 That O'Brien has to threaten physical torture (such as the inquisitors merely showing Galileo the dread instruments), shows that "Newspeak" in Winston's case has not worked. Therefore Winston is the "winner" in that he forces his tormentor to mere brutalism and implicit admission of ideological failure.

3 De Quincey says that the word objective was "almost unintelligible in 1821". *Confessions of an English Opium Eater*. Wordsworth Classic Edition, 1994, p. 242. It is certainly not in Dr Johnson's Dictionary of a hundred years previous.

4 Fort, *op. cit.*, pp. 725–6

5 Fort, *op. cit.*, p. 726

6 Fort, *op. cit.*, p. 962

7 Fort, *op. cit.*, p. 963

8 Bishop George Berkeley (1685–1758) is known for his principle *Esse est percipi* ("to be is to be perceived"), discussed in his influential work, *Treatise Concerning the Principles of Human Knowledge* (1710), which set out his idea that reality consists of ideas in the mind of God. His conceptions of the relativity of space, time, and motion anticipated Mach and Einstein. Johannes "Meister" Eckhart (c.1260–1327) was pronounced an heretic for a similar view: "The eye with which I see God is the eye with which He sees myself." See useful discussion of this philosophical view in *Keats*

and *Shakespeare* by John Middleton
Murry, Greenwood Press, London,
1976 (originally published 1925).

HOLY
WAR

1 Fort, *op. cit.,* pp. 918–919
2 There is the opinion that he has been
replaced by the film star and the
advertising executive.
3 See the novel *Darkness at Noon* (first
published in 1941 by Macmillan)

GAS LAMP
THEATRE

1 From the short story *Property* in the
collection, *A Crown of Feathers.*
Jonathan Cape, 1974, p. 75
2 This was the pseudonym of the writer
F. W. Rolfe. For the wonderfully strange
story of this writer's rather Fortean life,
see A. J. A. Symons' *The Quest for
Corvo.* Penguin Books, 1934
3 Fort, *op. cit.,* p. 771
4 *Bright Star of Exile.* Barrie and Jenkins,
London, 1978, p. 214
5 Damon Knight, *op. cit.,* p. 54
6 Fort, *op. cit.,* pp. 155–6
7 Fort, *op. cit.,* p. 572
8 Fort, *op. cit.,* p. 154
9 Fort, *op. cit.,* p. 671
10 *Arcana Caelestia.* The Swedenborg
Society, 1904, Chapter XXV. 21–23,
p. 211
11 Fort, *op. cit.,* p. 251
12 *The Life and Opinions of Tristram
Shandy. Everyman's Library 617.* J.M.
Dent & Sons Ltd, 1959, p.59
13 *Ulysses.* The Bodley Head Ltd, 1960,
p. 745
14 Fort, *op. cit.,* pp. 506–507
15 Joyce himself credited the source of his
ideas about the interior monologue as
Dujarden's novel of 1888, *Les Lauriers
sont coupés.*
16 Fort, *op. cit.,* p. 56
17 Ibid., p. 56
18 Friedrich Chladni (1756–1827)
pioneered early researches into sound.
It is to be assumed that here Fort is
referring to Chladni's book on meteorites, whose theories that meteorites

fell from the sky were confirmed by
the French physicist Jean Biot
(1774–1862).
19 Fort, *op. cit.,* p. 57
20 Fort, *op. cit.,* p. 601
21 Jean Joseph Leverrier (1811–1877)
was Director of the Paris Observatory.
See the *Hutchinson Dictionary of
Scientific Biography* for an excellent
short account of his life and achieve-
ments.
22 Fort, *op. cit.,* pp. 201–2
23 Fort, *op. cit.,* pp. 200–1
24 Schwarzschild (1873–1916) was a
genius, unfortunately with a short
lifespan, having contracted a fatal skin-
disease in the Great War. He was
Associate Professor at Göttingen, was
the first to apply photographic photom-
etry, and also suggested in 1900 that
space was possibly non-Euclidean:
that is, sixteen years before Einstein's General Theory of Relativity.
His last papers also give the first
complete solutions to Einstein's field
equations.
25 Article by Roger Highfield in *The Sunday
Telegraph* August 26, 2001, p. 29
26 Fort, *op. cit.,* p. 192
27 Fort, *op. cit.,* p. 211

MOUNTAINS, TRIALS
AND LABORATORIES

1 *Metamorphosis and Other Stories,*
Penguin Modern Classics, 1975, p. 216

THE KAISER'S
DISC JOCKEY

1 See Roger Penrose, *Shadows Of The
Mind,* chapter 2: "Godel's theorem and
Turing Machines," and also chapter 3:
"The case for non-computability in
mathematical thought."(OUP, 1994).
2 Fort, *op. cit.,* p. 127
3 *The Disinherited Mind.* Penguin 1961,
p. 23
4 Fort, *op. cit.,* p. 127
5 *The Magic Mountain.* Penguin, 1969,
p. 214.
6 *Daily Telegraph.* August 19, 1996, p. 29
7 *Cancer Ward.* Penguin Modern
Classics, p. 100

NOTES FOR
PAGES
81–108

8   *The Magic Mountain, op. cit.,* p. 283
9   Fort, *op. cit.,* p. 126
10   *The Magic Mountain, op. cit.,* p. 283
11   Fort, *op. cit.,* pp. 207–8

MARKETING
BELIEF

NOTES FOR
PAGES
109–115

1   See *The Nature of the Physical World.*
     Everyman's Library 19
2   See this author's own novel, *The*
     Entertainment Bomb. New Futurist
     Books, 1996, c/o Turnaround Distribu-
     tion, Unit 3, Olympia Trading Estate,
     Coburg Road, London, N22 6TZ
3   For an interesting discussion of
     Newton's intense involvement with
     alchemy, see Richard Westfall's
     biography, *The Life of Isaac Newton.*
     Cambridge University Press, 1993
4   Alfred North Whitehead (1861–1947)
     is accepted as one of the great
     philosophers of the twentieth-century.
     The three-volume treatise *Principia*
     Mathematica, written with his friend and
     colleague Bertrand Russell, consider-
     ably influenced thinking about the very
     basis of mathematics. The book
     influenced the work both of Alan Turing
     and Kurt Gödel, the founder of compu-
     ter science and modern chaos theory
     respectively. Charles Fort would have
     relished the conclusion of both White-
     head and Russell in that it is claimed
     (by Roger Penrose, for instance), that
     they demonstrated conclusively that
     arithmetic, and hence mathematics, can
     never be proved to be consistent.
5   Pluto
6   *Adventures of Ideas.* Penguin, 1933
7   Fort, *op. cit.,* p. 59
8   *The Size of the Universe.* Pelican,
     1948, p. 142
9   Ticknor and Fields, *Bit By Bit.* NY,
     1984, p. 66
10   Fletcher Moulton's rather horrific view
     of an emerging techno-industrial
     infinity is mirrored by the disoriented
     state of mind of the character in
     Lamb's essay, *The Superannuated*
     Man (1833), and also gives us an
     insight into the state of mental shock
     of Bartleby, in Melville's short story
     of that name. Both characters reflect

the effects of the increased load and
pace of industrial tasking, and also
the emerging complexity of new
systems of industrialised commerce.
De Quincey too, in *Confessions,* sees
the same kind of disorientation, in his
vision of the South Kensington
Science Museum long before it was
built:
"Many years ago, when I was looking
over Piranesi's *Antiquities of Rome,*
Coleridge, then standing by, described
to me a set of plates from that artist,
called his *Dreams* and which record
the scenery of his own visions during
the delirium of a fever. Some of these
(I describe only from the memory of
Coleridge's account) represented vast
Gothic halls; on the floor of which stood
mighty engines and machinery, wheels,
cables, catapults etc, expressive of
enormous power put forth, or resistance
overcome. Creeping along the sides of
the walls, you perceived a staircase;
and upon this, groping his way upwards
was Piranesi himself. Follow the stairs a
little farther, and you perceive them
reaching an abrupt termination, without
any balustrade, and allowing no step
onwards to him who should reach the
extremity, except into the depths
below. Whatever is to become of poor
Piranesi, at least you suppose that his
labours must now in some way termi-
nate. But raise your eyes and behold a
second flight of stairs still higher, on
which again Piranesi is perceived, by
this time standing on the very brink of
the abyss. Once again elevate your eye,
and a still more aerial flight is described; and there again is the delirious
Piranesi, busy on his aspiring labours:
and so on, until the unfinished stairs
and the hopeless Piranesi are both lost
in the upper gloom of the hall."
Confessions of an English Opium
Eater. Wordsworth Classics edition,
1994, pp. 239–240
Fort often prompts us to look at
industrialisation as *a state of mind.* In
nineteenth-century fiction, such a thing
has been ignored completely by literary
critics. It is possible to read critical
texts on Mary Shelley's *Frankenstein*

for example, without a single reference to science, technology or industry.

11 Of course we should talk here of the Einsteinian frame, but we still say we *board* an aircraft, and ships still *sail*, although wood and canvas are things of a hundred years ago. In a similar manner, all distant astronomical events are referred to in the present tense. If we were to use the more suitable *past* tense for such events, this would be intolerably depressing, since it would mean recognition that no such events exist in the here-now. Hence at a stroke, modern astronomy would become an archaeology so completely dead that any study would perhaps be quite absurd. One can imagine the reaction of any scientist to any accusation that signals sent into outer space are not only an attempt to communicate with the dead, but are sent in expectation of an answer from the same! Thus verbal and metaphorical frameworks expressing how a group would *like* to see things are an essential part of rationalisations, showing such to be shot through with metaphysical assumptions concerning identity, purpose, and social relations. Similarly both the "Big Bang" and "gravity waves" are talked of as if they had some kind of locatable Euclidean centre "out there" (from the Earth) somewhere, whereas if we are to accept Einstein's space and time, the consequent Fortean comedy is that some other cosmic observer's Big Bang or gravity wave might well be located just outside Millwall Supporter's Club. Given the difficulties of changing the phallocentric tense, and the ethnocentric bias in metaphors of black and white, it is to be assumed that the use of syntax as protective psychological screens in scientific language and descriptions will continue.

THE
NEW SCRIPT

1 Fort, *op. cit.*, p. 424
2 Fort, *op. cit.*, p. 293

3 See account of Mantell's mysterious death after he chased a UFO in *The UFO Encyclopedia* compiled by Margaret Sachs, (Corgi, 1981), pp. 125–126

4 Fort *op. cit.*, p. 72

5 See the rather sinister manoeuvrings of the notorious Condon Committee in David R. Saunders and R. Roger Harkins, *UFOs? Yes! Where the Condon Committee Went Wrong.* New York, Signet, 1968.

6 See Patrick Huyghe, *The Field Guide to Extraterrestrials,* Avon, New York, 1996, also Charles Bowen's *The Humanoids,* Neville Spearman Ltd, London, 1969.

7 This metaphor is implied as regards the "depleted region" between collector and emitter of the transistor. The idea of "trinity" or "three in one" is of course is central to Western mysticism. The original Los Alamos test site was called Trinity. See a fascinating article on myth and technology in *Fortean Times* No 68 (April, 1993), by Dennis Stillings, editor of *Artifex*, entitled *Killing the Golden Calf*.

8 It is an idea expressed by that portmanteau word "psychosocial". This phrase seems to calm everybody down. If it means that things created by imagination alone can produce bangs on heads, then perhaps we should not calm down at all.

THE
ABSENT BRAIN

1 See James Gleick, *Genius*, Little, Brown, New York, 1992, for Richard Feynman's strange inspirations.

2 Quoted from J. B. S. Haldane's *The Marxist Philosophy and the Sciences*, London, June 1939 (hardcover reprint available from Ayer publications, ISBN 0836911377). Haldane was quoting in turn from Lenin's *Materialism and Empirio-Criticism*, London, 1934 (1970 hardcover reprint, International Publishers Co, ISBN 0717801268).

3 Bob Rickard, *Medical Curiosities,*

NOTES FOR
PAGES
115–127

Fortean Times 38, 1982, p. 30

4   "Dr Faustroll" article *Medical Bag, Fortean Times* No 60, 1991, p. 32

5   Ibid.

6   See article *Bad Medicine* in *X Factor* No 31, p. 866

7   Ibid.

8   For a definitive list of medical and psychiatric malpractice in the Western world since 1945 (including that of Walter Freeman), see *The Mind Manipulators* by Alan W. Scheflin and Edward M. Opton, Jr., London, Paddington Press Ltd., 1978.

9   Of late, we have the edifying Fortean tale of scientists mistaking sheep brains for cow brains in BSE research.

10 For many years the editor of *The Monthly Weather Review*. This was a popular and well-respected journal that often contained articles debating the main scientific issues of the day. Often it was open-minded enough under Proctor's influence to discuss weather, geographic, and astronomical anomalies. It was one of Fort's favourite journals, and he quotes from it frequently.

11 Rupert Sheldrake, *Seven Experiments That Could Change the World*. London, Fourth Estate, 1994 (discussed in *X Factor* No 39)

12 Article *Medical Curiosities* in *Fortean Times* 38, Autumn, 1982, p. 30

13 E. R. John, 1993 "Multipotentiality: a theory of recovery of function after brain injury", *Neurophysiology*, 1994

14 Despite modern attempts using computer modelling to show that the rod which entered Gage's skull avoided those areas associated with "emotions, social behaviour and aggression". See *Fortean Times* No 109, quoting article "The Return of Phineas Gage" from *Science*, May, 1994.

15 Fort, *op. cit.*, p. 771

16 *How The Mind Works*. Penguin, London, 1998. Pinker apologises for his "audacious" title in his preface. He does not offer any apologies for the title of his last chapter, which is "The Meaning of Life".

17 *Daily Mirror*, March 4, 1991

18 *Daily Telegraph*, January 8, 1997

19 Article by Joe McNally in *Medical Bag, Fortean Times* No 109, April, 1998, p. 19

20 *Medical Bag* in *Fortean Times* No 97, 1997, p. 19

21 *Phantom Limbs*, *X Factor* No 39, p. 1089

22 John Keel's underrated book, *The Mothman Prophecies*, Signet, 1976, is a good example of such a process.

23 See Arthur Koestler's discussion of the work of the biologist Kammerer in his celebrated book, *The Case of the Midwife Toad*. Hutchinson, London, 1973

24 But not even the brilliant radical Rupert Sheldrake (a review of his book, *A New Science,* in *New Scientist,* recommended that this work should be burnt), does not go so far as to equate his "morphological field" to metaphor. The dream I described was, after all, complex expanded metaphor; now there is an idea for a new computer!

25 Frank Rose, *Into The Heart Of Mind*. Century, London, 1985

26 That is relating to a pronoun.

27 See Arthur Koestler, *The Sleepwalkers*, Hutchinson, London, 1959, for the strange inspirations of Copernicus and Tycho de Brahe, and Koestler's analyses of Kepler's "fantasy-prone intellect".

28 Arthur Koestler, *Janus*. Hutchinson, London, 1978

29 Lyall Watson *Beyond Supernature*. Hodder and Stoughton, London, 1986

30 Douglas R. Hofstadter and Daniel C. Dennett, *The Mind's Eye*. Basic Books, New York, 1981, p. 145. These editors are quoting from Richard Mattuck, *A Guide to Feynman Diagrams in the Many-Body Problem*. McGraw-Hill, NY, 1976

31 Rickard, *op cit.*, ITV, May 11, 1982, 10:45pm.

32 Ivan T. Sanderson, *Things*. Pyramid, NY, 1969

33 Frank Edwards, *Strange People*. Pan, London, 1966

34 *Ibid.*, p. 64

35 *The Sun* (Reuters) Friday, July 14,

1989, p. 26

36 *Running on Empty*, *X Factor* No 43, p. 1186

37 Leonard Stringfield, *Retrievals of the Third Kind*, *Flying Saucer Review*, Vol 23 No 4, 1977

38 Steven Rose, *The Making of Memory*. Transworld Publishers, London, 1992

39 *The Sun* (Reuters), October 14, 1996, p. 11

40 Letter from Nick Warren, *Fortean Times* No 97, February, 1997, p. 51

41 *The Hounds from Hell*, *X Factor* No 33, p. 928

42 Dr Gustave Geley, in his book *From the Conscious to the Unconscious* (Paris, 1919), describes the case of a young girl whose brain was pulped in a railway accident. After light surgery, she quickly recovered. In *Strange World* (Bantam, 1969), Frank Edwards reports the case of the young girl Marie (a pseudonym), who contracted sleeping sickness and suffered terrible daily convulsions until half her brain was removed in Wesley Hospital in Chicago May 4, 1951. She made an almost complete recovery, and at the time of Edwards' report (five years after the operation), she was said to be a normal, happy child.

43 See *Anomalies and Curiosities of Medicine* (reprint available from Blue Unicorn Editions, 1997). The authors, medical doctors George M. Gould and Walter L. Pyle, describe the complete recovery of a Russian woman mill worker who had a large iron bolt driven into her brain.

44 In an address before the Anthropological Society at Sucre, Bolivia, in 1940, Dr Augustin Iturricha told of the case of a fourteen-year-old boy who was being treated for a brain abscess. The boy complained only of a violent headache, and was fully conscious and rational before his death. The autopsy showed that the brain mass was almost entirely detached from the bulb. The abscess involved all of the cerebellum and part of the cerebrum. We are left to conjecture how the boy's physical co-ordination was achieved, and what he

did his thinking with.

45 Professor John Hastead, *The Metal Benders*. Routledge & Kegan Paul, London, 1981

46 *Medical Curiosities*, *Fortean Times* No 38, 1982 (no author credited)

47 For example, there are mercifully brief passages in the latter part of *Women in Love* (1916) that rival anything in Julius Streicher's *Der Stürmer*, or Hitler's *Mein Kampf*.

48 Richard Westfall, *The Life of Isaac Newton*. Cambridge University Press, 1993

49 Sir Cyril Burt, *ESP and Psychology*. Wiedenfeld and Nicholson, 1975. This book has become a classic in this area of interest, and was an influence on the work of Arthur Koestler. Recently however, both Stephen J Gould in *The Mismeasure of Man* and Leon J. Kamin in *The Science and Politics of IQ,* have cast serious doubt on Burt's statistical work on intelligence testing, accusing him of fraud. Strangely, these two writers make absolutely no mention of Burt's work on parapsychology. Given very similar accusations against the mathematician Samuel Soal, a sometime President of the British Society for Psychical Research (see *The Unexplained* No 1, Orbis Publishing, London, 1980), and also certain people who worked under Rhine, see *New Frontiers of the Mind* (Pelican, London, 1937, p. 80), and also article *Animal Psi Revisited* by John L. Randall (*The Paranormal Review* No 6, April, 1998), discussing the dismissal of Walter J. Levy by Rhine himself in 1974. There is something very odd about such perverse actions by undoubtedly brilliant men. As far as I know, no one has yet researched the connection between the famous "displacement effect" described by G. N. M. Tyrell in *The Personality of Man,* Pelican, London, 1946, and the suspect statistical arrays of the accused. Rhine himself was accused of cheating by G. R. Price in a notorious article in the American journal *Science* in 1955, only to

NOTES FOR
PAGES
145–161

apologise in 1972, in another article in *Science* entitled *Apology to Rhine and Soal.* One can hear Fort's laughter from beyond the grave.

50 Samuel A. Goudsmit, *Alsos,* American Institute of Physics, Woodbury, NY, 1996 (originally published in 1947)

51 R. V. Jones, *Most Secret War*. Hamish Hamilton, London, 1978, p. 306

52 Should their involvement be doubted, both Hahn and Heisenberg closely supervised the manufacturing and design on the shop-floor of the Krupp works in Essen, prior to final assembly of the reactor in the medieval castle-town of Haigerloch. Here, whilst waiting for the pile to reach critical mass (which it never did), Heisenberg went to the half-Gothic half-baroque church and played Bach fugues on the organ. Had his work been successful, one is left to conjecture whether he would have chosen a suitable piece in celebration as convoys containing nuclear warheads trundled their way to the newly-constructed underground V2 bases.

KNIFE-EDGE SYSTEMS

1 Fort, *op. cit.,* p. 389
2 Proctor was also editor of *Knowledge.*
3 Fort, *op. cit.,* pp. 239–240
4 Fort, *op. cit.,* p. 66
5 Scott Corrales article *Vanished!* in *Fortean Times* No 96, January, 1997, p. 22. Scott claims his sources are the American Tracers Company for the first figure, and "different law enforcement agencies" for the second.
6 These figures are taken from *Moonwalker,* an article in *X Factor* No 35, in which the former Apollo astronaut Edgar Mitchell describes his research into what he calls "black budget" funds. In this same article, the connection of the New Reconnaissance Office with the CIA is stated in the context of a discussion of a unspecified report by Whitley Strieber about a Congress investigation into the finances of the New

Reconnaissance Office.
7 S. K. Runcorn, ed., *Physics in the Sixties*. Oliver and Boyd, London, 1963, p. 23. Essay "Matter and Force after Fifty Years of Quantum Theory" by L. Rosenfeld.
8 Fort, *op. cit.,* p. 67
9 Fort, *op. cit.,* p. 141
10 Bart Kosko, *Fuzzy Thinking.* HarperCollins, 1994
11 Fort, *op. cit.,* p. 736
12 Fort, *op cit.,* p. 333

COSMOLOGY AS CONSUMERISM

1 Quoted from *History of the Warfare of Science with Theology in Christendom.* D. Appleton and Co., 1897, p. 9. For a complete account of Bishop Ussher, see Colin Groves' *Archaeology in Oceania* 31, 1996, pp.145–151.
2 Lancelot Hogben, *Science for the Citizen*. George Allen & Unwin Ltd, London, 1938, p. 979
3 Article by Robert Matthews in *The Sunday Telegraph*, Oct. 6, 1996, p. 19
4 Fort, *op. cit.,* pp.142–143
5 Fort, *op. cit.,* p. 530
6 Ibid.
7 "Primitive sac-like animal consisting of two layers (ectoderm and endoderm) of cells." *Concise Oxford Dictionary*
8 Fort, *op. cit.,* p. 531
9 For examples of such, see *The Pursuit of the Millenium*. Paladin, London, 1970, by Norman Cohn, also his *Europe's Inner Demons*. Paladin, London, 1976
10 Fort, *op. cit.,* p. 531
11 See *The Murder of TSR2* by Stephen Hastings, M. C., M. P.
12 Fort, *op. cit.,* p. 428
13 Fort, *op. cit.,* p. 265
14 Fort, *op. cit.,* p. 389
15 Fort, *op cit,* p. 905
16 *The World of Ted Serios*. Jonathan Cape, 1968, p. 290. This book is about the experiments with Ted Serios, who could produce images on sealed film of concealed targets.
17 Wykeham Professor of Logic at Oxford. Arthur Koestler warns us (in *Roots of Coincidence*) not to get this Price confused with the "controversial"

spiritualist Harry Price, who wrote the book, *The End of Borley Rectory*. This shows that Koestler, one of the great fighters for intellectual freedom, could distance dangerous "extremists" as readily as anyone.

18 Preface to Whateley Carrington's *Matter, Mind and Meaning*. London, 1911 (reprinted by Ayer & Co)

19 J. P. Chaplin, *Rumor, Fear and the Madness of Crowds*. Ballantine, NY, 1959

20 George Allen & Unwin, 1982, p.160

21 He wrote *Water and Dreams* and *Psychoanalysis of Fire*.

ACCURACY AS MYTH

1 Ed by Peter Dale Scott, Paul L. Hoch, and Russell Stetler, Penguin, 1978

2 *Assassinations*: *The Proof of the Plot* (p. 135), and *The Zapruder Film* (p. 185)

3 Ibid., *From Dallas to Watergate:The Longest Cover-Up* (p.337), and *The Death of Kennedy, Vietnam, and Cuba* (p. 340)

4 Ibid., *CIA activities and the Warren Commission Investigation* (p. 411)

5 *Assassinations COINTELPRO* (p. 304); this is J. Edgar Hoover's own internal department instruction hinting that Martin Luther King might have to be "removed." See also Robert Blair Kaiser, *The Case is still Open* (p. 309) on the shooting of Robert Kennedy, and the convincing evidence that Sirhan Sirhan was almost certainly hypnotically programmed.

LEE HARVEY OSWALD AS FORTEAN MAN

1 *Assassinations, op. cit.,* p. 401

2 Oswald completed a pretty stiff US Marines radar and electronics course,

and became a qualified radar operator guiding U2 reconnaissance planes and also nuclear-loaded aircraft from the American base at Atsugi in Japan. During his military service, however his behaviour became increasingly strange. According to Anthony Summers, he shot himself with his own pistol, and assaulted a fellow Marine. These were court-martial offences. but Oswald was not charged, serving only disciplinary sentences in the "brig". For a detailed account of other strange incidents during Oswald's military service, see *Legend: The Secret World of Lee Harvey Oswald* by Edward J. Epstein, Hutchinson, 1978

3 See Anthony Summers, *The Kennedy Conspiracy*. Warner Books, 1980

4 *Ibid.,* p. 377

5 *Assassinations*, p. 84: *The Murder of Patrolman Tippit* by Sylvia Meagher.

6 *Ibid.,* p. 229: *Physical Evidence* by Josiah Thompson

7 General Walker was one of Patton's WWII commanders, and had an American tank named after him (the "Walker Bulldog").

8 *Assassinations*, p. 197: *The Case for Three Assassins* by Lifton and Welsh.

9 Which appear just as mysteriously as do the documents in another Borges story, *Tlon, Uqbar, Orbis Tertius*. Here indeed is history imitating literature.

10 *Avatars of the Tortoise,* from the short-story collection, *Labyrinths*. New Directions, 1964

APPENDIX: SCEPTICISM AS MYSTIQUE

1 *I Was Elvis Presley's Bastard Love-Child*. Critical Vision, Manchester, 2001, p. 11

NOTES FOR
PAGES
161–181

index

ABSOLUTELY ESSENTIAL
Fortean Times

HEADPRESS RULES!
Spectator

HEADPRESS *The Journal of Sex Religion Death*

23: FUNHOUSE

David Kerekes, Editor

CULT FILM SPECIAL! This twenty-third edition of **Headpress** is devoted to seventies horror classic **Last House on Dead End Street**, a visceral cult obscurity inspired by the Manson murders and fuelled by the copious intake of drugs. We track down the reclusive director, Roger Watkins, several of the film's stars, and also cast on eye over Watkins' post-**Last House** career in the porn business.

PLUS: An heretic looks at JACK KEROUAC; Lap Dancing in Greece; The Day I Punched the Anti-Christ; An interview with artist JOE COLEMAN; Readers on the BBC's GHOSTWATCH; The Italian Scandal of Horror Fiction for Children; Reviews and more!

ISBN **1-900486-18-0**   ISSN **1353-9760**   Price UK **£8.99** / US **$14.99**

Pages **176pp**   Market **Pop Culture**   Published **Available Now**

www.headpress.com

Send a first class stamp
(or 2 x IRC) for the latest
Headpress/Critical Vision
book catalogue

HEADPRESS
40 Rossall Avenue
Radcliffe
Manchester
M26 1JD
Great Britain

Or visit

www.headpress.com